"In this powerful and necessary book, Harper does something truly unique. By telling the story of her own family, she tells the story of America through a deeply Christian lens. As truthful as it is hopeful, this beautifully written book about resistance, healing, memory, place, history, justice, and identity shows how we are all still shaped by the stories we tell. This is a story that will stay with you."

—Sarah Bessey, editor of *New York Times* bestseller *A Rhythm of Prayer*; author of *Miracles and Other Reasonable Things*

"*Fortune* is an arresting, moving, and altogether remarkable book. The author—one of the most influential faith leaders in America and around the globe—deftly combines her own story with a broader narrative of race, theology, and our country's tragic history. This book is a triumph! It should be read in living rooms, classrooms, and anywhere else where people seek passion, purpose, and truth."

—Joshua DuBois, White House faith-based advisor to President Barack Obama; bestselling author of *The President's Devotional*

"Harper gives us a glimpse of her family's survival, resistance, and resilience through her bold storytelling. In this epic narrative, she reminds us that our stories aren't entirely lost to racial injustice. We can reclaim the richness and brilliance of our stories, our people, and our faith. *Fortune* will have your attention on every page and provoke each of us to explore our family history

and discover redemptive visions for ourselves and our family lineage."

—Latasha Morrison, *New York Times* and ECPA bestselling author of *Be the Bridge*; president and founder of Be the Bridge

"Harper is one of the most influential leaders in the US and across the globe. This is her most important book yet. She unifies her own family history with her insightful theology. She names the sinful, demonic force of racism, but she also casts a vision for how we can heal our wounds from it. Pure fire from beginning to end."

—Shane Claiborne, author, activist, and cofounder of Red Letter Christians

"A beautiful book of great spiritual and emotional depth. Through a mix of memoir and historical excavation, Harper conducts a unique, courageous exploration of America's original sin and its terrible toll on the physical, spiritual, and psychic existence of Black Americans through the struggles of her ancestors. This book will touch your soul."

—Obery M. Hendricks Jr., visiting scholar, Columbia University; author of *Christians against Christianity: How Right-Wing Evangelicals Are Destroying Our Nation and Our Faith*

"In *Fortune*, Harper helps us imagine how the sterile print of America's first race laws impacted living, breathing people. Particularly in chapter one, her analysis of the life of Fortune Game Magee and her descendants helps us consider how these laws and the constructs of race that they built shaped the course of our nation. You may not agree with everything, but you must consider this work."

—**Paul Heinegg**, author of *Free African Americans of Maryland and Delaware* and *Free African Americans of North Carolina, Virginia, and South Carolina*

"Harper is one of our generation's most important wisdom teachers. *Fortune* is a compelling invitation to receive the story that has shaped a nation through the story of her family. It makes clear how the stakes in our public conversations about race and justice are both deeply personal and universal: they touch us in the most intimate spaces of our lives."

—**Jonathan Wilson-Hartgrove**, author of *Revolution of Values* and *Reconstructing the Gospel*

"Harper is a gifted storyteller and one of the voices we need to listen to for America's future. In telling the story of her ancestors and her personal story, she shows us a deeper way of understanding our nation's difficult past and offers a way forward toward its diverse and equitable future."

—**Rev. Jim Wallis**, founding director, Georgetown University Center on Faith and Justice; founder and ambassador of Sojourners

"*Fortune* is a brave and brilliant meditation on the shameful legacy of racial injustice in America. This is a seamless narrative brimming with historical reflection, family lore, and spiritual healing. Highly recommended!"

—**Douglas Brinkley**, professor, Rice University; author of *Rosa Parks: A Life*

"With skill and love, Harper weaves together nothing less than an epic and true story of race, religion, history, and identity. A small number of books convey such soulfulness and richness with every word, and this is one of them. *Fortune* recovers the story not just of a single lineage but of whole eras, people groups, and nation-shaping events, and it reads like both memoir and exposé. It rewards the reader with insights and emotion on every page."

—**Jemar Tisby**, *New York Times* bestselling author of *The Color of Compromise* and *How to Fight Racism*

"Harper is one of our nation's most critical voices on the issues of race, gender, faith, and justice. In an era when the world feels unmoored, Harper anchors us in the truth of what brought America to the brink. Through masterful storytelling and deep spiritual reflection, Harper weaves together ten generations of her family story with the story of America. Then she points the way forward to a world where all can flourish. *Fortune* is necessary reading for us all."

—**Kirsten Powers**, *New York Times* bestselling author, CNN senior political analyst, and *USA Today* columnist

"'Whoever saves a life,' the rabbis teach, 'saves the whole world.' In this brilliant story of Fortune, which is also the story of America, Harper demonstrates how one who narrates a life also tells the story of the whole world. Take and read how one family and the whole world were broken by the lies of race, and how we might be part of repairing the breach."

—**Rev. Dr. William J. Barber II**, president, Repairers of the Breach; author of *We Are Called to Be a Movement*

"The magic of Lisa is this: she tells the whole truth of our historical existence as a nation built upon racist structures, ideologies, and laws. In *Fortune*, Harper lays bare the guttural facts about where America sits in the expanse between the bright promise of 'I Have a Dream' and the rayless reality of 'Make America Great Again.' In the end, she makes clear the work we must accomplish to see that our hope for true equality and justice never fades."

—**Jen Hatmaker**, *New York Times* bestselling author, speaker, and host of the *For the Love* podcast

"It is difficult to write a book on race, faith, family, reparations, and justice in ways that are compelling to people who are either tired of or resistant to thinking about these matters. Harper has written just such a book. Harper has the rare gift of speaking honestly in ways that remind you of Tom Skinner, and of speaking intimately in ways that remind you of Maya Angelou. There are few evangelical writers who match the power of her voice. I am very glad we all get to hear it in print."

—**Willie James Jennings**, professor, Yale Divinity School

"Harper is a masterful storyteller. In *Fortune*, Harper offers us a front-row seat to the intergenerational story of her family as they moved from being a community of enslaved Africans to free African Americans. With a sociohistorical scalpel and unflinching honesty, she unpacks the sound of her family's names, an African American family in White America where the bone of racism chokes the breath out of everyone and everything it touches, including democracy itself. Faced with the choice of becoming broken-winged birds from the weight of racism, the men and women in *Fortune* choose to both fly in it and above it. This is the magnificent breath of fresh air that we inhale from the genius of this African American family."

—**Ruby Sales**, founder of the Spirithouse Project, long distance runner for justice, social critic, popular educator, and Black folk theologian

"'How do we repair what race broke in the world?' This is what Lisa Sharon Harper challenges us to consider in her new book. She takes us on a journey of discovery using her family history as the vessel, and calls us to contemplate not only the cost and pain of racism but the promise of an 'America yet to be'—should we dare to confront our past, repair the damage, and demand a future that belongs to us all. A fantastic read and an important work in America's search for her authentic self."

—**Mitch Landrieu**, former mayor of New Orleans; founder of E Pluribus Unum

Previous Works by Lisa Sharon Harper

*The Very Good Gospel: How Everything
Wrong Can Be Made Right*

Forgive Us: Confessions of a Compromised Faith (coauthor)

Left, Right and Christ: Evangelical Faith in Politics (coauthor)

Catch: A Play in One Act

Evangelical Does Not Equal Republican . . . or Democrat

An' Push da Wind Down: A Play in Two Acts

FORTUNE

How Race Broke My Family and
the World—and How to Repair It All

LISA SHARON HARPER

BrazosPress
a division of Baker Publishing Group
·Grand Rapids, Michigan

Published by Brazos Press
a division of Baker Publishing Group
PO Box 6287, Grand Rapids, MI 49516-6287
www.brazospress.com

Printed in the United States of America

Library of Congress Cataloging-in-Publication Data
Names: Harper, Lisa Sharon, author.
Title: Fortune : how race broke my family and the world-and how to repair it all / Lisa Sharon Harper.
Description: Grand Rapids, Michigan : Brazos Press, a division of Baker Publishing Group, [2022] | Includes bibliographical references.
Identifiers: LCCN 2021033221 | ISBN 9781587435270 (cloth) | ISBN 9781493432745 (pdf) | ISBN 9781493432738 (ebook)
Subjects: LCSH: Harper, Lisa Sharon. | African American women—Religious life. | African American Christians—Religious life. | United States—Race relations—History. | Racism—History. | Race relations—Religious aspects—Christianity.
Classification: LCC BX4827.H326 A3 2022 | DDC 277.308/3092 [B]—dc23
LC record available at https://lccn.loc.gov/2021033221

The Author is represented by the literary agency of Ross Yoon Agency.

Baker Publishing Group publications use paper produced from sustainable forestry practices and post-consumer waste whenever possible.

22   23   24   25   26   27   28   7   6   5   4   3   2   1

To all my relations
Who struggled under the weight of oppression—
Stretching your necks to catch a glint of warmth from the sun:
Behold, the sun.

Contents

Foreword

Especially do I believe in the Negro Race; in the beauty of its genius, the sweetness of its soul, and its strength in that meekness which shall yet inherit this turbulent earth.

—W. E. B. Du Bois

Captured in the 1920 publication *Dark Water: Voices from within the Veil,* Du Bois continued his lifelong project of decolonizing false notions about people of African descent caught in the matrix of America's peculiar racial contract. It was Du Bois's calling to remind America of the *imago Dei* (image of God) applied to all humanity, especially those living behind the veil. He wrote the above credo as a declaration of belief and as a subversive act. When Blackness is viewed through the lens of humanity, the American mythos is disturbed.

Black people, according to America's mythology, must be framed by a lie for Whiteness to flourish. Du Bois made the claim that people of African descent are worthy, have a story, have self-agency, and bring to the table a spiritual and intellectual genius—for those invested in the Confederate mythos, such rhetoric was unpatriotic and probably socialist. Du Bois and his contemporaries found this accusation thrown at all who dared to offer an

13

alternative vision and account of America's history. Du Bois's declaration echoes in this publication you hold in your hand by Lisa Sharon Harper. She, not unlike Du Bois, has crafted a credo that upends the American racial mythology for a vision of what can be versus false narratives of being "great again."

Lisa Sharon Harper mines the extraordinary story of her own family tree through the eyes of Sambo Game, Maudlin Magee, and their daughter Fortune, who we would call Creole in today's verbiage. She held in her body the genius of Africa, the privilege of Europe, and the marginalization of gender, on the displaced colonial soil mistakenly called the New World. Lisa, like a modern griot, weaves a tale that is enlightening while simultaneously heart-wrenching. Hearing the story of Africans who survived the demonic cruelty of enslavement in America is to witness the brilliance and bruised grace of one's family tree. The spiritual ingenuity to survive while the demon of displacement attacks the psyche is a miracle academics and theologians fail to recognize.

We stand at a peculiar moment in history in this land Du Bois called the "yet to be United States of America," where Black visibility is at its highest. Beyoncé Knowles is a global phenomenon. Serena Williams and Simone Biles are some of America's greatest athletes. Ava DuVernay has risen to cinematic prominence as the nation's premier socially conscious producer and director. Kamala Harris and Stacey Abrams are arguably two of our most influential political voices. The largest global movement to elevate the issues of Black life was organized by Black women who declared "Black Lives Matter." But with this heightened visibility we are also in an unprecedented period of White backlash, where antebellum ghosts haunt both political parties, though clearly these electors have found greater aid and comfort in one. Black death recorded on social media is the norm, and the denial of Black pain is now a right of passage for conservative politicians and preachers who seek power.

Race or racialized thinking has fractured the global village, and specifically has poisoned the American democratic project. When I speak of race in this context, I am talking about the social construction of an idea that designated one group superior and another inferior. I am not speaking about ethnicity or culture with this statement. It should be noted that Black people often use the term "Black" interchangeably to describe a social construction or an ethnic connection. America's mythos banishes ethnicity and culture for our public discourse and replaces it with this nation's original civic sin of White supremacy, racism, and racial privilege.

What is extraordinary about this publication is Lisa's ability to weave history, family narrative, theology, and creative nonfiction against our contemporary scene. If you ever have the privilege of hearing Lisa speak, you will quickly recognize that she is a storyteller and a writer who is excited about serendipitous historical details, but she never loses sight of the main themes and characters of her story.

After reading this book, I was thankful. Thankful I had the privilege to go on this journey with Lisa's family. Thankful God keeps calling and inspiring gifted women and men to articulate a faith that is broader than Sunday rituals or Sabbath contemplation. Thankful I have a friend of grace and brilliance who is unafraid to speak truth in an era where lies, bigotry, and privilege are venerated. And thankful for the sacred synchronicity that created the tapestry to allow Sambo Game, Maudlin Magee, and a daughter named Fortune to produce a series of human resisters to the American racial contract, one being my friend, Lisa Sharon Harper.

Read from these pages, Beloved, and let this story of family, race, and resistance create anger in your spirit and ultimately inspire your heart to join the work to heal our nation and eventually our world.

Otis Moss III
Senior Pastor, Trinity United Church of Christ
Founder, Unashamed Media Group

Acknowledgments of Country

This book embarks on a pilgrimage through my family's story as a framework through which we all might sharpen our understanding of the story of race in our nation. Before we begin, I acknowledge the first nations of the lands we will tread in these pages.

I honor the first peoples of current-day Somerset and Wicomico Counties in Maryland. They were the Nanticoke, Wicomiss, Manokin, and Susquehannock Nations. They lived along the waters where they built villages, fished, hunted, and loved and cultivated the land. They traded with early settlers but were eventually enslaved, and many were sent to the Caribbean to slave on English plantations.[1] They were and are here.

I honor the first peoples of Ohio County, Kentucky: the Chickasaw (*Chikasha*) and Cherokee (*Ani'yunwi'ya*) Nations, and the Shawnee (*Shawanwaki*) Nation farther north. They were a woodland and mountain people who lived in log cabins, cultivated the earth for sustenance, and valued harmony above all else. They were and are here.

I honor the first peoples of Kershaw County, South Carolina: the Catawba, the Cherokee, the Cusabo, the Sewee, and the

Wateree Nations. They were water people who lived along South Carolina's middle- and upper-country rivers. They stewarded the land until they were "discovered," enslaved, and hoodwinked for their land. They were and are here.

I honor the first peoples of Barbados: the Taíno (Arawak) and Kalinago (Carib) Nations. And I honor the first people of Puerto Rico: the Taíno (Arawak) Nation. People of the sea and explorers, the Taíno are a matrilineal people who recognize both women and men as chiefs. The Kalinago are fierce warriors who fought for their land but were overwhelmed by those who claimed "discovery" of them and their land. They were and are here.

I honor the first peoples of New York City, New Jersey, and Philadelphia: the Lenni Lenape Nation of the Algonquin-speaking peoples. A matrilineal people, the Lenape women managed the land, cultivating the "Three Sisters": maize, beans, and squash. The men hunted and fished. When Giovanni da Verrazano made early contact with the Lenape in 1524, thirty familial clans thrived throughout the nation.[2] By the time William Penn claimed Pennsylvania in 1682, only three clans remained. The rest had been decimated by disease, war, and famine. They were and are here.

To the Nanticoke and Wicomiss and Manokin and Susquehannock and the Chickasaw and Cherokee and Shawnee and Catawba and Cusabo and Sewee and Wateree and Taíno (Arawak) and Kalinago (Carib) and the Lenni Lenape: I see you. I honor you. I thank you for laying foundations of harmony, balance, truth, and honor on this land. We thank you for stewarding the land where Creator settled your people. We bless you. We bless your elders: past, present, and emerging.

Prologue

"Have they come yet?"

"Have who come?" I was sitting on the patio of a retreat center in west Michigan with a new friend, Greg Ellison, professor at the School of Theology at Emory University. We had come to this center to be among spiritual leaders and discuss faith-based approaches to healing the world.

"The ancestors," he replied.

I had explained to Ellison and a few colleagues with deep roots in the mystic tradition that I was about to embark on a pilgrimage to the place where the first ancestors in my family were brought to the US as slaves from West Africa in the 1680s. Somerset County on the Eastern Shore of Maryland was not far from my home in Washington, DC, but it felt a world away. I told them I was terrified to unearth the story of my family. It felt like I was about to push into the heart of American evil.

I had heard rumors that this area in southern Maryland was like the Deep South, a breeding ground for hate groups holding onto racial caste systems. If you've ever visited Gettysburg National Park, one of the more striking things isn't the park itself or its famous landmarks. It's the locals who proudly display Confederate flags in their front yards or on their vehicles, or sell Southern trinkets in their antique stores, as if to dismiss the meaning behind the battle and the pivotal address that took place there. I had heard similar stories of Somerset County. Just south of the Mason–Dixon line, Somerset had pockets of Southern sympathizers.

All I could think was that I—a Black woman—was about to drive into the heart of hate to discover truth, beauty, and healing. I did not know what to expect or who from my past I might encounter.

"They will guide you," Ellison told me.

One week later, I sat in my living room remembering his words. Despite his reassurances, I still felt fearful about my trip. Cable news droned in the background. Something about Russia. Something about collusion. Something about America going to hell in a gift box from Trump Tower.

Then I felt it.

A presence.

In my mind's eye, I saw her: a Black woman with my shape—curvy, soft—a white apron over a dingy blue floor-length skirt, and a white head wrap. I don't know how, but I knew—it was Betty Game, my great-aunt going back eight generations. For many years, I had been researching Betty, her family and descendants. Betty lived in Maryland in about the 1750s; she was a mixed-race, emancipated indentured servant who had managed to buy land of her own. I had located tax records dating back to that era and found a single sentence explaining how Betty had refused to pay an extra tax required of free Black women landowners. Further record digging showed that Betty never paid the Black tax on that property.

Betty stood in my living room like an eighteenth-century Black Fairy Godmother.

"I will guide you," she said without words. As Ellison had predicted, my ancestors were helping me on my journey.

Days later, I moved closer to the land of my American origin with every revolution of the rental car wheels across the mighty Chesapeake. Suspended high above the water, this bridge was one of the longest I'd ever crossed. Crossing over the water, I moved toward the land from which my ancestors escaped.

Records show that three generations of my family lived on the Eastern Shore of Maryland: some of them enslaved, some indentured servants, and some free. The fourth generation likely crossed the Chesapeake as indentured children, separated from their family by the movement of masters. They eventually lived free in Virginia. How they got there, the substance of their struggles, and how those struggles affected the generations that came after has been my journey for the last three decades. This book is the product of their pain and their push.

Introduction

My mother, Sharon, leaned over my seven-year-old body as I lay
on my side, curled up in bed. Eyes closed, I had just watched the
first episode of the television series *Roots*, based on Alex Haley's
novel, huddled near the television set in our West Oak Lane neighborhood row house in Northwest Philadelphia.

Mommy sang to me:

> Wade in the water
> Wade in the water, children.
> Wade in the water
> God's gonna trouble the water.

I didn't understand it then, but my mother's generation was
made up of baby boomers whose parents had transplanted to the
North during the Great Migration and had infused them with a
power that Dr. King called "soul force." It was gleaned from the
blood-soaked earth of the South. They refused to be crushed by
northern oppression. Moreover, Black boomer women and men
were the first generation of people of African descent to live on this
land with legal and systemic protection of their civil rights since
the Civil Rights Act of 1875 was overturned and Reconstruction
crumbled. Now under the cover of the Civil Rights Act of 1964

and the Voting Rights Act of 1965, which they had fought, bled, and died for, there was space to look back and re-member.

There in my flower-wallpapered bedroom on East Walnut Lane, a sleepy suburban street where middle-class African American children played hopscotch, Mother May I?, Red Light–Green Light, and hide-and-seek from morning to night on sloped lawns in front of our row houses—there in the final hours of the day, once I'd had my bath and been tucked into bed, my mother sang "Wade in the Water" over me. With a hum that rose from deep within her soul and words passed down through generations, she knit me together with my family's 289-year struggle on American soil.

Previous generations did not have the luxury of memory. Under constant threat and suffering from constant trauma, family separation, and death, many attempted to bury the past. My mother's mother, Willa, had suffered Jim Crow degradation as a child and escaped to the North as a teen. Tucked on the second floor of a three-story South Philadelphia row house owned by her mother, my great-grandmother, Lizzie—a home that offered northern shelter for three generations of her family—Grandmom Willa sang my seven-year-old mother to sleep with a song that attempted to lift her from the entanglement of Black struggle into the world of make-believe. Willa leaned over Sherry's bed and sang, "I'm a little teapot, short and stout. This is my handle. This is my spout." But in the daytime hours when daily trials and memories haunted mundane tasks, my mother remembers her mother's voice filling the house with the songs of Billie Holiday and Bessie Smith like background prayers. Holiday's cover of George Gershwin's "Summertime" was her favorite. Willa sang of the morning her children would spread their wings and fly:

> But till that mornin', there's a-nothin' can harm you
> With daddy and mammy standin' by

Willa's mother, Great-Grandmom Elizabeth, was born in 1890 in Camden, South Carolina. I remember her at ninety years old, learning to walk again after breaking her hip and living with her daughter—my grandmother—Willa. I don't remember her ever uttering a word, but the elders say they remember a much younger Lizzie, the first in her family to seek asylum in the North, circa 1920. They say she moved through her days with a hum on her lips—often humming or singing "Precious Lord," a song written in her youth:

> Lead me on, let me stand
> I'm tired, I'm weak, I'm lone

Lizzie left the South and never returned—intentionally dismembered from her past.

On that night in January 1977, in the comfort of my mother's nest in our Philadelphia suburb, listening to my mommy sing me into the wading waters of sleep, remembering Alex Haley's *Roots*—Kunta Kinte and Yaisa, Binta and Omoro Kinte, and the last scene of episode one where Omoro presents baby Kunta to the heavens—I was awakened to a truth that lodged itself deep in my marrow: I have a past and a people and a soul force that extend far beyond my life.

The seed of this book was planted that night.

For most of my childhood I gleaned stories from my grandmother and my mother, but never wrote anything down. Then I saw *Dances with Wolves*.

When I was a child, every week we visited Grandmom Willa and Grandpop Junius Lawrence in South Philly. As we entered their row house, I hugged Grandmom and asked her, "Where's the brush?" She would point me to her dresser-top in her bedroom. I'd run and get the brush, then climb behind her and sit against the wall on the back of the couch. Willa sat with her back between my legs. Then I ran the brush through her bone-straight hair. Brushing Grandmom's hair was like brushing the head of my 1970s hairstyling doll.

I always wondered how her hair got that way. When I asked what she was, she got mad. She said with definitive finality, "We're Black. That's it."

But one day in fifth grade, on the school playground, several friends shared that they were part Cherokee. I thought of my grandmother's hair again. The next weekend when we visited, I waded into the troubled waters of identity again.

"Are we part Indian?" I asked her with trepidation—not wanting to offend.

But this time she answered with a secret: "We're part Indian, but don't ever tell anybody. They'll think you're trying to pass for White."

When my grandfather died, she gave me a beautiful Native American beaded necklace that she said he wanted me to have. I cherished it like a gift from the ancestors. I didn't understand the politics of passing at that time. I didn't know that Willa's mother, Lizzie, had passed at one point in her life. I didn't know what I understand now: that the political constructs of race in the US are made up, illogical, and devised for one purpose—to determine one's place in a human hierarchy of belonging. All I knew was that I didn't want anyone to think I was trying to pass. I knew enough to know that would be bad. So, I told no one. I never wore that beaded necklace in public, and I held my grandmother's secret until 1990.

In the first moments of Kevin Costner's award-winning 1990 movie, *Dances with Wolves*, Captain John Dunbar attempts suicide. His desperate act opens an opportunity for the Union army to attack. His bravery is commended with the opportunity to be posted anywhere he wants. He chooses the western frontier. From the moment I watched him step foot on the prairie—hands skimming tall prairie grass—tears streamed from an unknown place deep within my soul. A sense of longing rose from that place—longing for a home I'd never known—longing to be re-membered with my people and my land. But I didn't know who we were—only that we were "part Indian."

I called my mother when I got home from the movie theater. On that call, I sketched my first family tree. One branch reached back to Lea Ballard, Willa's great-grandmother—my third-great-grandmother—the last enslaved adult in our family. The other branch stretched back into the Lawrence family—my mother's father's patrilineal line—to Henry Lawrence.

"Henry fought in the Civil War," my mother explained. "He was Cherokee and Black."

That's all we knew. Later, my mother's brother corrected her: "We were Chickasaw," Uncle Larry said with his wavy gray hair tied back in a braid.

So, I came to understand, the Lawrence line descends from people who were African, Cherokee, and/or Chickasaw. I make no claim to be a member of any federally recognized tribe, be it Cherokee, Chickasaw, or any other. I only share the stories my ancestors shared with me.

Mystery . . . and bread crumbs.

I followed the bread crumbs and found they were enough to sustain life. I wrote an award-winning play inspired by those bread crumbs. Filled with my research and imagination of what might have happened, *An' Push da Wind Down* imagined how my Black and Cherokee family came together and ended up on the Trail of Tears, as family stories attempt to re-member.

In 2010, on the night I joined Ancestry.com, the doors swung open. I filled in the branches of our family tree as far as I could go. Hints popped up in the form of leaves. Those leaves led to an 1850 slave schedule for a Jonathan Lawrence with several "mulatto" enslaved children. There was no listing of their names, only their ages. The pre–Civil War census listed the names of free people. Enslaved people were listed according to their declared racial status (B=Black, M=mulatto, I=Indian). All of Jonathan's enslaved children had an M next to their names. I scanned the ages. According to my mother, Henry should have been born around 1842. There was an exact match.

On that slave schedule, listed as the unnamed property of Jonathan Lawrence, I was seeing likely evidence of the existence of the man who I had only heard spoken of, like the Greeks spoke of Hermes and Dionysus—mythical figures connected to their genesis. Here was the first evidence of Henry's reality.

Finding no more information about Henry that night, I switched to Jonathan's White daughter to uncover more information about the Lawrence family. White people were listed by name and had clear paper trails. My mother suspected that Jonathan was actually Henry's father. She imagined that he listed Henry as his slave to evade capture, because Jonathan may have been a passing Cherokee in Kentucky—after the Cherokee Trail of Tears. Jonathan's White daughter, Mariah Teresa Lawrence, married William Walter Lawton. Leaves kept popping up on Lawton's line. From generation to generation, I went further back until finally I was among the original settlers of the colony of Jamestown.

Suddenly I was connected to history. The colonial world seemed incredibly small. Truth is, there weren't many people in the US in the early colonial years. There's a good chance that if your ancestors were there, they had some connection with people we think of as mythical figures now.

More than a decade of research since then has filled in blanks through countless hours on Ancestry.com, FamilySearch, Geni, Fold3, and at the National Archives in Washington, DC, and on pilgrimage to the lands where my ancestors lived. DNA science has helped me, and all of us, make connections previously unfathomable. Ancestry.com, 23andMe, and African Ancestry have uncovered mysteries and secrets, correcting or confirming family stories while deepening my understanding of the lives of my ancestors and raising new questions.

The fleshed-out picture clarifies the profound costs of the political constructs of race and gender in the US and on my family and all those trapped in the talons of America's hierarchies of human belonging. Several times, while researching the lives of my great-grandmothers and great-grandfathers I found myself weeping—literally weeping. If only the constructs of race hadn't existed, Martha might have lived, Annie might have flourished, Augustin might not have been such a monster to his children, family fracture might not have been such a pathology on both sides of my family—and every woman in my matrilineal line might not have been molested or raped. How do we measure that cost? It is infinite, for it scrapes out the insides of the survivors and severely limits their capacity to flourish.

Mine is the first generation in more than four hundred years with enough distance from slavery and Jim Crow to try to assess the damage—and to demand repair. Not long ago, African Americans across the nation commemorated the four hundredth year since the first "twenty and odd"[1] Angolan men and women were forced off the English warship the *White Lion* and were received by John T. Rolfe, secretary of the colony. These men and women had been purchased in Luanda, Angola, and pirated from a Portuguese slave ship bound for Mexico.[2] The first enslaved Africans stepped foot in Point Comfort (present-day Hampton), Virginia, in 1619—in shackles. In the shadow of the four hundredth year since American slavery imposed itself on African lives—as scholars, documentarians, policymakers, and artists clarify the shape-shifting systems of control and confinement crafted to secure White supremacy on American soil and as White nationalist politicians seek to undermine the importance of 1619—we are compelled to ask one question, lest we find ourselves in the same controlled, confined, shackled space four hundred years from now: How do we repair what race broke in the world?

Reparation is about repair. To repair the world, we must first understand how the world broke. Any examination of racial injustice in the Western world must consider the theological grounds upon which legalized conquest and enslavement stood. Pope Nicholas V issued the *Romanus Pontifex*, which declared that explorers could claim the land of "uncivilized" peoples and enslave them. That papal bull laid foundations for the legal doctrine that fueled Europe's age of conquest: the doctrine of discovery.

This doctrine broke the world by mangling the proper power relationships between people groups. The theological lie of racialized human hierarchy became the fuel for Europe's age of conquest. The world cracked apart the moment the first European explorers looked at indigenous people who had stewarded land for thousands of years and declared them "uncivilized" and therefore unfit to exercise stewardship of their lands—or themselves.

If the break was fundamentally spiritual and relational, the remedy must heal our souls and repair the way we relate to each other in the world. While our relatedness has been shaped by conscious and unconscious beliefs, the power of belief does not stop with the mind. Belief is worked out in our bodies, practices, laws, systems, and structures. Belief shapes the world. But what shapes belief? Stories.

From Camelot to Beowulf to Mark Twain's *Tom Sawyer* and Jane Austen's *Pride and Prejudice*, stories born of European bodies shaped worldviews about European history around the globe. Even the story of Jesus, a Brown man, a colonized man, from a serially enslaved people, who lived in a time of occupation and colonization—that story was handed to the world through the sanitizing, White-ifying filter of European empires. Africa, Asia, Latin America, and indigenous people around the world received a White, blonde, straight-haired Jesus who always spoke with an English accent. If Jesus is White, then God is White. If God is White, then White people are closest to God. We must bow to them.

The varying perceptions of the Christian story divided our nation in antebellum times into two main camps: those who reconciled slavery and those who opposed slavery, both based on biblical teachings. Different interpretations of the Christian story divided our nation in the days of Jim Crow and the civil rights movement and culminated in the days leading up to the 2020 election when, in the face of racially disparate death rates due to COVID-19, Mayor Muriel Bowser, a Christian, ordered that "Black Lives Matter" be permanently painted on the street leading to the White House. And on January 6, 2021, the story of the ordained rule of White Christian men fueled an attempted coup and killed at least five images of God.

Nearly three-quarters of Americans identify themselves as followers of Jesus. How do we reconcile our faith stories? We bring disparate, competing narratives together by examining them, interrogating them, and most of all sitting at the feet of those who live and breathe and move in the same social hierarchy as those who first wrote and read and lived the biblical texts. Perhaps formerly enslaved ones, perhaps colonized ones, perhaps Brown ones in a White supremacist world can show White Christian Americans what they did not see in Brown, colonized Jesus. Any attempt to repair what race broke in our nation must contend with what race broke in our faith. In that space we will find the remedy for our nation's repair.

We have been deeply shaped by the stories we've told ourselves about God. We have also been shaped by the stories we've told ourselves about ourselves. The victor wrote our history. Celebrating the heroes of our nation's founding, the crafters of our national story marked its progression through a timeline of military conquests and economic exploits. The stories of the conquered and exploited have rarely risen to a height to be heard or seen beyond family and local community. These marginalized narratives must be pushed to the center. We must see them. We must reckon with them. These stories unearth the details of how and why and where racial hierarchy was built and protected. These stories reveal the details of the loss born of the practices, laws, systems, and structures created by human hierarchy. These suffocated stories raise a primal scream that cuts to the bone and reveals the depths and contours of our shattered national soul.

Fortune is divided into three parts. Part one explores the roots of our national story of race. Part two explores the toxic fruits of legal, judicial, legislative, and social decisions made that entrenched racial hierarchy in our nation. Part three explores what it will take to repair what race broke in the world. Along the way you will be introduced to my ancestors. They lived in the times when consequential history was made. Their Black and Brown bodies absorbed the trauma of laws and judgments passed to forge a White nation. This will be an emotional journey. Where I lacked details about my ancestors' lives, I have filled in their stories with context. I discovered through this process that often context is text.

Context often shapes the lives of the oppressed. Drought demands the choice be made to either hack it out on the land or migrate and live. Racial terror demands a choice: be brutalized, fight back, or run. Slavocracy demanded choices of enslaved children sold far away from their parents and families: be overcome by the trauma of the loss or find ways to protect your heart from attaching again. Context often dictates text. The details of context are usually erased from the victor's narratives. Sometimes discovering those details is enough to fill in the narrative.

My mother took me and my toddler sisters to see the classic a cappella Black women's quartet Sweet Honey in the Rock in Philadelphia back in the 1970s. I will never forget how their hums and beats called forth the spirit of the ancestors like Jesus called forth Moses and Elijah. In a Carnegie Hall performance about a decade later, they explained that Harriet Tubman used to tell the people she conducted on the Underground Railroad, "Wade on in the water. It's gon' really be troubled water."[3] You can't get through troubled times without wading in.

We are in troubled times. There is no way around it: we must wade in, face the realities and costs of the hierarchies of human belonging that we constructed in our nation's earliest years. We must face the cost and figure out how to pay it. If we don't wade into the water, we will find ourselves in this same place ten generations from now, with new iterations of control and confinement for people of African descent and others, exploiting their labor and justifying inaction on the basis of a Whitewashed Jesus read through the lens of empire.

In the same way that my mother leaned over my small Brown body and sang, "Wade in the Water," I sing:

> Wade in the water
> God's gonna trouble the water

I am here—in the water. Enter in. Let's get to the other side.

PART ONE

THE ROOTS

There is a tiny road that leads to a dead end, tucked back beyond the coniferous trees that line Mount Vernon Road on Maryland's Eastern Shore. The trees stretch to the sky, lining a maze of backroads that meander their way to the Wicomico River. I wound through the maze on my second full day on the Eastern Shore—the birthplace of Britain's second North American colony.

The previous day, Betsy McCready, a helpful clerk at the local assessments and taxation office, marveled as I explained my research and requested her help in finding any land records connected to Sambo Game, Maudlin Magee, or their daughter, Fortune Game/Magee. Betsy explained that the archives would have those records. But Betsy took out a map and showed me something we both marveled over. Game Road is located at the very top of the property once owned by Mrs. Mary Day, the woman to whom Fortune Game/Magee was indentured. Three of Fortune's children were also indentured by Mrs. Day. It's probable, Betsy said, that Fortune and her children lived on that road during the time of their indenture. It is a historically Black alcove. We both wondered aloud if Game Road was named after the Game family.

Seven lots line Game Road. One ancient, abandoned two-story house with an attic sits at the entrance to the road, flanked by several smaller one-story rentals. I parked my car at the top of the road. Black dragonflies the size of a truck driver's thumb swarmed the road. They were everywhere, as if standing guard, protecting the land from those who would encroach upon this sleeping part of the world. History happened here. America's first race and gender laws were lived out here. The cost of those laws was borne and born here.

I got out of the car at the street sign: Game Road. There it was.

Part one of this book begins with the story of Fortune, my likely seventh-great-grandmother. Her teenage body absorbed the wrath of the first race, gender, and citizenship laws in this land. In our national imagination, the experience of slavery is the singular link that binds all African Americans. We are a nation of black and white, winners and losers, cowboys and Indians, with simple morals attached to every story. We don't like shades of gray, nuance, and complexity. In submission to our culture's dualistic narratives, we have cast our nation's foundational stories as if they were sketched by Disney or John Wayne. Virtual cardboard cutouts of slave plantation caricatures separate field slaves from house slaves and paint them as warring factions. This two-dimensional, dualistic diorama of slavery in the US is at best inaccurate. At worst, it is insidious. This caricature of what it means to be African American oversimplifies the complex, textured, and nuanced creation story of colonial and antebellum America, as well as the current US economic system built on the foundation of 246 years of free and exploited labor.

The American economy was built on a foundation of exploited blacksmiths and carpenters and accountants and engineers and doctors and architects and chefs and coachmen and footmen and musicians and preachers, as well as planters and pickers and herdsmen and nursemaids and butlers and housekeepers. Each one exploited. Each one brutalized. Each image of God crushed or twisted or covered or violated or starved under the smothering blanket of slavery. Each one's sweat built this country. Each one's body controlled by the political and legal constructs of Whiteness in order to secure and protect global, economic, social, and cultural dominance for Europe and people of European descent.

Yet there is another dimension to the complex roots of America's racialized economy. There was something even before chattel slavery. Many of the earliest Africans in the US who were brought to the first colonies from the Caribbean, or born here before Virginia erected the first legal scaffolding of chattel slavery in North America in 1662, were indentured servants, not slaves. Indenture was not a race-based system. England's courtier class often received land grants and leased the labor of indentured European immigrants, Native Americans, and Africans to cultivate the land. Indentured servitude had a time limit of four to seven years, though people of African descent often did not benefit from time limits, because masters would fail to keep accurate records of their years of service, making it possible to hold Black servants indefinitely.

Lest the idea take root that indenture was equivalent to employment with labor protections, as we experience today, it was not. Indenture was slavery with an expiration date. Indentured servants were legally owned by their masters during the time of their indenture. They were property. Servants were beaten, pilloried, and whipped, tongues were bored, ears were cropped or nailed. Like the enslaved, escaped servants were hamstrung, hung on public display, or quartered as a warning for the masses. The women were raped. All with legal impunity. Courts added four to seven years to women's service as penalty for bearing children out of wedlock, and their children were indentured for decades—a punch to the gut for indentured women whose children were conceived as a result of rape by men in their indenturing families.

One thing I've learned in my research is that law is rarely, if ever, crafted in response to philosophical belief. Law is crafted to deal with real-time issues rising from common life in a society. Such was the case for the construction of race laws in the US. Through the story of Fortune we will encounter the initial system and its cost on Black and mixed-race bodies.

Next, we will encounter the Lawrence line, which is pure mystery with multiple possibilities and some I'm sure I have not yet conceived. In undertaking an African American family history you encounter a brick wall when you reach past the Civil War into antebellum slavocracy. Our family was fortunate that the Lawrence brothers were emancipated between 1850 and 1860, so we know something of their lives before the war. Still, the mystery overwhelms at times, and I have attempted to fill it in by tracing two possible narratives, given the evidence we have.

Finally, I will introduce you to Lea, who slaved in South Carolina—the last adult enslaved person in my family. Lea lived in the time of slavery, Reconstruction, and survived the deprivation of Jim Crow. She and her daughter Martha will reveal the particular burden of Black women attempting to survive race in America.

These are the roots of race in America. Political, legislative, and judicial decisions were made in this genesis era. They laid the political, economic, social, and spiritual foundations of America's slavocracy, Jim Crow segregation, redlining, and our persistent racial hierarchy. In the tradition of the Ghanaian Sankofa bird, our feet are faced forward—moving forward toward repair—but we cannot repair without turning our gaze back to understand how we broke. In part one, we encounter our genesis story—not the meta-story dictated by nobility and embedded in official narratives. No. This genesis story rises from court, tax, and military records and from the DNA of the oppressed. Hidden in these stories is the substance of the break—and the key to our collective repair.

1

Fortune

How Race Became Law

Mixed-race, eighteen-year-old Fortune Game/Magee stood alone in the quaint wooden courthouse in Somerset County, Maryland. Fortune lived and breathed and had her being in the exact days when English settlers built the legal framework that eventually enslaved more than four million people of African descent on American soil. Standing in that courtroom, Fortune's "mulatto" (mixed) body was used by the pioneers of our nation's legal framework to establish, enforce, and protect White supremacy. Their strategy? Snatch and suppress the flourishing of everyone else. This is the crack in our national foundation. Fortune felt that crack in her body.

I imagine Fortune sitting in the Somerset County courtroom having no control over her future. Her only crime was being born of a mixed-race couple. Black and White—that was the demarcation line between bondage and freedom in Fortune's days. But her court proceedings took place on ground layered with iterations of White nationalist subjugation.

The Somerset courthouse was built on land stewarded for thousands of years by the Nanticoke Nation and other neighboring

37

tribes. A tidewater farming nation, Nanticoke towns lined expansive swaths of rivers and creeks that flowed into the Chesapeake Bay, serving as main veins of transportation and sources of food. The towns were established deep in the surrounding marshes and swamps, where the people found emergent plants with edible roots. The land was plush with tall forest trees whose top branches seemed to weave together and touch the sky and whose roots stretched deep into the marshy earth.[1]

The doctrine of discovery was developed from a 1455 edict of Pope Nicholas V that granted the right of explorers to claim "uncivilized" land for the crown and enslave its people. Formally named *Romanus Pontifex*, this edict served as the legal foundation for the conquest of indigenous lands across the globe. In typical fashion, since the 1620s Virginia-based English traders conducted business with the Eastern Shore's indigenous nations, navigating a competitive market that traded guns, gunpowder, axes, hoes, Dutch cloth, and other goods in exchange for corn and fur. After more than a decade of trade, Lord Baltimore leveraged the doctrine of discovery to receive title to the land in 1632. He named it Maryland after Henrietta Maria, the wife of King Charles I, asserting the supremacy of England in the territory.[2] This was the way. Europeans landed on land and leveraged their own laws without respect to the laws of the indigenous peoples. They claimed the land and subjugated the people, leveraging their labor for White flourishing. For White men to flourish, Brown ones had to bow.

Over the next thirty years, Maryland's Eastern Shore went from a remote fur-trading outpost to a proprietary plantation colony of English courtiers, African and Native American indentured servants, Quakers, Ulster Scots (Scotch-Irish migrants), and a growing population of free men and women of mixed African, Native, and European descent.[3] Native tribes were removed to remote tracts of land and reservations. European racial logic was largely applied informally in these initial stages. Racialized hierarchies were imposed implicitly through the attachment of "Negro" or "Indian" or "Irish" to a person's name, and prejudice was largely exercised directly by individuals rather than in racialized systems, structures, and laws. The first official race laws developed in the colony of Virginia and then Maryland over these three decades. They took root in social and economic interactions, then through the courts, and finally through the legislature. Laws flow from and reveal the hearts of a society. I imagine Fortune's life before entering that courtroom. She knew the heart of that society. In her early colonial Maryland, race laws were in nascent form, born from the hearts of her neighbors and their White world. White supremacy and White privilege were explicit. They were assumed. And they were relentless.

Each word spoken by the prosecutor, the judge, and witness after witness wedged Fortune further away from freedom. Freedom— that condition ordained by God for all humanity on the first page of the Bible: "Then God said, 'Let us make humankind in our image, according to our likeness; and let them have dominion over the fish of the sea, and over the birds of the air, and over the cattle, and over all the wild animals of the earth, and over every creeping thing that creeps upon the earth'" (Gen. 1:26). God said all humanity bears the image of the divine. God said all humanity is called by God and created with the capacity to exercise dominion in the world. God said this of Fortune. She was human. She was born to run and laugh and love and flirt and be courted and marry and have children (or not have children) and help steward the world—to make choices that protect, serve, and cultivate her family, her community, her town, and her nation.

This is what it means to be human. This is what it would have meant for the law to see Fortune as human. But on that day in 1705, in the Somerset County courthouse, men of European descent spoke with conviction and agreed on one basic premise: Fortune Magee may be half-White, but she was not fully White. Further, she was a woman—designed for use by men. Three decades of ever-changing race codes that reflected increasingly hardened ideas of race and commitment to White supremacy brought Fortune to this moment. She stood amid White men who looked at her and did not see a human being. They looked at her mixed-race body and saw a challenge to their supremacy.

Fortune was the daughter of Maudlin Magee, a married Ulster Scots woman, and Sambo Game, an enslaved man likely from eastern Senegal. Fortune's parents were brought to Maryland on separate ships that swayed and swelled with the tides of the Atlantic. One ship from the north, one from the south. One brought Ulster Scots men and women to be indentured to English landowners as payment for their ticket from Belfast to the New World. The other ship dragged shackled men, some sold by their nations' enemies into a kind of slavery they had never known.

From slave castle to the putrid hull of a slave ship, a man named Sambo was forced aboard a ship in shackles. His name comes from the eastern borderlands of Senegal, at the intersection between Senegal, Mali, and Guinea. Sambo means "second son." Sambo was likely marched onto a slave ship in the colony of Gambia, warred over by the English and French for more than a century. Surrounded by Senegal on all sides except for its western coast, Gambia contained one major resource, the Gambia River—home to one of the earliest slave trading ports.

The race laws governing Fortune's trial were developed in direct response to an explosion of Black bodies in the Chesapeake from the 1670s through 1700. Until 1670, most enslaved Africans in the Chesapeake were brought by way of the Caribbean: Barbados, Nevis, and Antigua.[4] But conditions changed, and the Royal African Company incorporated in 1662. Leveraging technological innovations, the Royal African Company expanded England's slave trading capacity. Advances made it possible to bring enslaved Africans directly from Africa to the Chesapeake, with no need to stop in the Caribbean along the way. Middle Passage death rates declined, reducing the costs of shipping and purchase. In 1670, approximately two thousand Black people walked the Chesapeake shores. By 1700, that number had exploded to thirteen thousand.[5]

Between 1670—the approximate year genealogists believe Sambo was born[6]—and 1687—the year Fortune was born—only one single slave ship deboarded in Maryland. The *Speedwell* was a vessel owned by the Royal African Company and managed by Captain Marmaduke Goodhand. Goodhand guided his crew across nearly three thousand miles south from London to the banks of the Gambia River and docked there on March 7, 1686.[7]

The Middle Passage was hell—in every way, hell. Separated from his family and all who loved him, his homeland, his customs and culture, Sambo began his Middle Passage before hitting the water. It began when he was likely captured by a warring kingdom and traded to European traders in exchange for thick ceramic beads made by women in Europe.

The Middle Passage was a journey from human to unhuman—preparation for the complete subjugation necessary to undergird exclusive White flourishing. Bought as if no more than inanimate beads, Sambo was roped together with other purchased cargo. They marched like mules across hundreds of miles to slave ports along the lush banks of the Gambia River. There, Sambo, whom evidence suggests was my family's second son, would have been branded with the letter *G* to indicate his port of origin. The brand did not trace his tribe of origin, his lingual group of origin, nor his family of origin. No, it marked his port of origin. Sambo was in the process of becoming a thing.

He was then packed in a small dungeon or stockade with hundreds of other men. The women were stored separately. They sat in darkness for months with no toilet; excrement filled the space and became the mud they walked on. Occasional light poured in as they opened the doors to push more human cargo into this storage room that rivaled any European dungeon reserved for criminals. Sambo's only crime was to be born a strong Senegalese man from a region close to one of the great cities of the medieval world—Timbuktu, Mali, where the Sankore Mosque served as the Harvard of West Africa with multiple library collections dating back to the fourteenth century.

The *Speedwell* sat in port along the Gambia River for three months—until enough human cargo was purchased to meet Captain Goodhand's quota. Goodhand had intended to negotiate the purchase of 225 humans on this trip, but he fell short by eight souls. He set sail with 217 men, women, and children packed like toothpicks below deck.[8]

Like thousands before and hundreds of thousands after, Sambo's teenage body climbed the ladder out of the crypt-like bowels of the ship. He stepped onto the swelling deck where he stood naked, shackled to men from across the region—most likely from modern-day Senegal, Gambia, Mali, Guinea, and Niger. At the time, their lands had not yet been carved like European nation-states. They were kingdoms, dynasties, and tribal nations. The principal language of Senegal was Wolof. Sambo is a Wolof name. Other languages spoken between the captive men and women would have included Mandinka, Pulaar, and Diola, as well as nearly thirty-five other local languages from neighboring regions.[9]

White men stared back at them and barked orders they did not understand. The White men would have looked like ghosts to eyes accustomed to melanin-soaked skin.

I imagine sixteen-year-old Sambo looked past them, over the waters in the direction of home. He imagined his father, his mother, his siblings. He wondered if he would ever see them or his homeland or his boyhood crush again. He had no idea what awaited him on the other side of these four thousand miles and two months. He only knew he had to survive. Sambo did survive. Twenty-five souls aboard the *Speedwell* did not. Their hardened bodies were dragged from their excrement-filled slabs, hoisted above deck, and thrown overboard. Records indicate that the boat ran thirty-five tons over average capacity, so it's also possible that during the journey some who were still alive were chained together and pushed into the sea to reconcile the ship's weight or food supply. Over the course of the transatlantic slave trade, approximately two million souls, dead or alive, were tossed overboard and became one with the Atlantic Ocean.

We don't know exactly how Sambo and Maudlin came together. We only know they were brought to the English colony of Maryland within years of each other.

After the better part of a century partnering with Britain in its subjugation of the Irish and the exploitation of Irish land, Ulster Scots now sought escape from growing poverty, exclusion from civil society, and the shuttering of Protestant houses of worship anticipated to spike with the imminent ascension to the throne of Catholic King James II in 1685. Many Presbyterian ministers considered an exodus to the New World. George Magee boarded a ship bound for Maryland in 1682. Though not listed on the ship's manifest, Maudlin was likely with him.[10]

George and Maudlin's Ulster Scots exodus shares a common source with Fortune's subjugation: the British pursuit of exclusive flourishing. The force that threatened Fortune's future did not rise from American soil. It rose from the machinations of the British Empire, which traces its lineage to the Greek and Roman Empires. As with their imperial forebears, the British saw only themselves as fully human. Britain was for British flourishing. Non-Britons existed for the flourishing of the British Empire. British supremacy subjugated the Ulster Scots and the Northern Irish, because the empire asked a simple question: "Who is Irish land for?" Britain. In the New World, they asked the same question: "Who are the colonies for?" Britain. But sexual politics and the progeny of mixed-race relations complicated the question of British citizenship. Fortune stood before this British colonial court because Maudlin's love for a Senegalese man threatened White male supremacy—and Fortune's body was the evidence. Fortune fell within the crosshairs of decisions made four decades before, when Virginia's and Maryland's planter-class legislators placed race and sexual politics at the center of the question of British citizenship. Their foundational race and gender laws preserved their fortunes and built the legal scaffolding that entrenches and protects White male flourishing to this day.

In 1654, mixed-race Elizabeth Key legally challenged her enslavement on the basis of three points: (1) British law barred the enslavement of British citizens; (2) British common law established the citizenship of the child through the status of the father; and (3) British law barred the enslavement of baptized Christians. Key argued that her father was a British citizen, thus she too was a British citizen. Her father had recognized her as his own and had baptized her as a young girl. Therefore, Key must be set free. She won her case and opened the door for several more enslaved people in Virginia to win their freedom on the same basis in subsequent years.

The Virginia House of Burgesses was threatened by the prospect of losing legal claim to generations of free labor and incalculable wealth. So it moved to close the loopholes that Key's case revealed. It passed legislation in 1662 that was modeled after the Roman law of *partus sequitur ventrem*, which determined the citizenship status of the child according to the status of the mother, not the father. This shift allowed White slaveholders to continue raping enslaved Black women and producing mixed-race free labor with absolute impunity. British masters no longer had to acknowledge their children before the law, so their children had no claim to citizenship under British law. This single law laid the foundation for the legal construct of race in the US.

In 1664 the Maryland General Assembly followed Virginia's lead. But Maryland's slightly different context led its assembly to a slightly different legal strategy to maintain White male supremacy. That strategy shaped Fortune's future and the futures of all her descendants—myself included.

Maryland colonists enslaved Africans as early as 1640, but legislators did not begin to embed slavery into the colony's legal framework until 1664. Four elements converged to launch Maryland's quest to weave racial hierarchy into its legal structure.

First, the African share of the total Maryland population increased dramatically. In 1640 there were only 20 people of African descent in the colony with 600 Europeans. By 1660 there were 760 people of African descent in a population of 8,500 Europeans. White dominance was facing a demographic challenge.

Second, by the 1660s, Maryland was solidly a tobacco territory. The planter class needed more free labor to meet increased demand.

Third, the newly established Royal African Company offered the promise of increased access to enslaved labor.

And fourth, with more Africans in the colony, mixed-race children were causing a conundrum within the implied racial hierarchy—particularly the baptized children of European women and African men. Some six hundred mixed-race children were born in Maryland and Delaware in the colonial era. All of the free Black families descended from White women and their mixed-race descendants.[11]

These elements compelled the Maryland General Assembly to pass the first of a series of race laws in 1664. The first iteration transformed enslavement to a lifelong identity rather than a state of indenture or a condition that could be changed. The Maryland General Assembly kept English common law, which passed citizenship through the lineage of the father. Unlike with the Virginia House of Burgesses, Maryland legislators perceived their problem to be the mixed-race progeny of White women gaining their freedom. To boot, the assembly declared that the children of marriages between White women and enslaved Black men would be enslaved for life, and all their descendants after them. The White woman would also become the enslaved property of her husband's master until her husband's death. Finally, the children of married White women and enslaved Black men would be enslaved for life if born *after* the law went into force. But if born *before* the law passed, they would serve their father's master for thirty-one years.

Fortune's father was enslaved, but she stood in that Somerset County courtroom to face the prospect of indenture precisely because she was not enslaved upon birth. She likely had been able to live free until she was eighteen years old. Why? Because of White privilege.

Lord Baltimore Charles Calvert, grandson of the first Lord Baltimore, brought sixteen-year-old Eleanor Butler with him from England to Maryland in 1681—six years before Fortune was born. Butler fell in love with and married an enslaved man, identified in court records as "Negro Charles." She appealed to her friend Lord Baltimore to repeal the 1664 law, which required Eleanor's immediate enslavement and the enslavement of all her children for life, in perpetuity. Calvert immediately moved to repeal the original 1664 race law. It was rescinded and replaced with the 1681 race law, which acknowledged an unscrupulous practice that had developed since passage of the original law. Masters were forcing their White indentured servant women to marry the masters' enslaved African men. This practice reaped exponential increases in planters' free labor force over generations. Maryland's legislature limited the scope of the law to forced marriages between Black men and White women and dropped the requirement that their children be enslaved. The result? As of 1681, all newborn mixed-race children would be born free.[12]

According to Maryland State Park historian Ross M. Kimmel, Butler benefited only marginally from Lord Baltimore's efforts. She was still enslaved because her marriage took place before the 1681 law was passed. But as a White woman, she was afforded liberties not usually afforded to enslaved people. Still, her children and descendants were born after the 1681 repeal. They should have been born free.[13] The 1681 law provided the children free status regardless of which parent was White.[14] Butler's grandchildren were enslaved. They appealed to the courts in 1710. Around the time of the Revolutionary War, they finally won.[15]

Fortune's fate should have been equally clear. She stood before the judge in 1705. The eighteen-year-old girl listed as a "mulatto" in court documents should have been subject to Lord Baltimore's 1681 law. But in the interim, the Maryland General Assembly soured on Lord Baltimore and replaced his law with a harsher, more comprehensive, racialized legal structure in 1692—five years *after* Fortune's birth.

The new law protected White women and their children from slavery by removing the financial impetus for their enslavement. They would be indentured to the local parish, not enslaved by the master. The parishes were ordered to transact the sales of enslaved Black men and indentured White and mixed-race servants to White families. The proceeds of those sales assisted poor Whites in the parish.[16]

The 1692 Maryland Race Law

1. Any non-servant freeborn white woman who married a black man was to become a servant of her church parish for seven years. Her husband, if free, was to become a slave for the parish.
2. If the woman was a servant, she was to serve out her remaining time, with additions for time lost due to pregnancies, and then she was to become a servant to the parish for seven years, provided the match was not forced upon her by her master.
3. Children of mixed marriages were to be servants of the parish for twenty-one years.
4. If the miscegenating couple was not married, the woman was to suffer the seven-year penalty, the child was to serve for thirty-one years, but the husband, if free, was only to serve for seven years instead of life.
5. The same penalties befalling a white woman as detailed above were to apply to any white man begetting any black woman with child.
6. Any master forcing a marriage was to forfeit ten thousand pounds of tobacco.

Source: Ross M. Kimmel, "Blacks before the Law in Colonial Maryland" (MA thesis, University of Maryland, 1974), chap. 3, https://msa.maryland.gov/msa/speccol/sc5300/sc5348/html/chap3.html; Proceedings and Acts of the General Assembly, April 1684–June 1692, in *Archives of Maryland* (1894), 13:546–48, available at https://msa.maryland.gov/megafile/msa/speccol/sc2900/sc2908/000001/000013/html/am13--547.html.

In essence, at the turn of the eighteenth century, *the church itself became the primary auction block in Maryland*. The grotesque nature of this arrangement cannot be overstated. The church joined the banks, insurance companies, shipping companies, iron works, and other institutions in crushing the image of God on this land. The church was the principle protector and manager of White supremacy through the trade of enslaved and indentured human beings in America's second colony.

According to the 1692 law, a child of a White mother could not be enslaved. Period. The race of the mother became the determining factor of slave or free status.[17] But intolerance of interracial relationships hardened in this law. White women and their children could still be indentured as penalty for miscegenation—married or not. A penalty of seven years indenture was given to the woman and twenty-one years indenture to the child if the parents were married—or thirty-one years indenture for the child if the parents were not married.

Standing before the court, eighteen-year-old Fortune was born free and should have remained free according to Lord Baltimore's 1681 legal turnabout. But of course the application of law is different from the law itself. Fortune's fate was largely dependent on the judge, especially in this formative period of colonial race law. Would the judge see and honor the legislative merits of Fortune's fight to stay free? Or would his sensibilities align more with the racialized hardening of the times?

I imagine Fortune, awaiting the judge's decision, looking out a window to her left, just behind the prosecutor offering his closing argument for Fortune's indenture. Her heartbeat races. Beads of sweat form on her forehead as she wipes sweaty palms on her dress. She clasps her high yellow hands—the only thing she has to hold on to in this moment is herself. I imagine Fortune thinking of the woman who birthed her, Maudlin.

We know so little of Maudlin other than the fact that she was an indentured Ulster Scots woman married to an Ulster Scot, George Magee, with whom she bore three children. Maudlin's first child was John Magee, born one year before Fortune. The year after Fortune's birth, Maudlin and George brought Peter Magee into the world and three years after that she gave birth to Samual. Historian Paul Heinegg cites the judicial record of this court proceeding, as well as land tax records indicating that Maudlin was alive and living with her husband George as late as 1705—the year of this trial. Yet, there is no record of her presence.[18]

With possible moments left in her free life, I imagine Fortune's thoughts turning to her father, Sambo. He, too, was born free. He, too, was bound and sold as a teen. He, too, lived on the other side of Whiteness, daily surviving the branding iron of legal

Blackness. Enslaved to Constable Peter Douty, Sambo and his wife were willed free and given land upon Douty's death, five years after Fortune's trial. We know that he and Fortune were close. She would take his surname and later live with him on that land. Evidence suggests Sambo may have been a healer. His son, Harry, was a practicing doctor in 1750. He credited his knowledge to an "old experienced Guinea doctor"—likely Sambo, who was from a region that intersected Senegal, Guinea, and Mali, before national boundaries were drawn. Sambo was a learned man who passed down what he knew to the next generation. It makes me wonder what he passed down to Fortune that was in turn passed down to us.

Fortune stood at the precipice of bondage with only the memories of her freedom and her family to give her comfort. Indenture was just as brutal as slavery. Indentured servants were whipped and maimed as punishment. Fortune did not know what was in store for her, and she had no control over it—perhaps that combination is the essence of the terror of bondage, whether enslaved or indentured. She held within her both this unknowing and a complete lack of control over her own body, life, and family.

When I imagine eighteen-year-old Fortune in that courtroom, I find my own breath shortening in anticipation of the ruling. With short breaths, Fortune likely listened as the judge asked her if she understood her sentence. She was hereby ordered to retroactive indentured service to Mrs. Mary Day until the age of thirty-one years old.

Twenties gone.

Freedom gone.

Safety for herself and her daughters? Gone, gone.

***

Fortune served Mary Day for every one of her sentenced years. She bore two daughters before entering her court-ordered service to Mary Day on June 15, 1705. Rose and Sue Magee were joined by three more sisters born while Fortune was in Mary Day's service— Perlina Game, Betty Game, and Sarah Game/Fortune. No father is attributed to any of Fortune's children. Why? We do not know. Here is what we do know.

According to the 1715 race law and its 1728 amendment, if Fortune bore illegitimate children by a White man, the children would be indentured for twenty-one years. If the man was Black, the children would be indentured for thirty-one years.[19] Fortune indentured her first three children, Rose, Sue, and Perlina, to Mary Day as apprentices for twenty-one years—evidence that their father(s) were White.

In fact, the interdependent relationships between the Day and Fortune/Game families was, to an odd degree, like family. Fortune's daughter Betty Game inherited fifty acres from George Day Scott,[20] the grandson of Mary Day.[21] And Sarah's son, James, born in 1745, indentured himself as an apprentice to James Laws, a White man mentioned in Mary Day's deed. Laws helped James establish himself in a trade.[22] On the northern edge of Mary Day's land, in a remote corner of a historic Black community, sits Game Road. Game Road is likely where Fortune and her children lived when they were indentured to the Day family. The families were so intertwined, the Days likely named a road on their property after the Games.

But the law erected barriers to Fortune and her daughters marrying any man, Black or White. White men who chose to marry any of the Game/Fortune women would be indentured for seven years. If Fortune or her daughters married an enslaved Black man, they would be indentured for an additional seven years. In fact, women whose mothers and grandmothers were Black were the only women who bore no legal penalty for sexual relations with any man, nor did any man who exploited them and fathered children by them suffer any penalty. White men benefited from this legal loophole. The children of Black women provided them with free enslaved labor for life.

While researching, I learned to ask the question, Who benefits from this law? The answer was always the same: White men—planter-class White men. Always. These are our legal foundations.

It was common for mixed-race women, like Fortune and her daughters, to become pregnant while in the service of their indenturing families. No fathers were listed, likely because the fathers were in these courtier families and networks. The law required indenture for White men who bore illegitimate children by mixed-race women. But the law and its application are two different things. Planter-class legislators likely imagined enacting that law on poor White men, providing a bonus source of free labor. But when legal infraction implicated a White courtier or planter, the secret was kept and never investigated by the court. In the colonial hierarchy of human belonging, planter-class and courtier-class White men possessed the full image of God—all law existed to benefit them.

I got curious. I decided to check Ancestry.com DNA matching to see if I shared DNA with descendants of the families that indentured Fortune and Sarah. Sure enough, Ancestry.com DNA matching in 2019 indicated that I am likely a distant relative of both the Day and Fooks (and possible Fowke) families.

Fortune and Sarah were likely serially raped by members of the households they were ordered to serve. When they became pregnant, they were penalized with additional time added to their indenture. And their children were indentured for decades. They had no control over what happened to their children from birth to adulthood. It is a miracle that most of Fortune's children came back to her, living with or around her over the course of their lives. But it seems the vast majority of Sarah's children were lost to her.

Though Heinegg could confirm only one son of Sarah Fortune, he indicated that Sarah very well could have had more children not listed in court records, with those churchwarden records perhaps not surviving.[23] Plus, there are several other free mulatto Fortune relatives who appear in Essex, Caroline, and Hanover Counties in Virginia as early as 1769.[24] After her service Sarah returned to the Eastern Shore of Maryland, leaving her children with their masters in Charles County, which is just across the Potomac River from Virginia's Caroline, Essex, and Hanover Counties. It is entirely possible that the siblings were brought to Virginia by their indenturing families. They also could have simply chosen, upon release, to cross the river and move westward into Virginia, following the general flow of migration at the time. DNA clusters connect my family's line with one of these Fortune siblings—most likely Humphrey Fortune.

The Maryland General Assembly tried but did not prevent the mixing of the races through its race laws. The lives, indentures, descendants, and financial relationships of Fortune and her daughters are evidence that interracial sexual relationships took place after the passage of antimiscegenation laws. The laws eventually leveled penalties on both Black and White people, but they were not applied equally. While the law was levied with full force and even misapplied against women of color like Fortune, the law rarely if ever penalized planter-class White men.

Here is what the laws did prevent. They prevented many Black and mixed-race women from being protected by, provided for by, and committed to one man. They blocked Black and mixed-race children from knowing the shelter and full protection of parents for more than 250 years. Reverberations roll through the generations, taking up residence in our very bodies. Our bodies are the evidence.

And there is a broader cost. America's race laws laid foundations for antidemocracy within the world's first democracy. Democracy is inherently about equity and fairness—one person, one vote. Since 1662, thumbs were placed on the legal scales of this land. From that point forward we lived in a jerry-rigged democracy— held together with duct tape and Elmer's glue. Black people lost more and more freedoms over time until we were dangling from trees and being dredged from rivers. Why? To protect the 1662 supremacy of Whiteness.

We wonder how our nation has come to its present moment. We watch as today's courtier class—legislators, Fortune 500 businessmen, and celebrities—break every law with impunity. They bilk the system. They pay no taxes. They openly lie and cheat and steal. They even wage war on democracy itself through voter suppression and insurrection. These attacks on the core of American identity are swept under the proverbial rug. This 1662 law broke our nation—even before it began. That is our genesis.

By the time Fortune ended her service to Mary Day in 1718, she had adopted the last name Game, clearly identifying with her Senegalese father. Ten years later she owned land and lived with two of her children. Fortune's daughters chose sides in their choices of surnames, identifying with either the Senegalese Games or the Scotch-Irish Magees. But Sarah chose neither. She changed her last name to Fortune, likely lifting up her mother as the inherited treasure of her family. For more than 150 years to come—approximately eight generations—on Maryland's Eastern Shore and in colonial Virginia, the surname Fortune would spell f-r-e-e-d-o-m.

On the 1880 census, my second-great-grandfather Robert Fortune and his wife Mary J. Byrd lived next door to the Loving family in Caroline County, Virginia. Nearly a century after that, the Loving family challenged Virginia's 1662 race law in the Supreme Court case *Loving v. Virginia* (1967). Richard Loving and Mildred Jeter fell in love, got married, and were thrown in jail. Their Supreme Court win repealed Virginia's 1662 race law and knocked down laws that banned interracial marriage in seventeen states, effectively pulling up the legal root of American racialized hierarchy. The couple's daughter, Peggy, married a Fortune.[25]

2

The Lawrences

Fragmented Identity

A photo of Hiram Lawrence, my great-grandfather (my mother's father's father), peered down from her mantle, a protective and guiding presence. In the sepia-toned photo, Hiram leans back in his armchair, his left leg crossed over the right, his right arm resting while his left hand holds a corn husk pipe to a face creased with both worry and wisdom. Hiram's son Junius (my grandfather) took the photograph circa 1956. I always wondered what happened right before or after Hiram took that portrait. My mother recently shared that there used to be a sister picture with this one. It captured the moment after, when my mother climbed her eight-year-old body onto her grandpop's lap and snuggled up next to him in the same chair.

I never met Hiram. He died in 1958—cancer.

Hiram and the Lawrence line were always more mystery than certainty—and they still are. One of the greatest costs of the construct of race in the United States is how it severs people from their roots, their families, their people, their land, and their stories. Hiram was severed, but he tried. Oh, God, did he try.

Another picture of Hiram sat among the canon of family memories. In the photograph Hiram is an old man. He sits cross-legged on the bare ground with his two toddler grandchildren—my mother and her brother Richie. They are holding glass soda bottles. Hiram used to take them on hikes through the woods and marshlands on the edges of Philadelphia, Pennsylvania. He would sit them in a circle and tell them stories of the way things used to be. Decades after Hiram's passing, my mother shared with me one fragment of a memory she cherished: Hiram's favorite author was Daniel Webster.

"Webster," she said, "fought the Indian removals."

When my mother was a child, her older half-brother, Larry, told her a story: One day, circa 1940, Larry's ten-year-old hands gripped the front doorknob of his grandfather's house in the community of Elwood in Philadelphia. He turned the knob. As the door swung back, Larry found a tall brown man standing on the front steps. The man's name remained a mystery to little Larry. He watched his father, Junius, invite the man in. At the time, Larry was visiting his grandfather in a Black community on the edge of Philadelphia. Larry, Junius, and Hiram—son, father, and grandfather—sat with the stranger in Hiram's living room as the nameless man tried to convince Larry's Grandpop, Hiram, to join his Cherokee/Chickasaw family in Oklahoma. They had struck oil, the man said.

But Hiram liked the way his family was living. He owned land, a lot of it. He owned several houses on one block in quaint, marshy Elmwood. He rented his homes to families streaming north at the height of the Great Migration. Hiram did not want to leave Philadelphia, where he had planted roots after years in the Navy exploring the world. So, he didn't. He never left the border city between North and South—the City of Brotherly Love, even though that city ultimately betrayed him by seizing his property under the legal banner of eminent domain.

Continuity of people groups on particular land produces a relationship with that land. This is the nature of indigenous peoples' relationship with particular land across the globe. As the people sow into the land, so they reap. As they care for the land, so the land cares for the people. As they live and breathe and birth and bury on the land, so stories of community life and hardship and struggle and overcoming are tied to that land.

In this way, continuity of place also reaps strong family and community ties. Families and communities bond as they dream together of what life can offer on that land. Their common struggles, triumphs, and defeats encountered through time on that land build common identity and a sense of belonging, both to the people and to the land.

From Genesis to Revelation, the biblical Hebrews built a relationship with the land that we now call Israel and Palestine over a period of nearly two thousand years. They built memorials on that land to mark births, deaths, and marriages. Stories were passed down from generation to generation so that the next generation would know who they are—to whom they belong. War, colonization, plague, and famine disrupted life for the Hebrews, separating them from their land. We see them stolen from the land by Assyria, Babylon, and Persia. We see them migrate from the land to Egypt in search of food. We see the Romans occupy and colonize the land, pouring salt on the soil so that the land can no longer bear fruit. And we see references to the land in the stories, songs, and lessons that form the people, from the tree of life and the tree of the knowledge of good and evil in Genesis 2 to the psalmist's prophecy in Psalm 85 that truth will spring from the earth and justice will shine down from heaven and the earth will yield its increase to Jesus's calming of the storm, commanding the fish, and dying on a hill called Golgotha to the new Jerusalem and the tree of life prophesied in the last chapter of Revelation.

Likewise the Cherokee and Chickasaw people; the Lakota and Potawatomi; the Celts and Sami; the Taíno, Inca, and Aztec; the Yoruba, Igbo, Fulani, and Hausa; the Aboriginal, the South Sea Islander, and the Hawaiian; the Lano and Biak peoples of the Papuan tribe; and the Palestinian people—all are indigenous with thousands of years of struggle, triumphs, colonization, removal, and return to their ancestral lands. Their collective identity, communal lessons, and deeply rooted sense of belonging have grown over thousands of years in relationship with their lands, their people, and their stories.

In every corner of the world, a primary weapon of Western domination has been to cut off indigenous and other subjugated peoples from their lands, from their families and communities, and from the stories that tie them together. Colonization wields four crucial weapons of conquest in its arsenal of mass destruction: genocide, slavery, removal, and rape. These weapons hack people groups apart, separating them from land, people, story, and identity. These weapons yield for colonizers more land for production of wealth, fewer foes to threaten wealth, and low-cost or no-cost labor to grow wealth.

The impact of colonization on the conquered is fragmentation. Four generations after the conquest, memory itself is fragmented. Names of family members are often lost. Family and community stories are forgotten, forbidden, twisted, or hidden. Meanwhile, the colonized are forced to rehearse and remember their new identity, which is usually tied to the slave master's story—their surname, the name of the reservation, township, or favela to which they were removed, or (as in South Africa) the month of the year in which they were sold. These grafted stories usually begin at the point of colonization or enslavement. To seal the deal, subsequent generations were often educated apart from their parents and people. They were taught their people's story by the colonizers, from the point of view of the settlers, in schools with curricula established by those settlers.

Six generations have passed since the Lawrence family appeared out of nowhere on the 1850 census in Sulphur Springs, Kentucky. Only fragments of family memory remain. My mother remembers her father, Junius, telling me we were from the Cherokee and Chickasaw nations. My Uncle Larry explained to me that Grandpop Hiram told him we descend from the Chickasaw. My grandmother gifted me a Native American beaded necklace upon my Grandpop Junius's passing. She said it had been handed down in our family for generations. I cherished that necklace. Then one day, it unraveled in my hands. I remember the horror. I remember the beads rolling from my fingers. I don't remember how old I was or where I was. That moment is disconnected from time and space—standing on its own in my memory, rolling past my mind's eye as if in slow motion. Each bead dissembling from the others, the intricate handwoven pattern that had graced generations of Lawrence kin fell apart in my hands. Guilt and grief washed over—they still wash over. Surrounded by rolling beads, I cried hard in liminal space.

My father rolled away when I was nine, taken by divorce and remarriage. My mother moved us to Cape May, New Jersey when I was ten, drawn by love and remarriage. Separated from my Lawrence blood by hundreds of miles, my mother and sisters attempted to graft into the Harper family, but it's not the same. They could not replace blood. I spent my preteen and teenage years longing for that feeling of wholeness—completeness—we had when family who shared memory were together. When that necklace unraveled, I lost the only tangible connection to the family I never knew.

Fragmentation is a way of life for the colonized. From the genesis of imperial rule, settlers have uprooted themselves to procure land and people in pursuit of wealth and power for their empire. In Western civilization, citizens and subjects were not understood to belong to their families or to their land. Rather, the conquered ceded land to the conqueror. Both conquered and their land belonged to the republic—existing solely for the flourishing of the empire. In his treatise *The Republic*, Plato established the foundational belief that racial people groups exist to serve the republic in particular ways. Plato pontificated that race is the different metals that people groups are made of. He said some people are made of gold, others of silver, bronze, etc. He explained that a people group's race determines their contribution to the republic.[1] Flash forward to Virginia 1662 and Maryland 1664. Race in the British colonies distinguishes slave from free, citizen from noncitizen— the one created to flourish and exercise dominion on colonial land

and the other created to uphold White flourishing. But what of indigenous nations? What was their place in the racial schema?

In his groundbreaking documentary *Exterminate All the Brutes*, Raoul Peck explains settler colonialism: "As a system, it requires violence. It requires the elimination of the natives and their replacement by European settlers."[2] By this logic, indigenous peoples exist as a fundamental threat to the flourishing of Whiteness. They must be eradicated by either death or removal.

After decades of English settlers seizing land and on the heels of the discovery of gold in Dahlonega, Georgia, in the midst of an economic recession, President Andrew Jackson signed the Indian Removal Act of 1830. One year later, 15,000 Choctaws began a two-year-long walk to Indian Territory, now called Oklahoma. Approximately 2,500 died. Alexis de Tocqueville witnessed the removal and wrote, "In the whole scene there was an air of ruin and destruction, something which betrayed a final and irrevocable adieu; one couldn't watch without feeling one's heart wrung. . . . We watch the expulsion . . . of one of the most celebrated and ancient American peoples."[3]

From that point forward southeastern indigenous nations were removed one by one. The Seminole Nation, a creole nation principally swirling with native Floridian tribes, formerly enslaved Africans, and Muscogee (Creek) who fled the seventeenth-century Native American slave trade in Georgia and Alabama, escaped into Florida. In 1835, many Seminoles pushed deep into the Florida Everglades, refusing to leave their homelands. By 1837 more than one thousand American troops and Seminoles had died as the Seminole fought for their freedom. Their leader Osceola was captured in 1837. Some Seminole walked west. Others forged deeper into the Everglades—separated forever. From 1827 to 1838, twenty-three thousand Muscogee (Creek) were removed. Thousands died on their long walk to Indian Territory.[4] The Chickasaw took their first steps on the long walk in 1837.

The Tsalagi (Cherokee) people were rounded up in May 1838 and placed in open-air stockades in southeastern Tennessee. Many died in those stockades. Women were raped by soldiers while their men listened to their screams, divided from their wives and daughters in a separate holding pen.[5] Elders died of exposure while children wept from malnutrition and heartbreak. Then, in the dead of winter, in the middle of a blizzard, they were forced to forge their trail of tears. Sixteen thousand walked. Four thousand died. Many escaped. Others who lived along the route escaped into the mountains. They hid under assumed identities and listed themselves as White or Mulatto on the census—officially cut off from their core identity.

One or two trails of Lawrence blood that moved and lived and had their being in and around Sulphur Springs, Kentucky, are said to lead back to the Cherokee and Chickasaw Nations, according to family lore. We have little connection to the people—our people— anymore. We were cut off from them when forced to choose between dignity and death. Fragmented by settler colonization and our own survival tactics, memory itself is pockmarked with gaps, tangles, and confusion. All we have left of our people—our kin, who lived together for thousands of years before colonization—are shards of inherited memory and surviving pictures.

In 1926, at age forty-four, Hiram Lawrence received a phone call. The voice on the other end, I imagine, was his mother, Harriet. She spoke with a dialect painted with the twang of Kentucky mountain country but tempered by decades in Indiana's midwestern plains: "Your brother is dead," she said. "Come home."

Four years Hiram's junior, William died of a heart attack in Altoona, Pennsylvania, where he had settled in his adult years. He had never married and had no children. His body was making the journey from Altoona to his childhood home—Rockport, Indiana—where his mother and father fled after being chased out of Kentucky. William's body was on its way to Rockport to be buried in the Lawrence family plot.[6]

Barrel-chested, mixed-race Hiram knew not to risk entering a roadside restaurant to order off the menu on his way to Indiana— a northern state being settled by White southerners migrating to the Midwest in the wake of their own Great Migration from barren southern lands—monocropped to death. In Indiana's White mecca, Hiram's Black, White, and Cherokee/Chickasaw body (as he told it) would draw attention and invite violence like mosquitoes to water. Hiram likely loaded his truck with ham, cheese, apple butter, and bread prepared by his wife, Ella Fortune—Robert Fortune's granddaughter. He and his son, Junius, would make sandwiches and share stories on the two-day journey from Philadelphia to Rockport, Indiana. They would keep each other company on the road. This was Junie's chance to see his father's childhood home, to hear his father's stories of where they came from, to hear his memories of their people, and to meet, perhaps for the first time, his grandmother, Harriet Smith.

Harriet A. Smith is listed as White on the 1870 census. Nestled in the winding mountain-country of Sulphur Springs, Kentucky, Harriet lived in the household of Abraham Lawrence with his wife, Ava; Harriet's mother, Rosahana Barnett; and her little sister, Martha. Harriet's kin, Green and Finos Barnett, lived next door on either side of Abraham's house. Green worked as a sixteen-year-old farmhand for the Bennett family, while Finos was a nine-year-old boarder with another Bennett lot. Everyone was listed as White. Our family story corrects the record—or complicates it. They may have had some European heritage, but they were definitely not White, Hiram told his son, Junius, who then told my mother: They were Cherokee and Chickasaw. Abraham was Black and White. Why then was this mixed family living in a completely White community? And why were they all passing for White?

In the nascent years following the Civil War, with the stench of dead bodies hanging in the air, gaping holes in family structures where fathers and brothers would have occupied the space, some boys, girls, widows, and the lost and abandoned lived as boarders or workers in neighbors' homes. They cobbled together family frameworks out of family bits blown apart. The same is true for those who escaped the devastation of the Indian removals three decades earlier.

Cherokee and Chickasaw families had stewarded the lands of western Kentucky for thousands of years, and many never left

Kentucky's hill country. Even as their nations ceded land throughout the turn of the nineteenth century, numerous Cherokee and Chickasaw people stayed. In 1838, as US Army officers marched thousands of Cherokee westward from Red Clay, Tennessee, along the northern route of the Cherokee Trail of Tears, they passed Cherokee and Chickasaw people who were hiding in the hills to escape removal. Shrouded by thick forests in the highest hills of Sulphur Springs, we believe Harriet, Martha, Rosahana, Green, and Finos paid a significant cost to remain on their land. From the Trail of Tears through the Indian Wars of the West, my second-great-grandmother Harriet and her family and her kin likely presented themselves as White to the world as an act of resistance against colonial removal. Yet, who we really are was passed down from generation to generation. Their names are not on the Dawes Rolls, so we are not enrolled in either nation. All we have is the stories and the land, which bears witness.

Whites wanted the world—the whole world. They were determined to get it. Their strategy was to erase all color from the land. In the months following the Civil War, when unshackled men and women of African descent rose into full citizenship, White southerners cowered. They could not imagine a world where governance could be shared. They could not imagine a world without domination as the central goal of life. Free Africans, like free Cherokee, Chickasaw, Muscogee, Choctaw, and Seminole, presented an imminent threat to the flourishing of Whiteness. This was the same womb that birthed the Ku Klux Klan. Churning with fears of domination, delusions of ordained election, and the shame of weakened Whiteness, women sewed white hoods made of bedsheets to mask the frailty of their weakened husbands. The Thirteenth Amendment to the US Constitution ended chattel slavery in the United States. Ratified on December 6, 1865, that amendment dismantled much of the colonial foundations of racial hierarchy established more than two hundred years earlier by the Virginia House of Burgesses. Eighteen days after that ratification, former Confederate soldiers birthed the Ku Klux Klan in Pulaski, Tennessee, on December 24, 1865.

White sheets wreaked havoc for five years, terrorizing Black communities and White race traitors. Their ultimate goal was to establish a Confederate takeover of southern states. They failed. Congress passed the Fourteenth Amendment in 1868, establishing birthright citizenship. This provided the protection of citizenship to African Americans and signaled a sound rejection of Confederate politics in the new America. On March 30, 1870, Radical Republicans leveled the legal playing field of citizenship by passing and ratifying the Fifteenth Amendment, granting the vote to all men regardless of race, color, or previous condition of servitude.

Three and a half months after ratification of the Fifteenth Amendment—the ink still wet—Bunyon Duvall, assistant marshal of the census in Sulphur Springs, Kentucky, knocked on the door of thirty-five-year-old Civil War veteran Abraham Lawrence. Situated in this all-White Kentucky hill country, mixed-race Abraham was surrounded on all sides by White families. Duvall looked at Abraham, his family, and boarders—all light enough to pass—and wrote "W" next to each of their names—White.

In 1871, the US government signed the Ku Klux Klan Act. As the first iteration of the Ku Klux Klan died out and the government declared protection from its terror, at the age of sixteen or seventeen, Harriet Smith married Abraham's twenty-nine-year-old brother and fellow Civil War veteran, Henry Lawrence. I imagine the smiles between them at family gatherings. I imagine Harriet's longing for stability. At the time, she was the only Smith in a family of Barnetts who were living with the Lawrences. Her brothers were laborers living with the families on either side of her home, and the whole community was full of White-presenting families with White-presenting surnames. But a closer look reveals that nearly all the family surnames surrounding the Lawrence, Barnett, and Smith households were actually common Cherokee surnames. Bennett, Hunt, Morris, Daniel, Neighbors, and Davis are all surnames represented in the Dawes Rolls of 1890, the official registry of those whose families survived the Trail of Tears and settled in Indian Territory.[7]

The Cherokee adopted White-sounding names long before their Trail of Tears as one strategy to avoid removal. The nation's goal was to prove to the US government that they were civilized and thus worthy to remain on their land in proximity to multiplying White settlers. By 1824 one-third of Cherokees could read and write English. Sequoyah developed a syllabary and began to write the Cherokee language down. Eventually, the people created their own newspaper, the *Cherokee Phoenix*, printed in both Cherokee and English. No road was left untaken in the nation's desperate attempt to prove it deserved to stay on its own land.

Ancestry.com DNA matching indicates that I am indeed connected to both the Barnett and Smith families through third and fourth cousins, which would place our common ancestors in Rosahana and Harriet's generations. This is all consistent with our family stories and begins to unravel the knot of unknowing. It is nearly impossible to produce a hard connection. Our ancestors resisted removal and stayed on the land. That left them without documentation to prove their heritage or connection. The Cherokee had already intermixed with Europeans and some Africans for hundreds of years by the time of the removal. It is common knowledge within the native community that many tribes, including the Cherokee, adopted nonrelatives into their clans and considered them full members of the tribe. Most people on the Dawes Roll of 1890 report only a fraction of Cherokee blood. How much less would that be now? All we have now are the stories, the memory of the unraveled necklace, the story of the tall brown man from Oklahoma, and the bits of evidence we can piece together from intentionally obscured records. I wish I could pass on to the next generations one clear, documented story, but that could only happen if our ancestors had been supported and served by the government that ruled their lives. That is not our story. Bits of narrative are all we have. We try to fill in the pieces, but this is the cost of removal.

I imagine Hiram and his son, Junius, hitting hour six on their journey from Philadelphia to Rockport, Indiana.

Junius asks his pop, "What was it like to live in Indiana, Pops?"

"What do you mean?" Hiram says in my imagination.

"I mean, what was it like living in the sticks before you joined the Navy and traveled the world?[8] What was it like before you broke the color barrier at the Philadelphia post office and before you married Mom in Phoebus, Virginia?"

Hiram married Ella Fortune in the same area where the Fortunes had lived since the mid-1700s—in the region of Virginia where the earliest Africans were brought to these shores. They tied the knot in 1907, then moved to New York City, then found a plot of land on the outskirts of Philadelphia—in the little community of Elmwood.

In my mind's eye, flashes of violence, depression, terror, and love flicker in Hiram's mind in response to his son's question. He doesn't speak it all to his boy. Rather, he says, simply, "You'll see."

I want to paint a rosy picture of Hiram. I want my ancestors to be warm and kind and comfortable, but Hiram was a hard man, a misogynist who could be violent. According to one family story, Hiram hated Ella's cooking. From the line of well-to-do free mulatto men and women stretching back to Fortune Game and her parents, Sambo and Maudlin, Ella Fortune was a utilitarian cook. Her crown jewel at mealtime was mashed potatoes. But everything else was bland, like eating white paper. Hiram was known to raise his hand to Ella, holding her whitewashed food high above his head when he didn't like it. Then he would hurl it against the wall.

What caused this rage? Did Hiram miss his family? Did he miss Harriet's hominy and succotash? Did he feel unmoored with no homeland under his feet, under constant strain to push back White governments pressing in—groping for his land? Was he jealous of Ella's ability to trace her roots to the earliest Africans in America while he had been cut off from his Cherokee and Chickasaw peoples by the removals? He never learned the stories that would have anchored him to this world. Is that why he loved Greek and Roman mythology so much? Were the myths of Roman gods an adopted anchor—an attempt to survive the Christian God that justified the theft of his humanity and fashioned a world where he was not allowed to plant roots and grow? Is that why he named my grandfather Junius?

There are two possible Henry Lawrences that could be Hiram's father, Henry. I'm going to tell you the stories of both. Both reveal how race broke the world and both give us a taste of the cost. Here is the first Henry.

On a hot day in the middle of June 1880, census enumerator Mr. A. Hines mounted the steps of a quaint, sturdy home hidden in the wooded hill country of Sulphur Springs, Ohio County, Kentucky. Mr. A. Hines is likely Alexander T. Hines, who mustered into the Confederate army in Hopkinsville, Kentucky, in 1861.[9] About fifty miles southwest of Sulphur Springs, the cracked earth of Hopkinsville holds the graves of two Cherokee chiefs, Chief Flea Smith and Chief Whitepath, as well as many others buried in unmarked graves in 1838. They died of exposure and disease when the US Army forced the last wave of citizens of the Cherokee Nation to hold camp in an open field in Hopkinsville, stalling their long walk to Oklahoma's Indian Territory. Thousands waited for months for the river to thaw enough to cross. They waited outdoors in a fierce blizzard. Many died. Many escaped. The land that witnessed Cherokee agony also bore witness to the nascent rise of Kentucky's Confederacy that broke ranks with Union loyalists. Mr. Hines was there. He sided with slavery.

Now a man of stature—holding the power of the census record in his hands—Mr. Hines arrived, a man of dark complexion according to his Confederate Oath of Allegiance record.[10] Hazel-eyed Hines, raised in Sulphur Springs, was among the last of the Confederates to surrender in Washington City on May 6, 1865. Fifteen days later, he swore allegiance to the United States of America and was allowed to return home. Now he knocked on the wooden door of a home situated in the solidly White community of 1880 Sulphur Springs. Three years after the 1877 Harding Compromise, Reconstruction was dead. Federal troops had been removed from the South and lynchings were on the rise. Kentucky was the second most dangerous state for a Black man in 1880. Thirty Black men and boys had been lynched in Kentucky in the three years since federal protection was lifted. The only state to surpass this level of terror was Louisiana, where fifty-eight men, women, and children of African descent were lynched by mobs within those same three years.[11]

I imagine the first Henry Lawrence rounding the house with a bucket in his hand, having come from milking the cows or feeding the chickens. Hines would have known racially indistinct Henry Lawrence. They grew up at the same time in the same small mountain town. Hines would have known Henry was an emancipated mulatto man. He would have known that Henry fought on the side of the Union. He would have known Henry's brothers and sister. In this small and close-knit community, Hines would have likely even known Henry's former master.

Jonathan Lawrence, a White man, moved west to Kentucky from South Carolina or Virginia sometime between 1840 and 1850. With the question of slavery at a fever pitch—driving every Christian denomination in the United States to split—the Whig Party flailed as the Confederate States of America rose to prominence in 1850. That year Jonathan appeared for the first time on any Kentucky record with six "mulatto" children listed as his property: five boys and one girl. Family oral history and DNA matching tell us they were not only his slaves; they may have been his children.[12] Henry Lawrence, Hiram's father, was one of them.

At the height of King Cotton's reign in the 1840s and 1850s, with the transatlantic slave trade outlawed by Congress in 1808, breeding farms peppered the North, including Kentucky. Men and women of African descent were bred like horses to supply the Deep South with enslaved laborers. Millions were sold from Virginia and Kentucky downriver into Georgia, Alabama, Mississippi, and Louisiana. Abolitionists faced brutal retaliation for freeing their own enslaved people and aiding fugitives of the slave trade on the Underground Railroad. In that context, something had shifted for Jonathan. When the census taker came through Ohio County, Kentucky, in 1860, Jonathan Lawrence owned no slaves.[13] He had set his children free.

Three years later in 1863, as soon as they could, the four mulatto Lawrence brothers who were old enough to fight enlisted in the Union army. Their enlistment papers mark the first time their names appear in print—anywhere, anytime:

Lawrence, Abraham, 28, Colored, Laborer
Lawrence, Bob, 26, Colored, Laborer
Lawrence, Randall, 24, Colored, Laborer
Lawrence, Henry, 21, Colored, Laborer

All were born in Kentucky. The name Jonathan Lawrence is listed next to each of their names, indicating that he had been their owner and had himself previously served in the military. If they had been enslaved, their master's name would have been listed as the one serving. Masters often enlisted their property to fight in their stead. But the brothers' names stand strong on that page, declaring for the first time, "We are free. We have names. We fight for ourselves."

All four Lawrence brothers enlisted in the Civil War. Robert Lawrence fought with the 54th Massachusetts Colored Infantry Regiment—the unit featured in the film *Glory*.[14] This Henry enlisted, but it is unclear where he fought and unclear what he did immediately after the war. All we know is that he survived. He appears on no census or tax list in the years directly following the war. Then suddenly he appears, having married Harriet Smith in 1871.

On the 1880 census, Henry is a farmer. Harriet is listed as "Mary H." and their daughter, Eliza, as "Anne E."

I imagine Henry, with golden skin gleaming, walking with a wartime limp toward the similar-skinned census enumerator Hines.

"Welcome," Henry says, an arm outstretched for a solid handshake.

The men exchange small talk.

I can imagine Mr. Hines's mind racing. Standing in the shadow of thirty-five lynchings throughout Kentucky over the last three years, Henry is not safe living in White men's Confederate hills.

Harriet, light enough to pass for White, opens my imagination's screen door and asks Mr. Hines if she can offer him something to drink.

"No thank you," Hines clips. "I just need to get your numbers for the census."

Hines asks, "Names?" They answer. He takes the privilege of Confederate heritage in this White man's part of the world and inverts the women's names, placing their middle names first, thereby obscuring the record of their existence for White authorities who might search for proof of their Cherokee and Chickasaw presence. Harriet becomes Mary H. while nine-month-old Eliza becomes Anne E.

"Employment," Hines asks.

"Farmer," Henry says.

To list farmer is to claim ownership of the land. Field hands were farm laborers. Henry owned this land.

"Can you read and write?"

Neither Henry nor Harriet could read or write, according to Hines's records.

"Race?" Hines focuses on his ink pen as he writes "B" next to Henry's name before Henry can speak. This marks the moment Henry became "Black." He was listed on the 1850 slave schedule as "Mu" for mulatto in an era when accurate records of property mattered. In the years since the war, the power to determine racial identity had shifted from slave owner to government agent—in this case, the census enumerator. Race was not self-declared. Census takers scanned household members and bequeathed racial identities according to their racialized perceptions in the moment. Next to Mary H., Hines writes "Mu" for mulatto.

Hard boundary lines marking racial identity serve supremacy's purpose—purity. For this reason, Henry became Black and Harriet was exposed: she was *not* White. Why would Hines, a former Confederate of dark complexion in all-White Sulphur Springs, list Henry, a Union man of similar complexion, as "Black" in a town simmering with racial tensions? Wouldn't that implicate him, too? He was dark also. Here is one possibility. Hines is a surname found on the Cherokee Dawes Rolls.[15] It is possible that Alexander T. Hines was a Cherokee man who hid in the hills to escape the trail, much like Harriet and her mother, Rosahana. It is possible that this brown man sided with the Confederacy, following the lead of the Oklahoma-based Cherokee Nation, which also swore allegiance to the Southern slavocracy in exchange for cash and sovereignty. In the end, the Confederates might have lost the war, but in Sulphur Springs, Kentucky, they were the majority. And in 1880, in the post-Reconstruction era in Kentucky, they were the law. In a strange way, Hines won his sovereignty after all. In the sovereign act of census-taking, Hines declared Harriet's "subhuman" status. He did not out her as Cherokee. He could have, but he might have implicated himself. Rather, he went further. He played into the Black and White racial politics of Jim Crow Kentucky. Likewise, Hines obliterated half of Henry's story from the public record, distinguishing his brown skin from Henry's. Hines's skin may have been brown, but it was not Black.

What was the cost? According to the family story, White nationalists chased Harriet and Henry out of pure-White Sulphur Springs. They found solace across the river in Rockport, Indiana, where Hiram grew up. The Lawrences and Smiths were separated from their land again. But on the 1900 census Henry is living back in Sulphur Springs with Eliza. The census marks him as a widower. But Harriet is indicated as alive and in Hartford, Ohio County, Kentucky—minutes from Henry but also listed as a widow. Fragments of stories and racial trauma. We don't know what caused their separation. Racial terror likely had some impact on the stability of their marriage. The worst part of the race-imposed destruction is all of the hiding—hiding produces emptiness where narrative should bloom.

That is the story of the first Henry Lawrence. Here is the second.

The African American Civil War Museum identifies a man who might be *our* Henry Lawrence, who mustered in as second lieutenant of the 116th US Colored Regiment in 1863. He joined at Camp Nelson, close to home in Kentucky.[16] Camp Nelson was the third largest recruitment camp for African American soldiers. Not solely a military base, Nelson housed formerly enslaved families and opened its gates for abolitionists to teach those families to read and write in preparation for postantebellum life.

But this Henry Lawrence did not actually begin his service at Camp Nelson. Pension papers filed in 1882 reveal that Henry's military service began in the nascent days of the Civil War, on October 14, 1861. Mixed-race Henry mustered in as a private in company F of the 15th Michigan Infantry Regiment—a White regiment.

News of the outbreak of the Civil War compelled free Black men to rush to enlist. Black men had fought on both sides of the Revolutionary War and the War of 1812, despite a 1792 law that banned them from military service. But the law was invoked when the Civil War broke out and most Blacks were turned away from service. Henry was not. He fought, even though his complexion was visibly dark, and he had blue eyes according to a description of him scribbled on his pension papers.[17] Henry was a riddle. Riddles resist racialized boilerplates.

This riddle rose through the ranks of that White regiment, suffering war wounds in the Battle of Mount Sterling. In 1863, Henry was promoted to the rank of second lieutenant of the 116th US Colored Regiment. Under constant Confederate fire, Henry and his men dug a canal on the James River to open passage for Union troops to lay siege to Richmond. In two separate skirmishes, Henry was shot in the ankle and received a shell wound to his head. The James River canal initiative laid foundations for the final hunt and surrender of General Robert E. Lee at Appomattox.

On April 2, 1865, Henry marched with the 116th under the command of General Edward O. C. Ord as the Union army squeezed off Confederate supply lines between Petersburg and Richmond. Union General Ulysses S. Grant was joined by General Ord's army of the James in pursuit of General Lee. Ord led more than two thousand colored troops, representing seven separate US colored regiments—nearly every Black regiment in the Union army. Black men marched in lockstep by the thousands. They chased General Lee from Petersburg to Appomattox, Virginia. In Appomattox, they triumphed in battle and forced Lee's surrender. Think about that. Black men forced Lee's surrender. That is a bit of memory conveniently lost in Whitewashed paintings and history books.[18]

Henry continued in military service for two years following the war. I imagine that this space in the military, where he first saw his name written in black and white, where he was first permitted to exercise agency and to defend himself, where he bled for his country—and for his own freedom—was sacred space for him. In September 1865 the 116th traveled west to Roma, Texas. Grant was concerned about the situation in neighboring Mexico, where forty thousand French soldiers were propping up the puppet regime of Austrian Archduke Maximilian. Grant gave General Philip Sheridan permission to assemble a large Texas occupation force. Sheridan brought together fifty thousand men in three corps. They quickly occupied Texas coastal cities, spread inland, and began to patrol the US–Mexico border.

The 116th US Colored Regiment mustered out at Louisville, Kentucky, in 1867. There is no record of Henry's movements again until he marries Harriet Smith in 1871. But this Henry does not stay in Kentucky. He boards the first transcontinental railroad and travels west to Winnemucca, Humboldt County, Nevada—at that point an informal colony of dispossessed Northern Paiute and Western Shoshone people.

In the Humboldt County courthouse, Henry stood before a court and submitted his declaration for an original invalid pension in 1886. Up to 1885, the army had granted pensions only to soldiers who could present paperwork linking their wounds directly to the war. Twenty years after the war, requirements for approval were relaxed. It was no longer necessary to prove a direct link. Veterans only had to prove they had fought in the war and that they had a debility. According to a Brigham Young University study of pension approvals by race, White soldiers were two times more likely to be believed about the ailments they presented than Black soldiers.[19] The court described Henry as follows: "complexion, dark; hair, brown; eyes, blue." And in these papers Henry claimed to be German.

German? Henry was obviously mixed race with dark skin and blue eyes, so why would he claim German descent? Perhaps because this mixed-race man could not claim to be "White," even though his father was White. He could claim his father's national and ethnic heritage. Perhaps Jonathan Lawrence was of German descent. Perhaps Henry attempted to stave off the knee-jerk dismissal of Blackness in his pension papers by leaning on his White father's ethnic heritage to list his race as "German."

Still, for the next fourteen years Henry visited courtrooms, doctors, and lawyers—and his case was rejected every time. Nonetheless, he kept returning to the Humboldt County courthouse and making his case. Each year, his examinations revealed further deterioration. Each time, doctors' notes included minimizing words like "typical" and "normal," or they claimed to find no significant wounds. Henry's claims were rejected.

Then, in November 1899, from the soldier's home in Santa Monica, California, Henry sat for a surgeon's examination to be submitted to the courts one final time. The surgeon's notes read: "We find a typical case of paralysis agitans involving the right arm only. The tremor is almost continuous and cannot be controlled, making it very difficult for him to dress or undress himself. Cannot feed himself with right hand. Cannot sign his name without right arm is held by left hand, or another person."[20] On a scale of zero to eighteen, this doctor rated Henry's palsy deterioration at level six—less than 50 percent deterioration.

Regarding Henry's senility, the same surgeon wrote: "Senile Debility plainly exists; fibrosis of eyes and arteries noted. Movements are feeble, and he is easily fatigued, evidently unable to perform any manual labor except lightest chores." On a scale of zero to eighteen, the doctor rated Henry's senile debility at level seventeen.[21]

On January 6, 1900, Henry's pension was approved by the final signatory. He would receive ten dollars per month.[22]

Henry collected one month of his pension before he died on May 23, 1900.

According to the 2010 BYU study of racial discrimination in pension approval, the lax requirements that helped White veterans collect their pensions should have helped more Black soldiers

too. No longer would formerly enslaved men be required to produce birth certificates or previous medical records that they did
not have in order to prove their identities and veteran status. It
should have worked in Black men's favor, but it did not. Scrutiny
of Black claims increased until the turn of the century, when the
social climate shifted and more doctors began to believe their Black
patients. The shift was too late for Henry Lawrence and tens of
thousands of other Black Civil War veterans like him.[23]

Which Henry is ours? We don't know and that is the point.
Directly following the Civil War, both marry Harriet Smith. But
in the mid-1880s, one remains in Sulphur Springs, Kentucky, while
the other boards a train bound for the Western frontier. We hold
fragments of narratives. We have placed them together in the
ways they make the most sense, but the point is that we hold only
fragments—intentionally.

From the earliest days in the colonies meticulous records were
kept of European indentured servants' time served, jail sentences,
baptisms of White babies, European immigration lists, deeds,
wills, tax records, diaries, obituaries, newspaper announcements,
graveyards. Everything has been documented about White lives.
Certainly, there are people of European descent who lack pieces
of documentation because members of their families wanted
to disappear and live anonymously under assumed names and
identities. Likewise, there are fortunate Black, Indigenous, and
other people of color who discover the names of their ancestors in
writing—perhaps on a master's will or military record or plantation inventory list. I am among the extremely fortunate. On both
sides of Junius's family—the Fortunes and the Lawrences—my
family was free before 1860. That means we were able to find
a few fragments of their stories: military enlistment, land tax
documents, census documents—but only a few. They were not
well documented. And most of those fragments of documentation
only exist for those deemed Black or White—or Native Americans
who obeyed removal orders and adopted their colonizers' identity

frameworks—frameworks that parceled native identity into quarters and eighths or erased rebellious families altogether. After all, the point was to replace Native Americans with Whites. They disappeared from the land through forced removal. Fragmented families claimed Whiteness or Blackness. There was no social or legal incentive to reveal one's true identity. Revelation would mean permanent removal.

From its beginning, America has obliterated the stories—down to the very names—of Indigenous, and later Black, and other people of color through oppressive systems that either erased and changed the names of our ancestors or compelled them to do so in order to escape annihilation. Who benefits from the obfuscation of our stories? White nationalism does. As Black, Brown, and Asian stories are shattered, White narratives reign supreme.

Photographs from 1926 taken by Henry and Harriet's seventeen-year-old grandson, Junius, hang on my wall, stand behind cut glass in vintage frames, and sit next to me here, even now.

There is a picture of Harriet standing strong in front of her home with what we believe to be a pipe cradled in her right hand. There is a picture of Henry's son, Hiram, standing beside a waterfall and another standing in front of a brick building with a wooden door. Two barrels sit on the ground, one atop the other. Hiram stands in front of them holding a metal bucket with his right hand while dangling his pipe from his mouth.

On the drive home to Philadelphia from Rockport, Hiram and Junius, I imagine, shared more memories that were passed down, along with a few laughs. They did not know then that within twenty years, Hiram would own lots of land in the marshland community of Elmwood. They did not know then that Elmwood would become the place where Hiram would pass down the stories to my mother, Sharon, and her brother, Richie, on long hikes through the marshlands. They could not know then that Elmwood, too, would be snatched away by Whiteness under the pretense of eminent domain.

I imagine Junius sitting in the front seat of his father's car, sandwiches tucked away in sacks on the back seat. Junius holds the necklace that his grandmother gave him to pass on in the family. He touches the beads and imagines . . . in the same way that I touched the beads and imagined. As I am writing now, memories are coming together in reunion. They come from the seven sacred directions: east, north, west, south, up, down, and center. Soon after my pipe-smoking Grandpop Junius passed away from lung cancer, my grandmother handed me that necklace and told me he wanted me to have it. Those beads connected my grandfather to his people—a people he never knew.

3

Lea

Slavery and Oblivion

Lea Ballard did what she knew best. She mustered strength from every inch of her body and set forth a scream that shook the universe. Lea's primal cry focused her intention on one thing: staying alive while pushing new life into the world.

Lea knew that cry. This was not the first time she had dug deep and hollered through the pain.

Albert was the first scream on record, but surely not Lea's first child. Twenty-five-year-old Lea pushed Albert into the world five months after South Carolina fired the first seceding cannon shot of the Civil War. In the smoke, uncertainty, and hope that followed, Lea let forth a bloodcurdling scream.

The women in Lea's line, daughters, granddaughters, and great-granddaughters down to the present generation, all suffered near-death experiences in childbirth. We've come to understand that it's a family trait passed down from woman to woman. Our pelvises are small, says my mother, making birthing especially dangerous.

I imagine the crunch of the broken pelvic bone added to the torment of ripping vaginal flesh. In my mind's eye, Lea laid her head against the wall adjacent to her 1861 slave bed: a basic frame, wires strung across, and hay strewn over the wires, with a sheet crafted of scraps from Missie's dresses laid atop the hay. That is, if she had a bed or a cabin at all. Most enslaved women and men slept on the floor packed into a single one-room cabin, or they slept in the fields where they worked.

Only the midwife would have been present for Lea. Enslaved women had no doctors or hospitals. Only the midwife and God could save them if life began to slip away.

Lea had been of birthing age for nearly fifteen years when Southern states formed the Confederate States of America in 1861. Recorded births after the Civil War show she averaged a new child every two years. Given her age in 1861, Lea could have had five or more previous children before Albert, but these are nowhere to be found in the public record. Chattel slavery left us with two conflicting numbers: seventeen, the number of children the family story says Lea pushed into the world, and twelve, the number of children recorded by census data from 1880 forward.

What happened to the other five children is lost to public memory. Were they sold into nearby Georgia or Alabama? Did they die? Did Lea raise them, or were they snatched from her arms at birth?

Slavery was commerce. The core lie of slavocracy is that the economic flourishing of some is more important than the lives, safety, and flourishing of others. As discussed in chapter 1, this theological lie finds its roots in Pope Nicholas V's *Romanus Pontifex*, which declared that only the "civilized" were ordained by God to rule. The rightful dominion of the civilized extended to all land where no "civilized" government had been established and to all people who were found on said land. According to Pope Nicholas V, the rest of humanity was not fully human. They were not created in the full image of God. They were not given the divine call to exercise dominion on earth. Rather, they and their land were created to serve the flourishing of the "civilized."

Since the Babylonian, Egyptian, and Kushite Empires, the slave trade had proliferated in kingdoms throughout North and Central Africa. Men and women were most often captured and enslaved during military conquests. Enslavement was also used as payment for debt, for ritual prostitution, and as punishment for criminal behavior. Slavery was not race based, nor the inherited status of a human being. Most often, it was levied as penalty for one's transgression against the community.[1]

The institution of slavery extended into Europe through the Roman Empire, which many scholars believe carved a trans-Saharan slave trade route into North Africa. Even then, the sale of Africans into Europe was limited due to the strong kinship ties within and between African kingdoms.

In 1492, Christopher Columbus set out on his first exploratory voyage in search of a direct route from Europe to Asia. He would try four times to no avail. Each time, Columbus's search for a northwest passage to Asia was blocked by land masses, previously unknown to Europeans but inhabited by upwards of 100 million indigenous peoples between North, Central, and South America. Columbus landed four times in the Caribbean and South America by 1502. The first transatlantic slave ship voyage followed a little less than two decades later.[2]

In 1520, the Spanish ship *Santa Maria de la Luz* became the first slave ship to cross the Atlantic. The *Santa Maria* boarded enslaved men from Africa ("Portuguese Guinea," or today's Mauritania) and ultimately disembarked forty-four enslaved Africans on land that would become known as San Juan, Puerto Rico.[3] Over the next one hundred years the transatlantic slave trade would proliferate in the Caribbean, as well as in South America, Central America, and Mexico.

One century after slavery took hold in the Southern Hemisphere, the English war ship the *White Lion* pirated twenty-odd Angolan men from a slave ship bound for Mexico, and eventually landed at Point Comfort, Virginia, near Jamestown. Over the next two and a half centuries, those twenty and odd would become 1,000 then 10,000 then 100,000. By the end of the transatlantic slave trade in 1808 nearly 400,000 Africans had been bartered on the shores of West Africa and brought directly to North American colonial shores. They were sold onto slave ships from

Africa's western shores of Mali, Senegal, Guinea, Ivory Coast, the Kingdom of Benin, and Ghana. Many had been originally sold into the western slave trade by warring kingdoms as far east as Kenya, Sudan, and Eritrea, but the majority came from Cameroon, Congo, Nigeria, and Angola.

When my African Ancestry DNA profile came in the mail, I opened the packet, slid the certificate of identity from its pocket, and read: "Your matrilineal ancestors are from two Nigerian people groups: Hausa and Yoruba. This is Lea's line. Lea Ballard's mother's mother's mother's mother was from Nigeria."

"I am from Nigeria," I thought as tears welled up in my eyes.

As I scanned the documents, I saw that the Yoruba people are mostly from southwestern Nigeria, while the Hausa are from the northern region that borders Niger and Chad. The Yoruba are one of the largest ethnic groups in Nigeria. Overrepresented within the North American stream of the diaspora, Yoruba men and women were often sold to westerners by the Yoruban Oyo Empire throughout the eighteenth century. The people of Hausaland are a regal people: politicians and artists. They trace their lineage to Baghdad, Iraq—the eighth-century intellectual hub of the Islamic world. They were known for their ability to influence, their sculptures, their colorful fashion, and their religious ceremonies. They were a mixed people, descending from the Semitic peoples of the ancient kingdom of Kush. Abraham was a Kushite, from the same people as Nimrod, the Kushite warrior. Sunni Muslim, the Hausa people were and are a horse culture.

I am Yoruba. I am Hausa.

Men, boys, and eventually women—warriors, weavers, princes, architects, engineers, doctors, librarians, and scholars of the Yoruba, Hausa, Igbo, Fula, Mandinka, Kanuri, and other peoples— were packed like cargo below deck and deprived of sunlight, nourishment, and sufficient water. Once a day, they were hosed down on deck where they were forced to dance. Historians estimate that 10 to 15 percent of captives died on the walk from inland Africa to the western coast. Another 15 to 25 percent were fed to the surging waters of the Atlantic. As it was with Sambo Game, this was a breaking process. They boarded western death ships as shackled human beings. They disembarked as property.

Forty percent of enslaved Africans entered the US through the Port of Charleston, South Carolina, the largest slave port in the US. Approximately 80 percent of all African Americans have at least one ancestor who was forced off a slave ship in shackles on Sullivan's Island, off the coast of Charleston.[4] When I began my search for Lea's roots, I expected to find generations of enslaved ancestors descended from Africans who entered the colonies or antebellum America through Charleston's Sullivan Island. But my Ancestry.com DNA profile showed no connection to the early South Carolina Black community. Rather, my DNA branch that stretches back through Lea is solidly rooted in the earliest Africans brought to Virginia's shores.

Camden, South Carolina, in Kershaw County, was settled in 1732 by Quaker and Scotch-Irish settlers migrating south from Virginia.[5] The Virginia-based Ballard family was among Kershaw County's earliest settlers. The minutes of a Quaker meeting in Albemarle County, Virginia, list David Ballard as one among many Ballards born in that area around that time. The listing says David was born in 1750.[6] As the first shots of the Revolutionary War rang, Quakers banned slavery. After the revolution, David picked up from Albemarle and hauled his family further south to South Carolina. They used the one major trail that cut through North Carolina and South Carolina's north country. When they reached the land that would become the seat of Kershaw County, the city of Camden, they laid stakes. His wife, Rebecca, bore their first child, David Ballard Jr., in 1793. By the 1800 Kershaw district census, David Ballard owned one slave.[7]

Genealogical narratives of the early Ballard settlers either paint them with a bucolic brush—describing them as "planters," "merchants," "a Justice of the Peace," or "a veteran"—or list their generations with forensic aloofness. There is never a mention that they were slavers. They were rapists. They bred laborers to plant their farms. They twisted justice to serve themselves. It is not mentioned that slavery was so odious that more than one thousand African rebellions rose up on plantations across the South, including in Kershaw County. Sixteen years after David Ballard recorded the purchase of one slave in 1800, enslaved men in Camden, inspired by their participation in the War of 1812 and Thomas Paine's soaring declaration of the natural *Rights of Man*, planned to rise up in armed rebellion on July 4, 1816. Their plot was found out when an enslaved African named Scipio informed his owner of the plan. The plotters were killed and the rebellion was squashed for the sake of slaveholders like David Ballard.[8]

Sin is passed down from generation to generation. As it goes, it snowballs. At some point, within five generations of Ballards in Camden, South Carolina, someone bought or was gifted Lea or her mother Hannah Reynolds. It is never mentioned that Lea certainly experienced the dreaded separation from her mother that came like clockwork to nearly every enslaved human being—either through death or sale. We don't know anything about Hannah Reynolds except that she existed. Her name is listed on Lea's death certificate: "Mother: Hannah Reynolds." That's it. There was once a Hannah Reynolds whose mother's mother's mother's mother was brought to Virginia's shores from Nigerian soil. She was Hausa. She was Yoruba. She was strong-willed and smart. She willed herself to live aboard that death ship. Then she survived countless indignities, but she also figured out a way to live and keep her children alive. Hannah was never listed with Lea on any census after the Civil War. They were separated, by death or sale in the antebellum era. Because Lea was listed as mulatto on the 1880 census, we know that Hannah suffered the violence of penetration, and that is how Lea came into the world. All of Lea's children are listed as mulatto on the same census. Like her mother, she would suffer that violence—again and again. That is all we know about Lea. These histories are never recorded. Instead, historians chronicled the mundanity of enslavers' lives. They made sure we knew that

David Ballard was born then and married so and so then and begat him who married her and died here, and so on.

White births and marriages and deaths were recorded with meticulous precision. Full names, dates, and locations help trace White life from South Carolinian soil to the homelands of Northern Ireland, Scotland, and England. Only the fortunate few people of African descent find listings of their ancestors in court documents, land deeds (if free persons), or among the beds and pitchforks willed to the next White antebellum generation. The early colonial race laws that shaped the lives of Fortune and her Maryland and Virginia descendants explicitly declared that the births of African-descended people (even those who were free) were not important enough to record. Likewise, Black deaths were not recorded, except as property loss.

On cotton, rice, and brick plantations across antebellum South Carolina, the muffled wails of mothers like Lea rose, the only testimony of their children's passing. One in every three children enslaved on cotton plantations died before their sixteenth birthday. It was even worse in the low country: one in three children passed before their first birthday in the malaria-laden swamplands of rice plantations. Malaria, dysentery, cholera, and neglect account for the majority of Black children's deaths in antebellum South Carolina.[9] Lea had seventeen children, but we have no record of five of them. The five born under the tyranny of slavery likely died or were sold or gifted deeper south, forced to follow the next generations of White Ballards into Georgia, Alabama, and Mississippi. Gone forever.

What will it take to heal the generational wounds of unknowing and separation? Reunion and story sharing. In *The Very Good Gospel*, I examine the Hebrew understanding of "very goodness" when God looks around at the end of the sixth day of the epic Hebrew poem we now call Genesis 1 and considers it to be "very good" (Gen. 1:31). The Greeks placed perfection inside the thing. Things themselves were thought to be perfect. That was the Greek project—to be perfect. That was not the Hebrew project. The Hebrew word for "goodness" is *tov*. The Hebrews understood *tov* to exist *between* things, not inside things. *Tov* was not about the perfection of the thing. It was about the wellness of the relationships between things. *Tov* is fundamentally relational. When God says "*tov m'od*," God is saying that all relationships in creation are radically good! The relationship between humanity and God, humanity with self, humanity with the rest of creation, all of creation and the systems that govern us—all work to bless all! There is no cursing—only blessing on the first page of the Bible. This is what God calls "very good." It is not that we are perfect. It is that our relationships are well. The word *m'od* means "forceful, abundant, overflowing." The relationships in creation were radically good, overwhelmingly good, forcefully good! We see what God considers to be good. It is not our perfection. It is our capacity to love God, love ourselves, love others, love the rest of creation, and love through our governance. It is our radical, interdependent connectedness. We were created for radical connectedness.

Now consider: If the essence of overwhelming goodness, according to the Hebrew conception, is radical connectedness, then the essence of sin is disconnectedness or separation. The chief sin of American slavocracy was separation. The institution separated parents from children, people from their homelands and communities, women, men, and children from their very identities—their stories. The chasm created in the souls of Black folk by slavery's brutal beating on Black families is as wide as the Mississippi River is long. Our relatives were sent away into oblivion.

But Black oblivion is not the only kind of oblivion within American colonial slavocracy. Mystery compounds mystery with the southeastern states' prolific investment in the Native American slave trade. Long before the first enslaved Angolans landed in Virginia in 1619, southeastern indigenous nations were pitted against one another and encouraged to sell their tribal enemies into slavery. The Cherokee, Chickasaw, Creek, Choctaw, and Seminole Nations were devastated when the British Empire placed the Native American slave trade at the center of its economic structure. Whole villages were captured and sold to imperial outposts throughout the Caribbean, New England, and New York, and to settlers throughout South Carolina. By 1695, South Carolina had become the hub of the Native American slave trade in North America. Between 1650 and 1730, at least 50,000 Native Americans were exported from South Carolina for enslavement in the Caribbean. Within that period, the rate of capture, enslavement, and exportation of Native Americans was greater than the rate of importation of enslaved Africans.[10]

South Carolina's layered slave trades grew in complexity. The multiplying African population increased the terror of White settlers, who codified their fear into law through new race codes in 1740: "All negroes and Indians, (free Indians in amity with this government, and negroes, mulattoes, and mestizos, who are now free, excepted) mulattoes (African/European) or mestizos (African/Native) who are now, or shall hereafter be in this province, and all their issue and offspring . . . shall be and they are hereby declared to be, and remain hereafter absolute slaves."[11] In other words, from that point forward, slavery once was slavery forever—for all future generations, in perpetuity.

Less than a century later, the recession following the Revolutionary War collided with the promise of Georgian gold, the invention of the cotton gin, and the rising reign of King Cotton across the South. Andrew Jackson had all the justification he needed to order the removal of all five southeastern nations from their ancestral lands. But not all walked.

In the one hundred years since they were brought together on plantations across the South, Cherokee, Creek, Chickasaw, Choctaw, and Seminole peoples had intermixed and intermarried with enslaved Africans. These enslaved Native Americans would not walk with their peoples. They would continue to toil with their darker-skinned families, suffering the whip, the chain, the rapes, and the dehumanization of slavery.

A few years ago, I traveled to Philadelphia to visit my elderly cousin, Sheila, in the hospital. I remember Sheila's slow, high-pitched voice that always sounded glad to see whoever she encountered that moment. She was born in 1952 to my grandmother's sister, Martha—named after Lea's daughter Martha Ballard.

Sheila shrieked as I entered her hospital room, "Liiiiiisaaaaaa! So good to see you!"

She was recovering from surgery and had all the time in the world to talk. We remembered my grandmother, Willa—our common link. Grandmom Willa and her mother, Great-Grandmom Elizabeth, raised Sheila after Sheila's mother died. Sheila is a current-day flesh-and-blood link to stories passed down directly from Lea to her grandchild, Elizabeth, and great-grandchild, Willa, both of whom she raised. Sheila heard the stories from them and she remembers them all.

In that hospital room, she told me something I'd never heard before. She said someone on Lea's branch traced back to Muscogee Creek Indians. I corrected her, explaining the Native American line came through the Lawrence side of the family, but she corrected me back.

"No," Sheila insisted, "we are Creek."

I asked her where she heard that.

She looked at me and her eyes narrowed, as if to say, "Believe me."

"Grandmom Lizzie definitely told me," Sheila said. "We are Creek."

According to Sheila, somewhere in our line, possibly stretching back to and past Lea, we are Creek. Yet because of the slaughter and chaos of colonization and slavery, we likely will never know.

Still, this interaction helped me understand the complexity, the mystery, and the misery that is the American story. Like Lea, we hold Yoruba, Hausa, European, Muscogee Creek, and scores of other people groups' stories in our national body. These are stories of conflict and subjugation. They hold enormous pain and heartbreak. They hold unimaginable shame and blame. Thus, they live beneath the surface of our discourse: their only evidence is our vast diversity. Black, White, Native American, Latinx, and Asian American alike contort to avoid touching the pain, facing the shame, standing naked before the world like a woman with her baby on the auction block. Worst of all are the machinations of people of European descent to maintain the clear, clean narrative of their supposedly inherent nobility, goodness, and integrity.

Lea's story—her blood alone—shows us how deep and winding the rabbit hole of slavery's sin goes. It is a winding root that wrapped itself around everyone, everything, and every generation—from the shackles of enslavement to convict leasing and Jim Crow lynching to the Bracero program and mass incarceration to the Trump administration's family separation policy and the forced hysterectomies on asylum-seeking women reported in 2020.[12] Slavery echoes through the ages and its death grip is strangling us. But it is more than strong. It is sly. It diverts our attention to avoid capture and extraction.

Americans like to contain racism by thinking of it as a problem of hatred. But it is rarely about hatred. Fortune's story shows us the roots of American racialization. Race was fundamentally a project of law, to enforce a political view of the world, one where White men inhabit the top rung on the ladder of human hierarchy. But that ladder is not merely about status. It's more than that. It is about control through the acquisition of land and money. The sin of slavery is domination. Motivated by insatiable lust for power and status, European men acquired power through the acquisition of land and cash. Slavery was simply the means to their desired end.

Repairing our broken world will require people of European descent to repent from striving for godlike control of all creation. People deemed "White" have warred against God for supremacy, declaring that they, too, have the authority to define human beings, land rights, even God. They declared some people to be "savages" and so they were, according to the law. They declared some people to be "three-fifths of a human being" and so they were, according to the law. They declared some to be "chattel" and so they were, according to the law. Europeans' domination of images of God across the planet has waged a world war against the dominion of God.

The ancients considered images of royalty to be markers of where that royalty ruled. Consider Pharoah's statue at the entrance to an Egyptian city or Nero's face on Roman coins that circulated throughout the kingdom. Where images of royalty were plentiful and in good condition, it was understood that the kingdom was present and strong. Where images of royalty were toppled or melted down, it was understood that the kingdom was at war. On the first page of the Bible, in Genesis 1:26, we read that all humanity is made in the image of God. With the words, "Let us make humankind in our image, according to our likeness; and let them have dominion," the biblical text breaks rank with precedent and tradition. Up to that moment, only royalty could possess the image of God—the supreme creator and ruler of the cosmos. But Genesis was now declaring that all humanity is made in God's image. All humanity marks the domain of God. All humanity is imbued with the inherent dignity usually reserved for kings and queens.

Thus, when the image of God was crushed, broken, twisted, distorted, covered, or erased, the ancient Hebrews originally hearing this text would have understood these acts against humanity to be acts of war against God. European conquest of land and people throughout the Enlightenment period was actually a period of European wrestling against God for control and dominion over the planet. For a time, Whites won. Enslavement was not the prize. Control was the prize. Status was the prize. Empire was the prize. Black, Native, and Brown bodies were simply the collateral damage of war waged against God—in the name of God, with the blessing of the church under the legal shelter of Pope Nicholas V's *Romanus Pontifex*.

Repentance will require people of European descent to face this truth. Repentance will require people deemed White to lay down distorted lenses, crafted for them by parents' and grandparents' stories, history books, museums, and media. Repair for the ones who broke the world will require that they renounce the lie that Whiteness is inherently good, inherently noble, and inherently right. Repeated lies distort perception, making it difficult to see reality. The lie of White goodness wore down the capacity for empathy, moving people deemed White into a series of knee-jerk justifications crafted to cordon off emotion from the requirements of progress. White progress.

Speaking with Bob Zellner, veteran organizer with the Student Nonviolent Coordinating Committee, I asked, "What drove White people to fight to the death to maintain White supremacy?"

He shared with me his theory of the shrunken heart.

"First of all, slavery was an act of war," he said. "It had to be carried out every day against Black people. In order to maintain the kind of plantation systems that we had under slavery, you had to commit acts of war and violence every day against Black people."

Slavers used frightful iron shackles, dehumanizing torture masks, branding irons, and they cut off ears and limbs for obstinate behavior and committed serial rape—because this was war.

"For centuries," Zellner said, "through slavery and later through Jim Crow and the sharecropper economic system in the South, White southerners had to constantly suppress their own feelings of sympathy and empathy for another human being. . . . In the same way that farm children had to steel themselves when the chicken had its neck wrung or the calf was killed or the rabbit was knocked on the head so you could have it for supper, they had to have no feelings for that animal. In the same way, they had to have no feelings for that enslaved person or that person of color. For centuries, White people have shrunken their own hearts."[13]

Distorted lenses offer a cover for licentiousness.

David Ballard was a Quaker. He and his descendants went against their own Quaker conscience to build their southern empire, or else they abandoned Quakerism altogether in exchange for status. Ballard and his descendants bought and sold people. They separated babies from their mothers and fathers. Children, mothers, and fathers were raped in the process of securing comfort for Ballard. Children, mothers, and fathers died doing Ballard's work.

Lea bore down and screamed her first daughter, Martha, into the world in 1865. Martha passed through the contractions of both mother and country. She breathed her first gulp, then a scream burst from her body—a scream that equaled the terror of moving from the safety of the womb into a world ablaze. Martha Ballard was born to a woman who had known only slavery. Martha and her descendants would know only freedom—to a point.

Born as the Civil War folded to a close, there is no listing of Martha's exact date of birth. The 1880 census only discloses the year of her birth, 1865. Listed as one of nine mulatto children of Lea Ballard, neither mother nor child can be found on any census before 1880. Martha's first fifteen years of life and Lea's plight directly following emancipation remain shrouded in mystery.

Lea Ballard Ancrum Williams was a woman for whom the putrid taste of antebellum loss had become familiar. That loss followed Lea throughout her first nineteen years, and its ghost haunted her in every generation till the day she died. The same year that Lea gave birth to Martha, our nation pushed the Thirteenth Amendment from passage to ratification within twelve months: "Neither slavery nor involuntary servitude, except as a punishment for crime whereof the party shall have been duly convicted, shall exist within the United States, or any place subject to their jurisdiction." These words catalyzed the reversal of the original Virginia laws established in 1662, as well as every race law that bound Fortune and her descendants, the laws that bound Henry and his brothers, and the South Carolina laws that shackled generations of Lea's family and would have bound them forever. I can only imagine Lea's tears and dancing on the day she learned she was free. To think of the joy now, my body cannot contain it.

Lea would taste loss again. But, for this moment, I imagine Lea standing still on the land she and her people had slaved for generations. On the day she hears that she is free, Lea raises her face to the noonday sun. She looks up to the trees—the leaves blowing and swaying overhead. Lea remembers the sound of the spirit songs in the brush arbor. She remembers her mother's voice in the trees. She listens close and soon she hears the harmonies of her foremothers,

all the way back to the Yoruba and Hausa women. They sing to
her from the trees: *Put on your crown, child. Put on your crown.*

> I came this night for to sing and pray,
> Oh yes! Oh yes!
> To drive old Satan far away,
> Oh yes! Oh yes!
> That heav'nly home is bright and fair,
> Oh yes! Oh yes!
> But very few can enter there,
> Oh yes! Oh wait 'til I put on my crown
> Wait 'til I put on my crown
> Wait 'til I put on my crown
> Oh yes! Oh yes!
>
> If you want to catch that heav'nly breeze,
> Oh yes! Oh yes!
> Go down in the valley on your knees,
> Oh yes! Oh yes!
> Go bow your knees upon the ground,
> Oh yes! Oh yes!
> And ask your Lord to turn you 'round
> Oh yes! Oh wait 'til I put on my robe
> Wait 'til I put on my robe
> Wait 'til I put on my robe
> Oh yes! Oh yes!

PART TWO

DEGRADATION AND RESISTANCE

White gravel crunched under our feet. I shifted my body weight to stabilize myself while beholding evidence of history that destabilized the world.

Participants of African descent on a 2019 Freedom Road pilgrimage joined me in a special ceremony at the edge of a field directly across from the Bryant Market in Money, Mississippi.

We walked across the two-lane highway and across the parallel train tracks and stood at the midpoint of our journey through the story of the control and confinement of African bodies on US soil. Nascent corn stalks blanketed the earth for miles. Deep in this field once stood a four-bedroom house, the home of sixty-four-year-old Rev. Mose Wright, who was the uncle of fourteen-year-old Emmett Till. Rev. Wright was a sharecropper, a farmworker who turned over a portion of his crops to the plantation owner, G. C.

Frederick, each season to remain on the land. The southern system forced sharecroppers to borrow money from the plantation store to access the tools and equipment necessary to harvest the crop. These emancipated families were enslaved again by debt.

My family lived in South Carolina and the Caribbean decades before Emmett Till's fateful trip to visit his uncle. Lea, Annie, Lizzie, Charles, and Willa contended with the same racialized brutality as Till did. Reinaldo and Anita faced a colonized Caribbean where people of African descent lived on the receiving end of the economic and social sledgehammer of eugenics. All of them found ways to survive prolific Black poverty at the turn of the twentieth century. Their stories preceded Till's and the Supreme Court's decision in *Brown v. Board of Education*. They were subject to the Compromise of 1877, which stripped Blacks of federal protection of their civil rights, and the Supreme Court's 1896 ruling in *Plessy v. Ferguson*, which entrenched Jim Crow segregation across the South. Two years later, in 1898, the US invaded and annexed Puerto Rico, bringing Jim Crow sensibilities and structures in tow.

Emmett Till boarded a bus in Chicago, bound for Money, Mississippi, in August 1955. Only three generations before, his ancestors likely slaved in the same field or one close by.

According to Charles McLaurin, a civil rights veteran who was our pilgrimage guide in Mississippi, Till had survived polio as a child and had a speech impediment. He was a stutterer and a visitor to the South, unfamiliar with the abject brutality of southern White supremacy. He was trying to impress new friends who are rumored to have dared him to ask Carolyn Bryant for a date. With typical early-teenage bravado, he said he could get a date with her. But when he entered the store, this stuttering young boy simply bought a piece of candy and left. Thinking he had made advances, his daring friends ran away, leaving the impression that he had just done something wrong.

According to Timothy Tyson's *The Blood of Emmett Till*, Carolyn Bryant, her husband Roy, and his half-brother J. W. Milam, who carried an Ithaca-brand, US-Army-issued .45 caliber semi-automatic strapped to his hip, drove their pickup truck along the

gravel road to Rev. Wright's home on August 28, 1955—days after
the incident at the store. Wright came out to meet them. They
demanded the boy and eventually barged into Wright's home and
snatched Emmett from his bed. Carolyn identified him. They tied
him up in the back of their truck and took him away into the darkness. They pistol-whipped him. They beat him for nearly an hour.
They gouged out his eye. They ripped off part of his ear. They
broke his femur and crushed his skull. They drove his stripped
body ten miles across the county line to the Tallahatchie River
where they tied a seventy-pound cotton gin fan around him with
razor wire and shot a .45 caliber bullet into his head.

Carolyn confessed in a 2008 interview that she had lied. Emmett
had done nothing to her.[1]

My father was fourteen years old when Emmett Till was
lynched. My mother was seven. Theirs was the generation lit on
fire by Till's death. Theirs was the generation that said "No more!"
Planted in the North after their parents had escaped the brutality
of southern segregation and Caribbean colonization, they survived
the brutality of northern redlining, segregated schools, and White
dominance.

Throughout 2019 I pilgrimaged to the lands where my mother's
and father's families lived. I also intersected with their work in
the civil rights movement. My father attended Congress of Racial
Equality meetings in New York, and my mother was a member of
the Student Nonviolent Coordinating Committee in Philadelphia.
My time on the Freedom Road pilgrimage, standing at the edge
of the field where Till saw daylight for the last time, was an act
of leaning in to understand my parents and what drove them to
break ranks with previous generations. It was as much a moment
to grasp what led them to believe they could halt the snowball of
subjugation from rolling over them—as it was to honor Till's life
and death, which catalyzed the push itself.

Our group stood there, gravel beneath our feet. Beneath the
sea of corn before us lay soil. Mixed in with that soil was the
blood of Emmett Till, the sweat and tears of his ancestors, and
the cries for freedom of centuries of enslaved Africans. One by

one, we gave thanks to these ancestors. We acknowledged their struggle. We thanked them for struggling. We acknowledged our accountability to them. Then we walked to the field and poured libations, pouring out water—a symbol of life for those whose struggle gave life to us.

It is impossible to count the ancestors' tears or to quantify the value of each drop. But part two of this book will seek to lean into those ancestors' stories and understand their tears, their resilience, and their various strategies of resistance. Finally, we will begin to reflect on what it will take to make the flow stop.

4

Lizzie

Like Dust

Lizzie's hands scrubbed the dishes clean of the last bits of rice and chicken left on her grandmother Lea's plate. Or at least that's how I imagine her in the nascent hours after Lea passed away in 1917. Lea had lived a life of horror and loss and glory and struggle and victory and family and exploitation and betrayal and heartache and love. And now she was at rest. I imagine Lizzie leaning over the washbasin like she had in White men's homes her whole life as a domestic servant. Surrounded by news clippings pasted to the wall, a stand-in for wallpaper, news of the US entering the Great War surrounded Lizzie as she moved grains of fresh South Carolina rice that clung to Lea's plate into the murky water. The cash crop was submerged as if baptized. As the water welcomed the rice— washing away centuries of sins—it pulled her out of the melee of early-twentieth-century convulsion and it consumed time itself.

One generation stood between Lizzie and enslavement to the Ballard family who lived down the road. Lizzie's mother, Martha, was born free mere months after the last cannon was shot at Appomattox in 1865. Now, Lizzie had just been sitting by her grandmother's bed alone. She said adieu to the last woman in her family who never got to kiss her children goodbye before they were sold deeper south—who never got to say goodbye to those children whose lives likely slipped from their famished, diseased bodies in the middle of the night—or maybe they dropped of malnutrition in the fields where they cut their hardened hands on cotton. In any case, Lea never got to say goodbye.

This was an era of reckoning—an era when people of African descent in the US watched White men claim to fight for freedom in a foreign war deemed "great" while waging a race war at home that stripped away the freedoms of people of color. Layered beneath the wallpapered headlines detailing the atrocities of World War I likely were headlines that detailed the deaths of loved ones and friends of the family in the Charleston race riot of 1876 and the Wilmington, North Carolina, race riot of 1898. Yes, these and many other moments of collective Black grief and trauma were pasted to the walls. But they were also seared into the intergenerational memory of my family.

The racial reckoning of the early twentieth century traces back to three decision points in American life in which Black life had been bartered in legislative deals that brought White harmony in exchange for Black evisceration. The first came when the concept of race was established in the colonial days of Fortune's time. The second came the day the first Congress of the United States compromised two-fifths of Black humanity away in an attempt to coax the South to play nice with the North. Southern legislators had balked at the injustice of their situation. In their Southern slavocracy, Blacks far outnumbered Whites. Southern White legislators argued to include the enslaved as full persons when calculating the number of House representatives apportioned to Southern states. The North argued that Blacks should not be counted at all, a position designed to give the North the clear numerical advantage in Congress. They compromised. Thenceforth, Congress would count enslaved people of African descent as three-fifths of a human being.

The third decision point helped close the election of 1876. Since the beginning of English rule on North American soil, compromises between men deemed "White" had always compromised Black life. In 1917, Lizzie Johnson, daughter of Martha Ballard and granddaughter of Lea Ballard, faced a decision—like the millions of other people of African descent heading north in the Great Migration: Would Lizzie continue to compromise her own life? Or would she exercise her agency to search for freedom?

I imagine Lizzie's eyes raised from the dishwater, looking out past her aunts and uncles' homes, which were flanked by White Ballard homes—a constant enforcement of the strict human hierarchy in Camden, South Carolina, under the oppression of Jim Crow. Lizzie was an octoroon—a person who is one-eighth Black by descent. Her father, who she never knew, was a White man—likely Jewish, according to the family story. She could pass for White, but not in South Carolina, not feet from the family who had owned her grandmother. Jim Crow kept tabs. If Lizzie stayed, she would continue to suffer the subjugation of Jim Crow laws and structures that permeated the South after the last compromise.

As the Civil War became recent memory, South Carolina crafted its Constitution in September 1865. Sections 5 and 13 reserved for White men the exclusive right to serve in public office. But the Radical Republican Congress passed the Civil Rights Act of 1866 to enforce the Thirteenth Amendment's abolition of slavery. The act outlawed all forms of law and practice that echoed the characteristics of slavery, including segregated housing. South Carolina acquiesced, but soon after, it rejected the Fourteenth Amendment, which granted birthright citizenship to all, including African Americans. Still, the amendment was ratified and became US constitutional law.

These were the flourishing years. With South Carolina's Jim Crow legislation outlawed, Black South Carolinians registered to vote in droves. Ten Black men were elected and served in public office in South Carolina between 1868 and 1877. An estimated two thousand Black men were elected to public office across the United States during that nine-year period called Reconstruction.[1]

Martha watched Blackness rise throughout her earliest years. She witnessed the joy-filled whispers in the cotton fields every time news filtered through of one more Black man rising. She was five years old when African American Alonzo Jacob Ransier rose to the rank of lieutenant governor of South Carolina. As Ransier rose, they all rose.

I imagine Lea, Martha, and all of Lea's children sitting in church hearing the times interpreted from the pulpit. Black rising fulfilled the biblical promise of Jubilee—that year that came once every forty-nine years. God, the leader of embryonic Israel, established Jubilee. Every forty-nine years, God declared in Leviticus, all slaves would be set free, all debt would be forgiven, and all land lost to debt over the previous forty-nine years would be returned to the family it was originally apportioned to when the Hebrew people first crossed the Jordan. Jubilee was the context of Martha's toddler years. I imagine her leaning against her mother's leg while Lea snapped beans with the other women on the front porch, marveling that the biblical promises were all coming to pass.

Then came one of the most consequential compromises in American history—the Compromise of 1877. Black personhood would be traded away. Ten years after the ratification of the Fifteenth Amendment and federal occupation of the South, the tension between North and South had shifted from the Civil War's battlefields to the realm of Reconstruction politics. Tensions lifted to a fever pitch as the 1876 election results came to a standstill based on disputed returns from the three southern states with Republican Reconstruction-era governments: South Carolina, Florida, and Louisiana. Congressmen called a closed-door meeting and hammered out the compromise. Anti-Reconstructionist Republican Rutherford B. Hayes would accept the presidency and would order federal troops to leave the South. Southern Whites would be free to deal with the southern race problem in their own way. With the last federal soldiers gone, hell broke loose.

White legislators purged state houses and the US Congress of Black members and senators. They set about the business of crafting a stranglehold of laws on Black bodies, limiting everything.

In her 2020 masterpiece, *Caste: The Origins of Our Discontents*, Isabel Wilkerson explains that South Carolina enforced its caste system by explicitly limiting employment opportunities for all people of color to domestic service or farm work.[2] Wilkerson adds that throughout the Jim Crow regime, African Americans, like Jews in Nazi Germany, were prohibited by law from walking on the sidewalk. They were compelled by the force of law to walk in the gutter, ensuring uninhibited movement of White bodies, purity of White space, and the reinforcement of the idea of the inferiority of Blackness.[3] Along with segregation of jobs and public spaces, Jim Crow carved out pure White housing space.

At age eighteen in 1883, Martha navigated Jim Crow South Carolina as Christian White nationalist paramilitary groups, such as the Red Shirts, rose around her and partnered with the Daughters of the Republic to reclaim southern territory for White rule. That year, the US Supreme Court ruled that housing markets were exempt from the provisions of the Civil Rights Act of 1866, which prevented discrimination. Banks and realtors drew red lines on maps marking the boundaries of Black and Brown communities. They made a pact to not sell homes to people of color outside those red boundaries of Black existence. This practice—called "redlining"— was declared constitutional and was enforced throughout the South and the entire United States for the next century.[4]

Plus, peonage caught millions of Black boys and men in the web of convict leasing by leveraging the freight-sized loophole in the Thirteenth Amendment, allowing enslavement in the case of imprisonment. Jim Crow politicians made an end run around the rising labor movement's demands by resurrecting slavocracy and sweeping Black men and boys off the street for infractions as trite as sitting on a park bench for too long, looking at a White man in the eyes, or attempting to steal a pig. They were sentenced to fifteen to twenty-five years in prisons, where they were leased to wealthy local business owners and forced to do hard labor on farms, on railroads, and in coal mines. The men got nothing. The states got bank. By 1898, 73 percent of Alabama's GDP was provided by convict leased labor.[5]

As David Oshinsky explains in *Worse Than Slavery*: "During the railroad boom of the 1870s and 1880s, convicts laid most of the 3,500 miles of new track in North Carolina."[6] Of the South Carolina–based railroad company, Oshinsky adds: "At the prison camps of the Greenville and Augusta Railroad, convicts were used up faster than South Carolina authorities could supply them. Between 1877 and 1879, the G&A 'lost' 128 of 285 prisoners to gunshots, accidents, and disease (a death rate of 45 percent) and another thirty-nine to escapes."[7]

That is only the death rate. There was also the torture that Black men endured at the hands of White South Carolinian and Georgian men on death's gangplank: scurvy covered the men's skin because they slept and washed and worked and ate in absolute filth.[8] Oshinsky tells the story of an old Black man named Foster, leased in Alabama, who was brought to the prison hospital after being beaten nearly to death. He was too old to keep up with the younger men:

> "Oh, they have nearly killed me . . . ," Foster told the chaplain. ". . . They stripped my britches . . . off and whipped me and then sprinkled sand on me and whipped me again and then made me climb a tree that was covered with ants and they got all over me . . . they bit me all over." Foster died the following week.[9]

According to our family story, Lizzie's future husband, Charles Jenkins, died in a "railroad accident" circa 1921. No records of the death of a Charles Jenkins in that era have been found. The Greenville and Augusta Railroad serviced the region where my second-great-grandfather likely met, fell in love with, and married Lizzie Johnson, in Camden, South Carolina. If Charles had been swept into the convict leasing system, his death would not have been recorded. Reginald Moore, founder of the Sugarland Convict Leasing and Labor Project outside Houston, explained to me the mortality rate of convict-leased men: boys and men ensnared in the system of peonage worked for three to five years until they died or were declared unfit to work in Texas. The policy was to bury them where they dropped.[10]

But in 1917, Charles was still living, likely walking with his three-year-old daughter Martha, named after her grandmother, hoisted on his shoulders in the adjacent woods. Eight-year-old Willie-Belle perhaps walked next to her father while six-year-old Charlie Jr. ran ahead as the four cut through the woods to visit nearby family. Lizzie would have the house to herself. She would have space to mourn the death of her grandmother who raised her from birth.

And she would have space to remember her sister.

I imagine Lizzie standing over the dishwater where bits of Lea's last meal float to the surface of troubled waters. Lea was gone . . . Lizzie's older sister Annie was gone . . . and though a small part of Lizzie spent every day of her childhood hoping her mother, Martha, would open the cabin door and step into her life, Martha would never come.

Martha slipped from this world just as she screamed Lizzie into it. Only the midwife was present. As with the generations before and since, childbirth in this line of my family was a deadly proposition. There were no hospitals that would accept Black people in the Camden area. Complications often equaled death.

In my mind's eye, Lizzie moves from the washbasin to the doorway of Lea's cabin, situated on the outskirts of town, near the swamp. Her eyes rest on one spot on the porch, where I imagine her older sister Annie sat for hours on Lizzie's tenth birthday in July 1900. As Lizzie turned ten, I can imagine Annie leaning in with almost a whisper, so as not to disturb the ghosts, and sharing bits of impressions of their mother, Martha; impressions lodged in the three years that Annie had a mother—the three years that nascent Annie could rest her head on Martha's shoulder—before her mother passed while giving birth to her sister. Annie held the memory of Martha for them both.

If Annie held the memory, I like to think Lizzie held their dreams. The two girls, thirteen and ten years old, respectively, likely escaped the oppressive heat of the potbelly stove that sat in the middle of

Lea's small cabin by sitting in their favorite corner of the wooden-planked front porch. Leaning with backs against the house, I can see them sitting cross-legged and watching the swarm of mosquitoes dance with the moths.

Annie and Lizzie were the only two Johnsons in Lea Ballard's home at the time. With their mother dead and their White father absent, the two were taken in and raised by Lea, who also took in Laura, her daughter from an earlier marriage to Mr. Ankrum, and Laura's four children. Annie and Lizzie's grandmother's house was packed with children and an anxious single mother who was not theirs. Surrounded by family, in truth they had only each other.

In my mind's eye, light from inside the house spilled onto the porch and attracted the moths. Two gold-lined, white-silk-winged moths flitted above their heads. They landed on the window directly above the girls' heads. The invisible pane drew the moths to the light but blocked them from its warmth. They could see the light but could not be warmed by it.

I like to think that on that summer night, Lizzie and Annie dared to dream of a world where they could experience the warmth of the light. They dreamed of living together in Philadelphia or New York, and perhaps they would reunite with cousins in Virginia and Washington, DC. Perhaps Annie would join the theater or sing in a traveling minstrel show. Perhaps Lizzie would become a rich landowner working and saving and bringing everyone else up north in time. In their dreams, Martha was with them. In that dream world, the mother they never knew would scold them for dreaming too much or getting their handmade dresses dirty in the woods. But no amount of scolding could make them less grateful to have Martha with them.

Seventeen years later and Lea having entered her final rest, I imagine Lizzie holding the doorpost as she stares at the spot on the porch that used to be hers and Annie's.

Nine years earlier, when Lizzie was eighteen and Annie was twenty-two, the sisters likely sat in their spot watching the relentless tropical depression of October 1908 roll over Camden. The ground was likely still soaked through from the floods of August that same year—the most severe on record in South Carolina's history. Across the state, rivers rose from 9 to 22 feet in August. Fresh memories of that trauma likely made hearts race as pools of rain converged with the Wateree riverbed and blanketed swampy earth.[11]

Lea Ballard's home was near the Wateree. As the Wateree rose, I imagine Annie Johnson sat on her grandmother's porch with her back against the cabin where she was born, the cabin where she was raised, the cabin where she knew all the uncles and the aunties living in surrounding cabins; formerly enslaved—all. Former owners surrounding them—all. Constant threat. Constant reminder of caste in the Jim Crow South. But on this day, the rising waters were the common enemy. The waters would not discriminate between White and Black Ballards.

Lea was seventy-two years old at the time. No men were present in her household to chop wood for the potbelly stove, so the mulatto women of the Ballard house chopped their own.

I imagine Annie's white mocha hands wrapping her bone-straight hair while perched on the front porch. With each wrap she gained determination to brave the rains to help Grandmom Lea with the firewood. Lizzie was likely inside helping Lea to skin the chicken for dinner. What follows is how I imagine the final moments before all of their lives changed forever.

Annie stepped off the porch and into the mulch of the riverbed, which had flowed over and mixed with rain and earth. The water was likely high enough to seep through Annie's shoes. She sloshed through the familiar woods with ax in hand, braving run-ins with orb-weaver spiders and water moccasins escaping from the Wateree.

According to family oral history, one of Martha's brothers followed his niece Annie into the woods that day. Martha was not there to protect Annie. Lack of healthcare had claimed her life during childbirth eighteen years before. Now, slavery's ghost was riding her brother's back. We don't know why he did it. We don't know what he was thinking. We don't even know which brother it was. Several of Lea's sons lived nearby. Annie would have known them all well. She might even have welcomed the help of a familiar man to help chop firewood in the rain. But slavery haunted the present, even if emancipation had been declared.

For 246 years, Black women's bodies were owned—not by themselves and not even by their husbands, because for much of that time enslaved Black women could not legally marry. Black women were the property of their owner. They existed to increase the owner's wealth through free labor and increase his sense of power through sexual domination.

Neither woman nor man had the power to determine whether their families would stay together or remain clean of the imposition of other men. Lea might even have been forced to breed children on her owner's farm. Imagine living your preteen, teenage, and young adult years being forced to sleep with multiple men—to birth babies that you would not get to raise. What does that experience do to one's spirit? What does that family arrangement do to one's understanding of family? What does that do to one's relationship with one's children? What does that do to Black women's relationships with their sons? What does that do to sons' understanding of, respect for, and capacity to honor Black women?

In *Post Traumatic Slave Syndrome*, Joy DeGruy explains that the history of Black American families reveals that, unlike in White America where stress tends to bring unity, within Black American families layered trauma mixes with stress to bring fragmentation.[12] DeGruy explains: "Many of our ancestors had to start from scratch to develop the necessary skills to maintain family."[13]

She adds: "For their part, the men suffer from a kind of inner psychic assault, demons emerging from a mythical masculine world of their own making, a world they create to endure their status of invisibility and impotence. He [the Black man], in subduing her [the Black woman], begins to feel a hint of power that vanishes more swiftly than a shadow when he returns to his white-male-dominated world."[14]

Lea's son, Martha's brother, Annie's uncle raped Annie in the woods that day. He likely used the ax to threaten her into submission. He likely chased and cornered her. He likely pounced and punched her down. He likely ripped off her head wrap, pushing her hair and body into the flooding mulch as he ripped her body and soul. Then he left her there to die in the mud, under unrelenting sheets of rain.

With Annie covered in filth and curled in a ball, I imagine Lizzie back at the house becoming irritated at first, then nervous when Annie did not return with the wood. They searched for her and found her beaten and bruised body deep in the woods. They carried her back and nursed her to consciousness and never-ending tears. Wailing rage and confusion filled the house and family. Annie never recovered. Nine months later she screamed her own child into the world and, like her mother, Annie slipped from this life soon after. Lea named the baby Snake. And according to the family story, the offending uncle was banished from the family forever.

Lizzie gave birth to a baby girl, Willie-Belle, the same month that Snake was born, July 1909. Willie-Belle was my grandmother. Now that I understand the context, I believe Lizzie found comfort in the arms of Charles Jenkins soon after her sister was attacked. Willie-Belle was the fruit.

Lizzie, never having known her mother or father, now suffered her sister being raped by her now-banished uncle. The family that had been so tight-knit was shattered. Lizzie bore three children by her husband Charles Jenkins: Willie Belle, who later changed her name to Willa Belle, Charles Jr., and Martha (named after the mother who Lizzie never knew).

Lea died in 1917 at the age of eighty-one. She lived eight years with her great-grandchildren—the third generation after slavery. Snake, Willie-Belle, and Martha were held by, scolded by, disciplined by, and loved by a living monument to American history—and they had no idea. To them, Lea was just Great-Grandmom.

With her strongest family ties in Camden gone, I imagine Lizzie stood on Lea's porch in the spot where she and Annie perhaps swapped dreams some seventeen years earlier. I see her look down at the weather-worn planks. They seem so small and rickety now that Lizzie is an adult, not like the foundation of a life full of gold-trimmed white moths. There was no more magic here—only loss.

Here Lizzie lost her mother, her sister, and her grandmother. And in four years she would lose Charles Jenkins too. The "railroad accident" took away her only love.

Widowed and without options under the snake-filled blanket of Jim Crow oppression and terror, Lizzie made the break. I like to believe she decided to follow her childhood dream. She would establish herself up north and send for family when ready. To have the best chance, she would leverage her octoroon skin to enter the graces of high-end restaurants where she could work as a waitress and make good money. She chose her lightest-skinned child, Martha, to travel with her. Martha and Lizzie joined the approximately seven million people of African descent who walked, filled trains, and packed cars heading north and west—outside the reach of southern Jim Crow terror. She eventually landed a job waitressing on the floor of the Grand Hotel in Philadelphia's Center City. In those days, Black people were relegated to kitchen jobs with suppressed wages in the North.

Willie-Belle and Charles Jr. were left behind, too dark to pass. Aunties and uncles received money from Lizzie to provide food and clothing to her children. But Grandmom said she never saw a penny. When she was finally called north to join her mother in Philadelphia a few years later, Willie-Belle boarded the train in near rags. She and her brother Charles had been forced to work in the cotton fields of Kershaw County to earn their keep. Grandmom refused to talk about South Carolina with anyone, and she never stepped foot in the South again.

When Lizzie fell in love with Cyrus Gillerson, a dark-skinned man, she was found out. Her boss discovered that she was Black, and he immediately put her in the kitchen with the other Black workers. She worked there as a baker for the rest of her working life. I believe that moment was bittersweet for Lizzie. She lost the vested assumption of goodness, competence, and rightness that comes with White-presenting skin. But Lizzie gained something greater— reconnection to the experience of her African American community. Throughout the Great Depression, my great-grandmother Lizzie became one of the most renowned bakers at the Grand

Hotel. She gained enough favor that she would take sweets home every night and pass them out to her hungry South Philadelphia neighbors—most of whom were also from Kershaw County, South Carolina.

Slavery fragmented our families. Jim Crow pulverized us through housing segregation, job limitation, medical racism, and assumptions of criminality that we paid for with our lives. These subjugation strategies have continued to cost Black families nearly 150 years of wealth accumulation. Generations of families were fragmented through death, migration, and prison, ripping gaping holes in our souls.

But a secret source of power has been passed down through the generations of African American families. That which should have gutted us did not. We reached down deep and touched our own souls. We connected to God. And like Lea, we looked up and listened to the ancestors sing over our tears. And still . . . like dust . . . we rise.[15]

5

Reinaldo y Anita

Bomba

Uncle Donnie twirled me around, then pushed out and pulled in, then showed his dazzling footwork, then swayed—and swayed. I was about seven years old, and magic was erupting in my paternal grandparents' living room again, as uncles, aunts, nephews, and nieces did the Hustle through the night. Dancing always seemed to break out at Weeks family gatherings. The Weeks family gushed with loud love. By contrast, my mother's Lawrence side was quiet, stoic, filled with the kind of love that served each other in their family system. Unlike the Lawrence line, which featured four siblings who visited sporadically throughout the week, the Weeks family came together as a collective. Aunties and uncles made grand entrances followed by beloved cousins who congregated and played at the feet of their adults.

Childhood visits to Grandpop Austin and Grandmom Ethel Weeks's house were filled with movement. I remember moving through their house, never sitting down. A velvet chartreuse couch and love seat beckoned me. Its high back and lion's claw feet tempted visitors to feel like royalty. But covered in a bulky layer of protective plastic, to sit on the couch created sounds that rivaled the trombone section of a marching band. Cold in the winter and boiling in the summer, the couch caused a discomfort that I avoided by mostly never sitting down. Instead, I moved through the house, from kitchen to living room, upstairs to bedrooms, and back again. Every time I visited, there was always dancing. I learned the Hustle at a family dinner.

Love flowed between the seven Weeks children, including one who passed away as a baby and one who died of sickle cell anemia the same year I learned the Hustle. To watch them dance and laugh and be loud and to smell the stewed oxtail, black-eyed peas, plantains, and white rice that filled their St. Albans, Queens, New York home, one would think they lived without care. But the Weeks siblings were master survivors. They survived Caribbean slavery. They survived poverty and disenfranchisement in Puerto Rico at the time of its US annexation. They survived their family's incremental migration to New York City in the era of Ellis Island. And they survived the bold act of integrating a Jewish community in the South Bronx at the height of the Depression.

What we didn't know in those hustling days is that our family danced to survive. Body movement was an act of defiant self-actualization in the hurricane of oppression that swept our ancestors from the shores of Africa to enslavement on the island of Barbados, and then carted them between islands and masters. Like their ancestors, who danced the defiant Bomba in the Black Caribbean postabolition settlement of Santurce, Puerto Rico, my father's generation of Weeks siblings hustled out oppression passed down from brutal English and Dutch owners and bosses and given to each generation by the last like a family heirloom. Violation and separation became the Weeks's keepsake. So they employed the powers of the Hustle and later the Electric Slide, just like our ancestors called forth the Bomba. These strong aunties and uncles donned dashikis in an attempt to give voice to some sense of self. Dance and dashikis both healed them and masked generations of pain.

Like the mangrove trees of Puerto Rico, Weeks family pathologies are like the leaves and branches that sway in the winds of current events. But intertwined beneath the surface, roots reach deep to the shores of West Africa and the indigenous peoples of South America through centuries of separation, displacement, exploitation, and abuse on Caribbean islands.

The Caribbean islands are shrouded in stories of pirates, shipwrecks, and coconuts. Never, in all the fables passed on from the Caribbean, did I hear the stories of genocide and slavery. But those two stories are the context within which pirates pirated, ships were wrecked, and coconuts were split. Exploring the Weeks line called me to dig under and around the roots to understand their context.

Around 1200 BCE, Taíno (Arawak) explorers boarded canoes off the coast of Venezuela's Orinoco Valley and rowed east.[1] They came upon the island we now call Barbados. More followed until several settlements were established on the island by 800 CE. Five hundred years later, the Kalinago (Carib) peoples landed on the island, and some speculate that they wiped out the Taíno. In 1536 the first Portuguese explorer Pedro a Campos landed on the island. For the next fourteen years, Spanish raiders unleashed a reign of terror, pilfering from the island and enslaving its people. They sold the Kalinago and remaining Taíno to neighboring regional plantations. The Kalinago abandoned the island.[2]

The English were the first Europeans to claim the island in 1627. Within decades, Barbados became the primary receiving port for British prisoners and indentured servants. In 1685, eight hundred West End men were banished to Barbados after they joined an attempted coup against King James II.[3] Nearly seven thousand Irish were banished to the island in the Cromwellian era, making Barbados the hub of White life in the British colonies. Barbados played a key role in the settlement of both Jamaica and the Carolinas. From Barbados, White owners, traders, indentured servants, prisoners, and enslaved Africans flowed to and between other British colonies in the New World.

Britain increased its participation in the transatlantic slave trade in 1670 when it developed technology that allowed its ships to successfully transport enslaved Africans directly from their home-land to the American colonies—a far longer trek than to Barbados. Still, Barbados was closer. The island received the lion's share of traffic for decades. By 1750, enslaved Africans were the dominant population, and the island had become Britain's first 100 percent slave-based economy.[4]

The only Weekes plantation in the Caribbean was situated on the far eastern tip of Barbados. The Mangrove Plantation of St. Philips Parish was owned by Ralph Weekes in 1680.[5] The Weekes family were Quakers.[6]

Ancestry.com DNA estimates that my first African ancestors deboarded an English slave ship in Barbados circa 1750.[7] The thick shackles clinked as they walked onto land in the colony's capital city of Bridgetown. From there, they were likely taken to a hold-ing pen near the auction square in the center of town. Under the pounding Caribbean sun, a descendant of Ralph Weekes, likely his grandson, lifted his hand to bid on the first African ancestor of my father's line to enter the Western Hemisphere. The British Weekes descendant likely examined my Yoruba ancestor as the auctioneer opened my ancestor's mouth to show his teeth. Weekes scanned his Black body, rubbed with grease to hide sores and to glisten under the tropical sun. And he lifted his own hand enough times to win my ancestor. I can imagine Weekes then carting my ances-tor to the Mangrove Plantation, where they branded him with the family surname and seared their initials into my ancestor's back.

Between 1662 and 1807, Brits bought and sold 3.1 million Africans to the Caribbean and American colonies through the transatlantic slave trade.[8] Nearly 400,000 were removed from their homelands and forcibly carried to Barbados alone. By 1684, Af-rican descendants made up 66 percent of the population of Bar-bados. One hundred years later, it was 79 percent. Through the mid-1700s, mortality rates for enslaved Africans on the island were so high that fresh boatloads of their kin regularly replenished the enslaved population. In the second half of the eighteenth century

increased gender parity allowed natural birth to exceed importation as the leading cause of population growth among the enslaved
in Barbados.[9] This was not the case on other Caribbean islands
like St. Kitts and Nevis, where the average enslaved person only
lasted eight to twelve years in the fields of St. Kitts. Two-fifths
died within one year of arrival. Twenty-two percent died on the
Middle Passage.[10]

I am baffled by the strength of my ancestors, my great-great-
grandfather John Weekes and my great-great-grandmother Mar-
garita Lucas. Their families were among the survivors in St. Kitts
and Nevis. The trauma their parents likely endured is unspeakable.

Testimonies shared by the International Slavery Museum in
Liverpool tell the story of the horrors of slavery on Caribbean
plantations: "If a Mill-feeder be catch'd by the finger, his whole
body is drawn in, and is squees'd to pieces, If a Boyler gets any
part into the scalding Sugar, it sticks like Glew, or Birdlime, and
'tis hard to save either Limb or Life."[11] In another account: "An
enslaved woman called Mimba, who was in her late 30s or 40s
had her 'hands ground off,' probably when feeding canes into the
mill, on William Stapleton's plantation in Nevis."[12] Mimba lost
her hands to increase the comfort quotient in a cup of English tea.

Ancestry.com DNA traces the movement of my Weekes family
across the Lesser Antilles in the Caribbean from about 1750 to
1925. Each move separated family members, deepened grief, and
further isolated men, women, and children. The movement of my
family's DNA reveals the complete disregard for enslaved African
descendant families. My West African family was deemed "Black"
by the state. As such, it was deemed chattel—like chattel homes
on the island of Barbados, each family member was able to be
picked up and moved when conditions deemed it necessary. Being
cut off from roots became a norm within my Caribbean family.

John Weekes's great-grandparents likely slaved on the island of
Barbados, where Ancestry.com places the greatest concentration of
Weekes/Weeks family DNA. Within one generation of its arrival
circa 1750, this line of the family was separated and shipped to
Grenada, Trinidad, Tobago, St. Vincent, the Grenadines, St. Lucia,

Antigua, St. Kitts, Nevis, St. Croix, St. Thomas, Guyana, and Su-
riname. West African descended Weekes family members were
owned by four separate colonizing nations: Britain, Spain, France,
and the Netherlands. By 1800, at least one ancestor was extracted
again and enslaved in San Juan, Puerto Rico.

St. Kitts and Nevis declared emancipation in 1833 and 1834,
respectively. Drought, hurricanes, and decades of economic in-
stability followed on emancipation's heels, pushing newly freed
men and women to move from island to island again, this time in
search of work, food, and shelter.

My great-great-grandfather, John Weekes, was born in 1843.
According to a 1904 manifest of alien passengers entering New
York City, John's son, my great-grandfather Reinaldo (b. 1873),
lists his birthplace as Barbados. Likewise, Reinaldo's daughter,
Lilian, lists her birthplace and both her parents' birthplace as
Barbados on the 1920 census. It seems after more than a century
of being carted around the Caribbean, John had found his way
home to Barbados and to the social stability that comes from
being rooted in a place among a people. Two generations knew
that stability until the Caribbean economy went bust.

With the abolition of slavery, the sugar industry dried up and
the economy crashed throughout the Caribbean. Two generations
of my family moved from island to island seeking stability in the
wake of emancipation. In 1908, Reinaldo's brother found his way
to the Panama Canal, the epic work project that employed thousands of Caribbean men desperate for work. Each one left family
yet again to make colonizers' economic dreams come true.

In the midst of Puerto Rico's annexed and crumbling economy,
Reinaldo Weekes found work in the capital, San Juan. By 1923, he
was a Black servant, likely working in the household of a White
land baron or politician. Situated solidly at the bottom of Puerto
Rico's racialized hierarchy, in an era permeated by eugenics theory,
at a time when Jim Crow America won the Spanish-American
War and consequently claimed Puerto Rico as its own—in this

era, Reinaldo married Anita de Richarson, a Black maid from Anguilla, on April 5, 1923. They lived in Santurce, near San Juan, with their nine-year-old son, Austin—my grandfather. Austin communed around a Bomba drum with his Santurce neighbors all of them annexed Americans without the full rights of citizenship. He watched adults dance out the oppression heaped upon their Black backs by San Juan's White ruling class. He bore witness as his neighbors offered their bodies to the Bomba beat for cleansing—for healing.

Santurce is one of three major hubs of Black culture and community life on the northeastern coast of Puerto Rico, along with Carolina and Loiza. Much like South Philadelphia was the first northern destination for freed men and women in the post–Civil War era, Santurce became a primary destination for emancipated people throughout the Caribbean.

When Reinaldo y Anita returned home from serving their White masters each day, they likely returned to a wooden home built on stilts atop Santurce's swampland. According to their marriage certificate, Reinaldo y Anita lived on Calle Loiza (Loiza Street), a main boulevard that flooded each time it rained and washed out when hurricanes passed over.

I imagine my little grandfather sitting cross-legged on the floor at Reinaldo's feet, huddled in a room with fellow Caribbean migrant neighbors, the rhythm of Santurce's Bomba Sicá (walking) filling the air. Like a Black man's strut, the rhythm has a groove—a swagger—an elegance. It reminds me of my grandfather.

Black Puerto Ricans under Jim Crow rule could not determine where they would live, where they would work, and how much their labor would be worth—and they could not protect their bodies from exploitation or molestation. They were subject to the racialized boundaries placed on housing, vocation, and rights. But in the Bomba circle the beat beckoned their bodies to move at will, where they willed and how they willed. In the Bomba, the men could plant their feet where they wanted, for as long as they wanted. The women could shake their hips how they wanted. The dancers could freeze when they wanted. And the women would extend their arms like eagles' wings, gripping their handmade crinolines, and they could move each side as if telling the story of their soul's triumph that day with each beat. Chests faced sky as shoulders bounced and arms pounded air compelled by the drum. The Bomba is pure power and dignity exercised by people stripped of both. They pounded out their pain in the midst of the community, encircled and supported by all.

Calle Loiza shares its name with the town of Loiza, named after the female chief of the region, Loaíza or Yuíza, who is fabled to have married the free African conquistador, Pedro Mejías, who settled the region. The town of Loiza was reserved by the Spanish crown as a settlement for Puerto Rico's enslaved Africans in the early 1600s. As a result, Loiza became the center of Black life and culture in Puerto Rico.

The Ayalas are one of three families that preserve the tradition of Bomba in Puerto Rico. Tito Ayala's uncle, Raul, runs the family's one-room, bright Yellow House that sits on the edge of Loiza's main road. The house is home to artifacts, paintings, pictures, and videos documenting the town's history. In the carport next to the house, Tito hosts Bomba drum and dance lessons each weekend. Around the corner from the Yellow House, cousin Wilcelino Pizzaro carves from coconuts the masks for the Festival of St. James. Across the road is the two-story wooden home and studio of Ayala cousin and renowned fine artist Samuel Lind, whose paintings and sculptures capture the spirit of Loiza and the Bomba and are featured in museums and galleries across the globe. I visited Loiza and spoke with these Ayala family members in June 2018. They taught me about Loiza, and without realizing it, they taught me about my grandfather Austin and myself.

Tito Ayala sat back on his folding chair in the carport next to the Yellow House. Soft-spoken and powerful, Tito explained, "Loiza is one of the first places we find the Bomba. When the slaves were brought to Puerto Rico, they were spread around the coast of the island on sugarcane plantations. The enslaved people around the island had something in common. It didn't matter if they were in San Juan, Carolina, or Loiza, they had the same drum. Each area had different rhythms, but it was all Bomba played on the Bomba drum."[13]

Africans brought to Puerto Rico were generally from present-day Nigeria, the kingdom of Dahomey, and Guinea.[14] The vast majority were Yoruba and Igbo. Though dispersed across the island, their home culture was the same. The drums were the same. Life in different parts of the island influenced the rhythms, but the Bomba drum and West African souls were the common source of those rhythms.

Tito continued, "When the people finished their work, their masters gave permission to do their festival. There they played the Bomba. . . . The Bomba is a conversation—between dancer and drummer. It does not stand on its own, but is everything: It is the dance. It is the drum. It is the festival and the mask."

When the Spanish claimed Loiza in the sixteenth century, they brought with them the annual Festival of St. James, the patron saint of Spain.[15] According to Loiza lore, an enslaved woman found a statue of St. James in the root of a tree in Loiza. She came back a second day and found it again. On the third day she returned and found it again. The people considered this a miracle, and from that time on they celebrated the Festival of St. James in Loiza. But the people subverted the meanings handed to them by their Spanish captors. Instead, they overlaid the traditional festival characters with West African meaning drawn from legends of their own people's military might and human dignity.

Three figures of St. James are featured in the festival: the patron of men, the patron of women, and the patron of children. The figures are embodied by three characters: the Vejigante who represents the African Muslim Arabs (Moors) who conquered Spain in the eighth century, the Conquistador who represents the Catholic Spaniards who pushed them out, and the Tricksters, akin to the trickster of African folklore, Anansi, the spider who outsmarted opponents with wit and craft. According to Tito Ayala, the figures also represent the Trinity. In this creole society, where Spaniards colonized and enslaved Taíno and African peoples, culture and meanings are layered.

According to the original legend of St. James, the saint appeared in a vision and promised to push the Muslims out of Spain. When the Moors were eventually pushed out, St. James was established as the patron saint of Spain.

"But the damage was done," quipped Tito Ayala. By the time the Spaniards told their African captives this story, African Muslims had already conquered Spain. So, when the enslaved West Africans heard the story, they identified with the Moors. They saw the Moors' power and were reminded of Chango, the conquering king from their own Yoruban heritage. More powerful in death, Chango inspired enslaved Yorubans who saw his power in St. James.

Tito explained: overt rejection of the master's message could lead to death, so the people accepted the message on the surface but changed its meaning in their communities. For the enslaved, St. James became Chango—the African warrior, strong enough to save them.

Samuel Lind explained further: The Vejigante was the best personification of African culture in Puerto Rico. Demonized by the Spaniards, the Vejigante walked through the street with a mask in bright colors and looked menacing from far away. But, Lind explained, "when he comes near, you feel happy. He talks with the people." Thus, in Loiza, the Festival of St. James developed as a subversive celebration of African power, complicit with the worldview of their oppressors on the surface, but defiant and empowered at its heart. The Bomba drum and dance permeate the festival. In the same way that Loiza legend tells the story of enslaved Africans who escaped into the mangrove trees and became the mangrove trees, those who stayed behind escaped into the Bomba and became the Bomba.

From his Brooklyn home, fortysomething Austin Weeks cast aside the weight of the White American dream, pumpkin pie, and

New York pizza to conjure his Caribbean soul and draw from his childhood Santurce community. There, in the memories of the Bomba, he mustered the strength to strut past pre-civil-rights-movement, mid-twentieth-century oppression.

With Austin and his parents having emigrated to New York City in 1925, all of his brothers and sisters had joined them in the South Bronx by 1930. My Aunt Najuma Weeks shared in an interview that her father graduated high school and attended Brooklyn College. He married Jamaican and Guyanese American Ethel Gemon, the daughter of Rev. Hubert Nicholas Gemon and Helier Eugennie LeSague. Rev. Gemon was an itinerant preacher who hailed from the Dutch quarter of a French area within British Guiana. Though we do not know his father's name, we know one thing about him that speaks volumes: according to the 1920 census, Hubert's father was from Holland and spoke Dutch. Originally from Kingston, Jamaica, Ethel's mother, Helier, moved with her husband from state to state until their family settled in New York City by 1930. Ethel bore Austin seven children, two of whom were stricken with sickle cell anemia. Austin wanted to be a lawyer. It took everything he had to hang on in school for two years, but bills hounded him. He dropped out of college, released his dream, and entered public service working for decades with the New York Housing Authority, advancing to the position of foreman of caretakers and eventually retiring with honors. Austin worked second and third part-time jobs to supplement his income, including as a retail clerk at the Abraham & Straus department store and as a driving instructor.

But performance was his love and second vocation. He often sang in nightclubs in the evening and composed his own music. Austin played the piano and the drums—especially the conga and bongo drums.

Aunt Najuma remembered those days with a smile: "Whenever the family came over to visit, our entertainment was each other," she said. "We had singers, dancers, musicians, and drummers."[16]

They danced with each other. They taught each other the steps. They taught each other the beats. Reinaldo—now called Grandpop Reginald—and Anita, always dressed with dignity, taught the young ones the old ways—what they would need to survive the oppression sure to come. They never talked about the racism they encountered in life with their children, nor did Austin or Ethel talk about it with their children. Rather, the adults locked White supremacy outside of the cocoons of their homes. Inside the home, Black dignity and excellence was the focus—taught through the Bomba and the arts.

And the children learned. Aunt Najuma became an actress, director, poet, and arts educator. Her sister, my Aunt Na'imah (born Ethelyn) became a lawyer. Aunt Najuma remembers her father beaming at Na'imah's graduation. Uncle Donnie became an advertising and marketing executive, while Uncle Richie loved poetry and took up learning the saxophone. And the baby, Aunt Linda, became a singer. My father, Dennis, became a known photographer in the vanguard of the 1960s Black theater scene in New York City—artists' souls, all.

Like the art of the Bomba and the festival, the force of the Bomba lifts the soul out of the mire of despair. Previous generations' despair was heaped on them by economic exploitation and the brutality it took to enforce it. The next generations passed down their survival tactics along with gashes begotten by rods wielded by their own broken souls.

Aunt Najuma told me the story of how Austin's inner rage let loose on her.

She had become a singer and was invited to sing for a cousin's cotillion, a formal ball. Cotillions were things girls did, so she asked her mother if she could attend. Her mother, Ethel, said yes and helped her prepare. Najuma sold tickets on behalf of her cousin while Ethel made her a special dress. Najuma threw herself into practicing her song for the big day.

On the day of the cotillion, Austin came home from work early and stopped her from going, because his daughter and his wife did not get his permission. Black patriarchy slams the lives of Black women. Economically stunted, socially hunted, and mentally isolated, castrated Black manhood lines Black women's souls with gashes the size of a machete. Each cut is a vain attempt to feel what it's like to wield some amount of power in a White patriarchal world.

But women are not the only victims. Children also bear the brunt.

Austin used to line up his children in a humiliating ritual on weekends and go through an accumulated list of each child's offenses from the previous week. Then he would whip them—all of them—one by one.[17]

Throughout his adolescent years, my Uncle Don shared with me in an interview, Austin beat him once per week—or every two weeks in a good stretch.

"I remember times when my dad hit me so hard," Don said, "that I'd wake up on the floor somewhere. I would actually pass out."

He added, "My father made a paddle with a handle so that he could hold it. I would get whacked with that to the point where there was blood on the paddle."

"That was not a one-time event," Don emphasized.[18]

Austin passed the Bomba down to his children; as it turns out, they needed it to survive him—and every ounce of racialized subjugation heaped on his back and the backs of his ancestors.

Centuries of fragmentation, separation, and abuse now play out as predictable pathologies from generation to generation. My father, Dennis, escaped his father's fury and forged his own way in 1959 New York City at seventeen. Don also escaped the beatings at age seventeen. He moved out before the end of his senior year in high school. I can only imagine the terror at home that would drive multiple seventeen-year-olds to abandon ship. The terror of being in the world without the cover or guidance of parents must have been less painful than the terror at home. Dennis worked odd jobs to pay for a room and make a way. Don joined a marketing apprenticeship program that offered housing and a living stipend. Other siblings left as soon as they could, eventually leaving Linda, the youngest, to fend for herself.

My father's generation is fragmented now, occasionally drawn together by their children's attempts to unite the family. To this day, unnamed pain festers beneath smiles and attempts to love. But that pain explodes upon the slightest provocation, taking away fragile connections in its wake.

To some degree, I understand it. Hurt people hurt people, and no one needs to tolerate abuse. But another part of me imagines what our lives might have been like if the British John Weekes had never enslaved a single human being—had never passed down people and property to his family—had never branded or sold a single member of my family—had never separated my family from their homelands only to be separated again and again and again in every single generation.

Today, fifteen Caribbean nations are forging forward, calling on Britain, France, and Holland to repair what their racialized greed broke in the world. In 2013 the Caribbean Community (Caricom) launched its push for reparations for Native American genocide and African enslavement. They called for reparations and an apology. Britain refused both.

In the wake of the May 25, 2020, murder of George Floyd by police officers in Minneapolis, formerly colonized peoples and nations marched for justice around the world. They recognized the knee on Floyd's neck as the same knee on theirs through the systems of colonization, enslavement, exploitative "apprenticeship" in the Caribbean, Jim Crow in the US, and apartheid in South Africa. They identified common current-day, policy-based pathologies that haunt the lives and stunt the flourishing of formerly colonized peoples around the world, including poverty, mass imprisonment, police brutality, environmental injustice, unequal education, poor housing, and lack of healthcare. In response, Black and Brown nations across the globe rose up to demand reparatory justice. In that context, in July 2020, Caricom pushed again, updating its call for reparatory justice via an online event hosted by the University of the West Indies and attended by heads of state and leading experts on reparations.[19]

The case for Caribbean reparations is clear (and will be explored further in part 3). For now, it is enough to know that those who lived it see it. Race broke us. It broke us all. None of us will ever find peace until we fix it.

In the early days of the COVID crisis, I got a glimpse of healing for my family. My cousin, Rich "Dred" Weeks (also known as DJ RTrane), leveraged his deejaying talent and resources to bring the family together online for Saturday night dance parties. DJ RTrane spun the oldies as Weeks cousins, aunties, uncles, nephews, and nieces clicked into the online party. Each one made an entrance and each was welcomed with loud love. Then we boogied down. We danced out the pain of COVID. We danced out the pain of separation, both forced and chosen. We danced out the pain of incarcerations and deaths and lost loves and lost jobs and no jobs within the family. And in the dancing, we felt the sacredness of the Bomba circle—the community that holds you as you dance out your pain with elegance and strength. I felt the Bomba spirit especially thick when DJ RTrane played our family classic, and Van McCoy beckoned us, "Do the Hustle."

Lea Ballard (ca. 1836–1917)

My great-great-grandfather Philip Fortune (ca. 1835–1907), father of Ella Fortune

Harriet Smith (ca. 1854–1930), photographed by Junius Lawrence after their trip to Indiana (chap. 2)

"Mother + Dad" "1943"

Hiram (1882–1958) and Ella (1882–1970) outside their home in Elmwood

Hiram Lawrence with his grandchildren,
Sharon (b. 1948) and Richie (1946–1975),
in the Elmwood community in Philadelphia

Hiram and Willa (1909–1993) fishing with Sharon (seated) and Richie
(standing)

Great-Grandpop Hiram and his son, Junius (1909–1973), next to their matching trucks for their hauling business

Great-Grandpop Hiram, photographed at the Delaware Water Gap

This iconic photograph of Hiram sat on my mother's mantle throughout my childhood

Richie Lawrence, my uncle

Elizabeth "Lizzie" Johnson
(1890–1980)

Reinaldo (ca. 1873–?) and Anita (ca.
1888–?) Weekes with their children;
my grandfather Austin is seated,
holding his brother Antonio (ca.
1926)

Willa Belle Jenkins (1909–1993) visiting Junius F. Lawrence (1909–1973) on a military base in Michigan during WWII

Grandmom Willa Belle Jenkins

Lawrence family outside their home in Elmwood. *Back row:* Junius Lawrence, Neil Lawrence, Catherine Robinson (Neil's daughter), Junius "Larry" Lawrence Jr., Neil Jr.'s girlfriend, Neil Lawrence Jr., Marshall Lawrence. *Front row:* Sharon Lawrence (kneeling), Ella Fortune, Hiram Lawrence, Richie Lawrence (kneeling)

Mom and me. Sharon Lea Lawrence (b. 1948) and Lisa Sharon Harper (b. 1969)

6

Sharon

Rebellion

My mother is a writer, but it took most of her life for her to know it. Following the rules of White patriarchy, she was conditioned to win a man and stay in her racial caste. To win the man she had to hold her tongue and shrink her mind and her will to fit inside his. To stay in her caste, she was told she had to diminish her own capacity to contribute to the world. Hers was the Rubicon generation—the generation that crossed over from the mores of Jim Crow and northern ghettos into a world where they could live anywhere, do anything—be anyone. But it was not without costs levied by the backlash of White patriarchy, ever present, ever devising more ways to subjugate and more ways to protect its own power.

At age seven, my mother, Sharon Lawrence, sat at the kitchen table in her family's three-story South Philadelphia row home on Dickinson Street. Sharon's feet swung in opposite directions as they often did when she had something on her mind.[1]

Sharon's father, Junius, held the September 15, 1955, issue of *Jet* magazine in his hand. It was one year after *Brown v. Board of Education* affirmed African Americans' constitutional right to equal protection of the law. Now, news of the dredging of Emmett Till's mangled body, dragged from a river in Mississippi, pulsated through Black communities across the country. The fourteen-year-old's beaten, mutilated, stripped body was wrapped in razor wire and tied to a seventy-pound cotton gin fan before being tossed off the side of the Tallahatchie Bridge. They dragged him from the river days later when his body surfaced, bloated and half-eaten by fish.

Emmett's mother, Mamie Till, defied the silence demanded by White patriarchy. Centuries of subjugation trained men, women, and children to hold their tongues to keep their lives. Mamie was Mississippi born in 1921; her parents had moved their family to the industrial North three years later in the midst of the Great Migration. They settled in Argo, Illinois, where they made a go of it for a decade, then split. Mamie threw herself into her schoolwork and became the first Black student to make the honor roll and the fourth ever to graduate from the nearly all-White public school.

I imagine it was that gumption that rose within her at the prospect of bowing to White patriarchy, aiding and abetting its existence by muting her screams, silencing her voice, and binding her own self in the hope that she could live another day—bound and gagged, but living. Mamie said "No." In the wake of Emmett's evisceration by White patriarchy that declared war on her son's body, she lobbed a bomb back. She opened his casket and forced the world to look full in his half-eaten face. Forty-three years after Jim Crow terror had seized the post-Reconstruction South, Mamie Till ignited a firestorm of mass resistance to its brutal hegemony.

My mother remembers her mother and father talking at the kitchen table in hushed tones and coded language: "Did you see that picture?" "How could they do that to that boy?" "My God. What that mother must be going through." "What is wrong with those people?" they asked in awe of White brutality.

Willa Belle and Junius would not allow Sharon and her siblings to see the pictures. Still, my mother caught bits and pieces about Till's demise and the pictures from local Black radio stations,

WHJE and WDAS, and from her friends on the schoolyard and in the neighborhood. Little Sharon's best friends, Linda and Ruby Mae, told her the picture was in *Jet* magazine.

Sharon knew where to find this issue of her father's weekly subscription: between the cushions of the couch. There, two literary gems of the Black community were kept safe: the *Jet* issue featuring pictures of Till and the *Dream Book*. Black families across America owned the *Dream Book*, a book like Sigmund Freud's *Interpretation of Dreams*, except Herbert Gladstone Parris's *Dream Book* listed things one might see in their dreams and translated those occurrences into lottery numbers—before the lottery was legal. Hence, my grandparents' *Dream Book* was hidden under couch cushions.[2]

Sharon left Linda and Ruby Mae and crept into her narrow South Philadelphia row home and crossed the living room, making a beeline for the couch. She knew where to find the magazine. She had seen it hidden under the couch cushion. She lifted the cushions and found the treasures. She flipped through the pages till she reached page eight. There she saw it, but she barely understood what she was looking at: Was it human? She put it back and covered it with the cushion so no one would know it was disturbed. But the memory stayed, and later she came back to see it again. Sharon kept coming back to view that image.

She remembered the image one day when she was taken out of class the same year. There were two elementary schools within two blocks in Sharon's Point Breeze neighborhood in South Philly. G. W. Child's Elementary was located across the street from her home on Dickinson Street. All of the Black children in the neighborhood went to Child's. All-White Drexel School was located two blocks away. Sharon's White next-door neighbors attended Drexel. In this 1955 northern city, segregated schooling was covertly practiced through administrative gatekeepers' claims that Black students were "out of district" and therefore could not attend the White schools.

High achievers at Child's were given the "privilege" of being drafted to supply free labor to White teachers by washing blackboards and beating erasers after school or offering free messaging service during school hours. My mother was a great student, so her little Black body was conditioned by the logic of White supremacy to do what it was created to do—offer free labor to increase White comfort. Like a mule, my mother was pulled from class—pulled from opportunities to learn more—to carry a message from one part of the school to another.

One day, Sharon sat on the scuffed wooden bench outside the principal's office. Secretaries sat behind the counter, click-clacking away on their typewriters. To her right was a box of books. Curious, Sharon's feet swung back and forth in opposite directions as she reached in and picked up one of the books. They had been originally stamped to Drexel School. Old and worn, pages were missing and there was writing in the margins. She picked up another book. The cover was missing. Another and another and another—all defective; all used, reused, and used again until they were ready for distribution to Black children. These books had been used by the all-White Drexel School for a generation. Now they were being handed down to the Black school—with the Drexel stamp still there.

According to my mother, this pattern repeated itself up through junior high. She watched and waited for new books, new desks, new supplies. Instead, each year her Black schools received the hand-me-down books, desks, and supplies from the White school blocks away. And each year she watched her White teachers spend more time in the teachers' lounge than inside the classroom. She watched them let Black children run rampant in the classroom while never really teaching them. This, too, is the logic of White supremacy: to go through the motions of teaching to appease the law, all the while never truly preparing Black students to flourish—to be competitive in academics, business, law, or governance. The country was in an uproar, shocked by the violence of Till's evisceration. Meanwhile, de facto segregated education was eviscerating the futures of Blacks in the North.

Sharon's grandmother, Lizzie, had forged north from South Carolina, in large part because by law she was not permitted to flourish there. By law, she was relegated to field or domestic work. Under Jim Crow law, Whites snagged exclusive rule and shoved all else to beg for scraps on their knees. Now Lizzie's granddaughter was the one shoved down, this time in the North. Not by explicit laws but rather by embedded policies, procedures, and budget allocations.

In Martin Luther King Jr.'s final manuscript *Where Do We Go from Here?* he exposes the economic disparities within northern schools during the years when Sharon was in high school: "Statistical evidence revealed in 1964 that Chicago spent an average of $366 a year per pupil in predominantly white schools and from $450 to $900 a year per pupil for suburban white neighborhoods, but the Negro neighborhoods received only $266 per year per pupil."[3]

Sharon suffered the violence of White nationalism—the commitment to preserve one's nation for White rule. It is the same violence exacted on the body of Emmett Till. The only difference was the means. The violence that Till absorbed was levied by the hands of individuals and protected by the courts. It inflicted unspeakable pain and ended his life outright. The violence levied on Black children by school systems structured to prepare White children to lead and Black children to be led is violence against Black futures. It is pure violence against the image of God within each Black body. Each time a Black child is taken out of class to carry a message rather than prepared to lead their family, their community, their city, their state, our nation—each and every time a Black or Brown child receives an outdated textbook or no textbook at all—each and every time a Black or Brown child is forced to learn from unqualified or underpaid teachers—each time Black and Brown children are herded into the vocational tech track—it is one more gash in the future prospects of that child and every single member of their family for generations forward.

Educational inequity is violence. One might argue it is an act of warfare against the flourishing of fellow citizens.

Where do Black and Brown children go? Where do poor children go—children who cannot afford private school? Children not lucky enough to win the chance to attend a charter school—where can they go?

"Sometimes I come across people of my age who have learning gaps," my mother reflected recently on the education that she and other Black children of her generation received. "Their grammar is bad or they cannot calculate or they do not know how to punctuate. It is often because their White teachers did not teach." And the White system did not prepare them to lead. It prepared them to offer low-cost or no-cost labor.

There was another kind of oppression exacted on children in segregated schools, particularly girls.

In the course of our interview, my mother's memory had been surprisingly sharp. Details like the placement of the books in the principal's office came with force and clarity. But Sharon's memory of one summer in her childhood blurs like a smudged blackboard. It was 1957 or '58.

The Philadelphia school district had instituted a free dental program for public schools. On the surface, this program was a progressive intervention. The school system partnered with Temple University and the University of Pennsylvania to provide free dental care in public schools throughout the city. The census began to track poverty rates in 1959, around the same time that Philadelphia's school dental program ran. At the time, while 18 percent of Whites lived below the poverty line, more than half of African Americans (55 percent) were living hand-to-mouth, not knowing where the next meal would come from, without healthcare—or any care.[4] So the school district pitched in to help.

But it is not enough to implement a program. How that program is administered reveals as much about the care, or lack of care, taken by those who govern toward the governed. The dental program at the G. W. Childs School was located in the school basement. It ran year-round, but few people were present in Philadelphia's boiling summer months: only two White male dentists and one Black female assistant.

Around age eight or nine, Sharon crossed Dickinson Street to enter Childs School where she had learned just two or three years earlier that she was inferior—unworthy of preparation to flourish. Today, she was to receive a different kind of lesson.

Sharon entered the school and walked through cavernous halls she knew like home. This had been her school her entire life. It was all she knew. All they had taught her was her inferiority. That was the familiar. She held the splintering wooden railing as her Keds skipped down stone stairs into the basement—a virtual cave—secluded from the world, set apart for dentistry performed on Black children.

Little Sharon sat on the wooden bench outside the dentist's office, feet swinging in opposite directions. The assistant called her name and guided her into the dentist's office. He stuffed her mouth with cotton and braced it to keep it open as he drilled into her teeth. As he drilled, he felt her nine-year-old leg. His hand was slow, methodical: below the knee, above the knee, mid-thigh, upper thigh under the skirt. My nine-year-old mother was frozen with fear. She could not move until the drill stopped. Only her feet could move. Her Keds flailed.

When I was a child, my mother opened her mouth and showed me all her fillings. "I probably didn't need all of them. I never had one toothache."

That was all she said then. I didn't understand it. As an adult, when I asked my mother how many times she was violated, she pointed to her mouth, full of unnecessary silver fillings. Each one a story of violation, yet it is all a blur now. Sixty-one or sixty-two years later, it is more a composite of several experiences that have melded into one life-altering memory than a detailed account of each filling's story. "It could have happened one time or ten. I don't remember," my mother strained.

Sharon buried this memory in the bowels of the terror trap called G. W. Childs School. She never told a soul about her dental horror until she was an adult. She told her best friend, Linda, who also attended Childs School. Linda said he did the same thing to her.

From Fortune's founding era forward, people of African descent on the soil we now call America had been legally banned from seeking recourse and economically, socially, systemically, and structurally banned from reaching beyond the basement of American life, where the brutality of oppression is hidden in the dark. The majority flailed in poverty. The Lawrence lot was among the fortunate who got to see the light of day in 1950s America. Working class with gainful employment, they lived and moved on the first floor of American life. They could breathe, but they dared not dream of more light, more space, more movement. They could look out of their windows on that first floor and see their neighbors, but they could not see the sky. And occasionally they were pulled into the basement where hidden things happened.

My mother's generation was the last in American history to endure this horror with little legal recourse. Though the Fourteenth Amendment guaranteed the rights of citizenship to all African Americans, regardless of previous state of servitude, and the Fifteenth and Nineteenth Amendments guaranteed all citizens the right to vote, northern cooperation colluded with southern racialized authoritarianism and effectively locked Blacks in the basement of America where torture, terror, and deprivation were the norm. Why? To preserve the bounty of Whiteness.

My mother's generation pushed en masse against that basement door. Rosa Parks, inspired by Emmett Till's open casket, trained to confront violence through nonviolent civil disobedience. A decade earlier, she had organized against the assumed ownership of Black women's bodies through her advocacy for Recy Taylor, who was gang-raped on her way home from church one treacherous September night in 1944 in Abbeville, Alabama. Taylor was kidnapped from a dirt road and gang-raped by six White men ten years before *Brown v. Board of Education* established African Americans' right to equal protection under the law. Since Virginia's establishment of race-based slavery in 1662, Black women had been legally and culturally claimed as the sexual property of White men. Reconstruction brought respite, but Jim Crow threw Black women back in the basement of any White man who would claim her body at any time, any place. To fight would bring death or severe hardship for her or her family.

My mother's terror was not the first in our family. Sharon's mother, Willa, told her about the unusual kindness of one White man who did not attempt to take advantage of her when she was working as a housemaid in the years soon after she had moved north to Philadelphia. The fact that it was unusual for this one White man to not take advantage indicates the likelihood that Willa was raped by one or more of the other White heads of the households under whom she served.

Forerunners—Frederick Douglass, Sojourner Truth, Frances Ellen Harper, Ida B. Wells, Paul Robeson, A. Philip Randolph, W. E. B. Du Bois, Booker T. Washington, Thurgood Marshall, and so many more—laid the foundations that later generations built upon. They won Black freedom. They built Black institutions. They raised Black consciousness. They organized Black unions and news-papers and businesses and legal strategies to win the protection of Black citizenship and the rights it affords. They made the road.

Then Ella Baker, Rosa Parks, Bayard Rustin, James Lawson, James Farmer, John Lewis, Diane Nash, C. T. Vivian, Fannie Lou Hamer, Ralph Abernathy, E. D. Nixon, Jo Ann Robinson, Stokely Carmichael, Malcolm X, Eldridge Cleaver, H. Rap Brown, Mar-tin Luther King Jr., and masses of other individuals rose up and marched on that road. Fueled and informed by their faiths and their communities, they rejected White supremacy and called forth the image of God within themselves and each other. They stood strong in the truth of their own humanity as they looked the crush-ing power of race full in the face and said "No!" in Montgomery and "No!" in Greensboro and "No!" in Nashville and "No!" on the Trailways bus and "No!" in Birmingham and "No!" in Mis-sissippi and "No!" in Selma. They sat down and rode buses, and children braved fire hoses and German shepherds and went to jail, and they died, and they painted the national vision of the Beloved Community from the steps of the Lincoln Memorial. And they lived with the poorest of the poor in Mississippi and registered Black people across the state to vote, and they challenged the White patriarchy of the Mississippi Democratic Party and cast the vision once again of a new America—one where the collective lives into the ideal of democratic governance that our mythology boasts. And they braved whips, batons, and horses on the Edmund Pettus Bridge, and they won the Civil Rights Act of 1964 and the Voting Rights Act of 1965.

Sharon watched it all from elementary school, then junior high, then high school. At fifteen, she begged Junius and Willa to let her board a bus and join the quarter million Americans bound for Washington, DC, on August 28, 1963. It was eight years to the day after Emmett Till's death and, in that time, civil rights organizations such as the NAACP, the Student Nonviolent Coordinating Committee (SNCC), the Congress of Racial Equality (CORE), and the Southern Christian Leadership Conference (SCLC) had organized the nation to stand up and say "No." Sharon desperately wanted to march, but she was too young to go on her own. So she watched the multiracial sea of citizenship on television and devoured every minute. She watched Black and White women and men pour onto the National Mall with signs calling for economic and racial justice. She watched rivers of people of all ages march and cheer and watch from tree limbs. She watched her people speak—clearly—demanding economic, social, civil, and political equality. And her teenage imagination was electrified by Dr. King's dream and pushed by John Lewis's cry: "To those who have said, 'Be patient and wait,' we have long said that we cannot be patient. We do not want our freedom gradually, but we want to be free now!"[5]

One day in 1965, shortly after Selma's "Bloody Sunday," Sharon and her best friend Linda rode the bus north on Sixteenth Street en route to Philadelphia Community College, where they planned to complete two years before transferring to Temple University. But Sharon saw two young men mounting a sign that read "SNCC Philadelphia" at the entrance of 521 South Sixteenth Street. Sharon and Linda got off at the next stop and ran back to the sign. SNCC was opening its first northern office—in Philadelphia—and they sought organizers and staff. Fresh out of high school, my mother became the church outreach organizer for SNCC's Philadelphia office. She was trained by Diane Nash, James Farmer, and Stokely Carmichael, among others, and befriended SNCC members like Ruby Sales while attending SNCC's first annual summer training in Atlanta 1966.[6]

On June 5, 1966, James Meredith, whose body had absorbed the trauma of the University of Mississippi riot when he integrated its campus four years before, set out on a one-man "March against Fear" from Memphis, Tennessee, to Jackson, Mississippi. Meredith wanted to encourage Black Mississippians to register to vote.[7] He was shot down on day two. Veteran Mississippi SNCC organizer Charles McLaurin recruited and partnered with Martin Luther King Jr. and SNCC's new chairperson, Stokely Carmichael, to pick up Meredith's march and finish in his name. Midway through the journey, McLaurin scouted a location in Greenwood, Mississippi, where the group could camp out overnight without harassment from local police. Tucked inside a close-knit Black community, Broad Street Park became the staging ground for Carmichael's most consequential speech.[8]

Organizers rode a pick-up truck to the edge of the park. Carmichael had been picked up by local police and detained earlier that day. He had just returned to the park when organizers called him to the truck, hoisted him onto its flatbed, and passed him the microphone.[9] He called the crowd to courage: "Don't let them scare you when you start opening your mouth—speak the truth!"[10]

After admonishing the crowd to love their Blackness, to define themselves, to reject the White view of Blackness, and instead to set the standards for all, Carmichael's voice raised with his fist as he zeroed in on the heart of the matter: "We have got to get us some Black Power! We don't control anything but what white people say we can control. We have to be able to smash any political machine in the country that's oppressing us and bring it to its knees."[11]

Carmichael's call for Black power was immediately interpreted by many Whites as a foreboding threat of violence or a call to become anti-White. It was neither. Carmichael, who later renamed himself Kwame Ture, seemed to cut time in half with his cry for

Black power. Before this moment, people of African descent had lived under the hegemony of Whiteness for 304 years, when the first race laws were passed in Virginia in 1662. That hegemony told us we were not human. We were not beautiful. We were not meant to determine our own movement or family structures or language or religion or future. We were not meant to steward land, only to work it for the benefit of Whites. We were meant to be ruled. We were created by God to lick White men's boots to make them shine, and like it. We were not even meant to have boots. This was the theological lie. According to Genesis 1:26–27, if a person is human, they are created by God with the call and capacity to steward the world—to make decisions that impact the world. The core sin of people of European descent has been to claim exclusive right to humanness—and thus the exclusive right to stewardship of the world.

Carmichael's call was rebellion against a lie. It was a clarion call for people of African descent to embrace their Blackness and their humanness—to embrace the truth that White people are *not* God. They are merely human. They do not get to determine the boundaries of beauty. They do not get to determine the boundaries of Black flourishing. They do not get to shape our own views of ourselves. We determine our worth. We determine the boundaries of our own flourishing. We determine how we will view ourselves. And this self-determination is not limited to the realm of cultural and social discourse. If we are human, then we are created to flourish and exercise agency in the world—economic and political, as well as social and cultural, agency.

At age eighteen, Sharon was drawn to this message and to this man. She was one of the few from Philadelphia among the charter members of the Philadelphia SNCC office. Sharon was assigned to orient Carmichael to the city when he came to town. The two walked the city. Sharon showed him landmarks and shared local history and politics. Eventually, they began to correspond, sharing personal family stories and dreams. Sharon, who won a citywide writing contest in elementary school, began to write and give speeches for Philadelphia rallies and would introduce Carmichael when he came to speak at the only church that would host him, Father Paul Washington's Church of the Advocate, an Episcopal Church.

As a little girl, Sharon was baptized and confirmed Episcopalian and looked forward to weekly children's Bible school at St. Elizabeth Episcopal Church in South Philly. But she lost faith in the body of Christ when Father Washington was the only pastor courageous enough to challenge White hegemony and welcome SNCC after Stokely's Black power speech. Immediately following the speech, Philadelphia police captain Frank Rizzo, a renowned racist, made it his mission to crush SNCC's Philadelphia chapter. And he did—to smithereens. Only two months after Carmichael's Black power speech, and one month after the Atlanta training, Rizzo unleashed eighty officers to raid the offices and homes of SNCC organizers. According to Sharon, they claimed SNCC possessed a bomb and sowed confusion among the young community. Four of her colleagues were arrested and imprisoned. SNCC fragmented, and the tight-knit community born in the crucible of Black struggle dispersed.

In late 1966, Sharon attended a SNCC retreat in New York's Catskills. The movement gathered to discern its future. Sharon had discovered her voice through SNCC. Speaking, writing, and advocating for Black empowerment unleashed a roar in the spirit of a young woman previously muted by White miseducators. With the Philadelphia SNCC office closed, Sharon drifted into the Philadelphia theater scene, seeking space for her voice on the stage.

In spring 1967, Sharon moved into a tiny apartment with roommates in New York City's Greenwich Village. She lapped up the New York arts scene, auditioning for a spot and nearly landing one in the Negro Ensemble Company. Douglas Turner Ward was interested. He told her to submit her résumé and headshot. She never did. She was distracted by a man.

Having run away from home at the age of seventeen, now-twenty-six-year-old Dennis Weeks, the son of Austin and grandson of Reinaldo y Anita, had married and divorced his high school sweetheart, and was now working odd jobs to make ends meet while breaking into the world of photography.

In fall 1967, nineteen-year-old Sharon entered the Record Hunter record shop on Fifth Avenue and Forty-Second Street. She was in search of the newest Richie Havens album, *Mixed Bag*. She hummed her favorite song, "Handsome Johnny," as she fingered through the album covers.

It's a long hard road, hey, before we'll be free

Dennis was a clerk at the Record Hunter. He approached Sharon and asked if she needed any help. Their conversation was light. They found they had similar musical taste. Dennis was smitten.

He asked if Sharon was a model. He wanted to photograph her. Sharon fell for it.

They dated.

They moved in together.

Months into their courtship, on April 4, 1968, Martin Luther King Jr. was assassinated. Nine months later, Lisa Sharon was born.

But nine years later, Sharon's voice was completely silenced under the weight of external and internalized patriarchy. Writing and acting in New York City gave way to homemaking and caring for three children back in Philadelphia, where she received the support of Willa and Junius. Sharon stuffed her own mouth with the cotton of everyday domestic concerns: paying bills, dealing with marital tensions, raising three young Black girls in a racially charged Philadelphia. She tried to stay connected to the part of herself she found in the movement. In 1976, she became the judge of elections in her West Oak Lane district. She held my hand as we walked across row house lawns on Walnut Lane, going door to door in our declining neighborhood. We knocked on each one to ensure everyone was registered to vote.

Sharon was born only three decades after passage of the Nineteenth Amendment and three years after World War II. She came of age in the midst of a shifting world dominated by men intent on keeping their supremacy. "Don't speak too much," Willa had warned Sharon as she came of age. "Men won't want you." Even within the civil rights movement, women organized the March on Washington, but only one woman was tapped to speak at its podium, and women were forced to march separately from the men.

Sharon met, fell in love with, and married Dennis, an abused son of violent patriarchy. Dennis wanted his wife to do as his mother had done—focus on the children and support him. That's it. He had reached for the vision of the (always White) male provider/protector. He had risen in the ranks of New York photographers. His photographs of Martin Luther King Jr.'s funeral were admired by the editor of *Life* magazine at the time. Dennis followed in the footsteps of his father when he laid down his artistic dreams in favor of the economic stability of the nine to five. Dennis became an insurance salesman. His Black body integrated White-dominant office space by day and attempted to rule Sharon and his daughters with an iron fist at night.

Black in an America at war with itself over the future and place of African Americans, Sharon and Dennis stood four generations from slavery. They were the last generation in both of their families to be born *before* their rights of citizenship were protected by passage of the Civil Rights Act and the Voting Rights Act. Their generation was the first to break out of segregation and forge a new path into a newly integrated middle class. Yet, in an attempt to survive White patriarchy, they both tried to appease it by shrinking and contorting themselves to live the White male American dream. They put their heads down, silenced their true selves, and donned the mask passed to them by parents who received it from their parents, and so on. Poet Paul Laurence Dunbar wrote about this mask, both a shield and a sword:

> We wear the mask that grins and lies,
> It hides our cheeks and shades our eyes,—
> This debt we pay to human guile;
> With torn and bleeding hearts we smile,
> And mouth with myriad subtleties.

Why should the world be overwise,
In counting all our tears and sighs?
Nay, let them only see us, while
We wear the mask.

We smile, but, O great Christ, our cries
To thee from tortured souls arise.
We sing, but oh the clay is vile
Beneath our feet, and long the mile;
But let the world dream otherwise,
We wear the mask![12]

When I was a little girl, I remember sitting on phone books so that I could reach my plate at our dining room table. My chair was pushed in close so that each scoop of peas made it into my mouth and not in a chewed puddle of green gush beneath my chair. My Keds swung in opposite directions under the table—hidden from view. I didn't know what racism was. I didn't know the cost of Whiteness and patriarchy on my mommy and daddy's lives. I only knew the anxiety of not knowing if the police would have to come to our house again that night.

7

Lisa

Light

My earliest memory is losing a sugar cookie to the Atlantic Ocean.
I was three years old, standing on fine Atlantic City sand. The sun
shone down on me and my family. I was playing with my next-door
neighbor, Bobby Griffin. We had just grabbed sugar cookies out
of their plastic packaging. I walked to the water with Bobby, and
the waves came and took my cookie.

I wailed.

And I never forgot it.

Loss is among the most human of feelings. But some are more
accustomed to the feeling than others. People of African descent
have been conditioned not to want, for fear of losing what they
have. It is not that we never get. We do. We built Black Wall Street.
We invented the cotton gin and the stop light and the Charleston
and the twist and rock and roll. My great-grandfather Hiram
owned a block of homes in Elmwood, Philadelphia. My great-
grandmother Lizzie built a beautiful family and cared for them
all under the roof of her three-story home in South Philly. My
mother, Sharon, survived domestic violence and bought her own

home in Mount Airy, Philadelphia. She bought us a Siamese cat, Sheba, as consolation for the loss of our father.

But Tulsa's Black Wall Street was looted, massacred, burned, bombed, and then razed to the ground. Eli Whitney patented the invention of the cotton gin and erased the name and memory of the enslaved people who actually invented that technology. The cotton gin made America filthy rich and deepened the degradation of African-descended people in the US. And even if he had wanted to credit the enslaved, according to the law he could not because the enslaved were not considered citizens.

Hiram lost his Elmwood land to eminent domain and died soon after. Lizzie lost her son Charles to medical racism when he died in a Black hospital in Brooklyn. When his Jewish wife showed up, they refused to continue to save him. They stood back and watched him die. Then Lizzie lost her grandchildren when Charles's widow married a Jewish man and he refused to let them see their Black family.

Sharon lost the home she bought as a refuge from abuse when she rented it out, leaving it in the care of a real estate agent who allowed squatters to trash it and burn it to ashes. And when Sharon moved me and my two sisters, Meredith and Hollie, from Philadelphia to Cape May, New Jersey, to blend our family with that of lifelong educator Ernest Harper, she lost me too.

I escaped into the White evangelical church. It was my safe place—separate from the subtle turf wars of blended-family-ville—separate from the space where my mother, who was so close to us in Philadelphia, was slipping into depression after having miscarried several babies in Cape May. In a recent conversation, my mother revealed that at least one of her miscarriages occurred because White medical staff did not believe her when she told them she was in pain. She, too, almost died. I knew none of this. I only knew my mother was distant—slipping away—and I and my little sisters had to fend for ourselves.

By 1982, my White evangelical youth group became the only space where I felt safe—safe from having to jockey for position, safe from having to contort myself to fit in, safe from the bullying

I endured at school, safe from the grief of being a daddy's girl who lost her daddy, safe from having to engage my sexuality which had been violated through abuse by a trusted one—at three years old—the same year the ocean took my sugar cookie.

In 1982, during my freshman year in high school, my friend Amanda kept asking me to attend her youth group. Every week I said, "No." It was more like "No way on earth," but I limited it to "No" to keep my friend. When I thought of youth group, I thought of church. When I thought of church, I thought "Grandma" and "boring." So, the answer was no.

The truth was, I was determined to be one of the popular girls, and I didn't think church was the way to get there. I was tired of being bullied. I'd been bullied the entire previous year by two poor White girls who mercilessly ridiculed and isolated me every day of eighth grade. So I melted into marching band, finding solace as a captain of the rifle squad. I could twirl with the best of them in eighth grade. But now I was in high school—a fresh start—and I was not going to repeat that torment again.

Amanda was adamant. She insisted I would love youth group. One day on a whim I said, "Okay." That word changed my life.

I attended youth group that week. I believe it was a Young Life chapter—a popular national ministry to high school students. To my surprise, all of the most popular people in the school were there! Popular cheerleaders and football players along with just regular kids. And Starla was there. Starla and I had sat together on the school bus every day of my seventh grade year. She was the only kid on the bus who invited me, the only Black kid, to sit with her. We became fast friends. Starla was one year ahead of me, so she went to high school when I advanced to eighth grade. I had to brave the school bus alone. When one of the mean girls would punch me in the back while walking from gym class, I would remember Starla's eyes. They seemed to gleam—literally. They shined with warmth and welcome. "Kindness exists," I would think, before absorbing another punch.

The room was packed—wall-to-wall teens, all White except for me. Starla sat against the wall with friends from her church's youth group. Her father was the pastor of a tiny local Wesleyan church. Their youth group had a handful of members, so they attended the local Young Life group to connect with other kids at school. After settling in with Starla's crew, I watched as the group's leader said they would start with a skit. One by one young people entered a clearing in the center of the room, saying "Me." Each one said "Me" independent of the others. Then they demanded: "Me." Then someone said "You?" and each of them questioned: "You?" Finally, without warning, they all stopped, looked up, pointed, and said "You." End of scene.

When I was a little girl, before my immersion into Whiteness, before Cape May, before my parents' separation and divorce, I remember lying on my back on the grass in front of our neighbor's house on Walnut Lane in the West Oak Lane neighborhood of Philadelphia. My friend Tracy and I lay on our backs next to the giant spruce in the center of her lawn. We looked up at the sky, watching clouds float above us. I imagined God sitting on one of those clouds. I wondered how to communicate with God. I wondered if God was good. I wondered if God knew that I had been molested. I wondered if God could do anything to fill the pervasive sense of emptiness that lived in the pit of my stomach.

After youth group the next week, I went to the skating rink with Starla and her friends from her youth group. Afterward we went back to Starla's place, where her mother served us donuts and milk. She asked us what Jesus had done for us lately. This was a foreign concept. Jesus was dead. How could he do anything for anyone? But that night I realized I had prayed once, on an eighth grade camping trip where everyone got lost. I sat freezing in a canoe that was trapped in mud. The tide had gone out and now one of my canoe-mates was stuck up to her hips in mud—quicksand. I looked up at the sky and screamed at the top of my lungs, "God, help!" It was the first time I had ever prayed. It was also the first time I didn't care what others thought. God answered my prayers.

My friend was pulled from the quicksand, and hunters found us in the woods that night.

I spent the next year learning about God and Jesus and prayer from Starla's parents. It was real. It was healing. Their love was real. It changed me.

I marvel now at how much I did not know and how much my mother understood when she looked at me cross-eyed about a year later, the night I came home and told her I had been born again—and that she needed to be born again too. I had found safe space in White evangelicalism. I had spent the past year doing walk-a-thons for Jesus and sing-a-thons for Jesus. I went to every Amy Grant, Michael W. Smith, and Michael Card concert, even the Christian heavy metal band Stryper. And on August 21, 1983, I walked down the aisle of a Sunday evening church camp meeting and I gave my life to Jesus.

But another thing had been gestating over the previous decade and a half since the civil rights movement—something I would come to learn many years after meeting the Jesus of White evangelicalism.

In the wake of the Supreme Court's 1954 ruling in *Brown v. Board of Education* and the enforced desegregation of the 1964 Civil Rights Act, White southern Christians removed their children from public schools and established "race schools"—segregated private schools designed to escape federal mandates against segregation in public space. Many of those race schools transformed into Christian schools.

Established in 1927 during the fundamentalist movement, Bob Jones University in Panama City, Florida, was an elder institution among Christian schools and had banned Blacks from the beginning. When the IRS changed its regulations in accordance with the 1964 Civil Rights Act, reserving tax exemption for private schools that do not practice racial discrimination, Bob Jones did not qualify. Rather than comply with the IRS, the university fought to maintain White space, justifying its position on the belief that the Bible mandates racial segregation. Church historian Randall Balmer notes that conservative movement organizer Paul Weyrich and Jerry Falwell, the fundamentalist firebrand founder of segregation academy Liberty University, advised Bob Jones not to fight for the right to segregate based on race.[1] It was no longer socially acceptable. Rather, they counseled to fight on the basis of religious freedom. Thus, Falwell and Weyrich launched the Moral Majority in 1979, and the Constitution's guarantee of religious freedom became the segregationist movement's best hope to push back the gains of the civil rights movement.

Three months after Bob Jones lost its Supreme Court case in May 1983—and me oblivious to the political stream I was about to enter and its political responsibility and alignment with policies that had shackled my family for three hundred years—I walked down the aisle of a Sunday evening church camp meeting and gave my life to Jesus. I was born again in the same era that the religious right was born from the womb of post-civil rights Jim Crow Christianity.

Michael Cromartie's *No Longer Exiles* recounts a 1990 meeting of religious right figures. In this meeting, attendees named abortion as the issue that could catalyze the rise of the religious right. Weyrich corrected them: *Roe v. Wade* did not catalyze their movement, he said. It was segregation: *Bob Jones University v. United States*.[2]

Balmer notes that when Bob Jones lost its case, Weyrich knew he could not achieve his goal—to build the conservative movement—by focusing on race.[3] Even with the evenly divided ideological makeup of the 1983 bench,[4] the court sided against racial segregation in protection of religious liberty by an 8–1 majority, establishing the firm judicial foundation of *Brown v. Board of Education*. While Weyrich hoped to build the conservative movement, Falwell's goal was always simpler: protect White patriarchy—a social order he believed was biblically ordained. He had established Liberty University for that purpose. I believe Falwell knew this Supreme Court loss represented a nail in the legal coffin of the southern segregation movement—a Supreme Court bookend to *Brown v. Board*. The only way to resurrect the South's uncivil war would be to overturn the court. To do that, they would need a movement.

In the years preceding that meeting, Falwell, Weyrich, and other religious right founders had reawakened the political force of the evangelical church. Self-exiled from political engagement since the 1925 Scopes Monkey Trial, fundamentalists had largely retreated from the public square, refocusing on personal holiness and missions. But since 1978, fundamentalist leaders had been led back into public cause by Falwell and Weyrich's fight to protect Bob Jones University and other White male-dominant spaces. They also stoked growing agitation among evangelicals to organize against abortion. When Bob Jones University lost its case, the Moral Majority and others turned their focus toward abortion.

Over the next decade, abortion was weaponized and wielded to wedge southern evangelicals from the southern-dominant Democratic Party and unite them in common purpose with the conservative movement within the GOP. It worked.

The pro-life movement catapulted to prominence in 1989, when the first major Supreme Court challenge to *Roe v. Wade* made its way to the high court.

Throughout my junior and senior years at Rutgers University, pro-life and pro-choice rallies proliferated across the New Brunswick campus. I attended pro-life rallies with my friends in Campus Crusade for Christ. Unfamiliar with the debate, I hung back on the edges, watching the mostly White crowd scream and chant. We felt important, like we were part of something bigger than ourselves, though I hardly understood what I was chanting for. Peppered throughout the speeches from the stage, speaker after speaker merely confirmed that abortion was wrong. Pictures of aborted fetuses plastered to picket signs waved as women and men stepped to the microphone and talked about the fetus's silent scream.

Two years after hosting a viewing of the 1972 cult classic *A Thief in the Night*, my Campus Crusade chapter sponsored a viewing of the 1984 agitprop film *The Silent Scream*, which debuted on Falwell's televangelist program. The room was packed with students silenced to a hush when Dr. Bernard Nathanson's narration interpreted the ultrasound of an abortion of a twelve-week-old fetus: "We can see the child moving rather serenely in the uterus." Nathanson characterizes the fetus as fully aware, able to sense danger and respond: "The child senses aggression in its sanctuary." Nathanson then imprints on the minds of viewers an image paralleled only by Edvard Munch's painting *The Scream*: "We see the child's mouth wide open in a silent scream." I will never forget it. It was like a horror movie. It was that image and the interpretation of the fetus's movement that tapped my deepest cry for justice and moved me to march "for life."

But four years before I marched and before my Campus Crusade chapter showed this film, CBS Morning News had sat down with five physicians recommended by the American College of Obstetricians and Gynecologists for their expertise in ultrasound analysis and fetal development to analyze that part of the film. The physicians explained that the cerebral cortex, the part of the brain that perceives pain, isn't functioning yet at twelve weeks. It's just not a factor. It's impossible that the fetus felt anything. So why did the video show the fetus suddenly thrash about? Because moments before the thrashing, the filmmaker slowed the film down to a crawl's pace. Then, just as the catheter suction tube is placed, the filmmaker turned the speed to regular pace.

Pro-life "experts" tried to rebut the physicians' analyses, but they couldn't. Instead, they dug in deeper. They admitted the cerebral cortex is not developed and minimized the fallacy by saying the abortion issue is not about pain. But *The Silent Scream* is all about pain. That's the entire point. The filmmaker intentionally misled viewers. He intentionally misled me. No one ever shared that CBS report with me. No one ever shared the testimonies of obstetricians. Instead, they showed the film to a room full of college students. They made young jaws drop with false testimony. Doctors who disagreed were demonized as "liberal." Then they gave us an opportunity to march.[5]

One day that year, my mother and I stumbled into a heated argument. Exasperated, I bent backward to convince her that her pro-choice position was immoral and un-Christian.

She asked, "What if the life of the mother is at stake? Should abortion be allowed then?"

"No," I countered flatly. I believed God was supreme. If God willed that the mother die, who am I to argue with God? I did not realize that was the exact same logic that the evangelical church used to justify slavery: If God ordained certain people to be slaves, who are we to argue with God?

"Lisa," my mother explained, "do you remember that time I was pregnant a few years ago, and I went into the hospital and the baby didn't make it?"

"Yes . . . " I scowled.

"I had an abortion," she said.

My heart stopped.

"I almost died, and the doctor had to take the baby to save my life." She paused. "I could have died."

I stood before my mother as a good Christian soldier. I was determined to win. With a heart of steel, I looked my mother in the eyes—my mother, the woman who almost died to bring *me* into the world, who worked nights to put herself through college while raising three small children, who would give up anything to make sure we were provided for—and I said, "They should have saved the baby."

Onward, Christian soldiers, marching as to war
With the cross of Jesus going on before
Christ, the royal Master, leads against the foe
Forward into battle, see His banners go

In war, there are no humans, only allies and enemies. Domination is the vision. If necessary, the death of the other is acceptable. That is war.

My own psyche was at war with itself. My parents planted roots of Black consciousness at an early age. They made me watch *Roots* every time it came on TV throughout the 1980s. I watched Cicely Tyson pull a cart meant for horses in her groundbreaking portrayal of Harriet Tubman in *A Woman Called Moses*. I cheered when the Equal Rights Amendment passed and states began to ratify it. I mirrored my mother's anger when southern states rejected it. I canvassed my Philadelphia neighborhood with my mother, watching her knock on doors and register our neighbors to vote. The foundation was laid.

But when I met White Jesus, all of that was challenged. And with salvation at stake—and adult community at stake—and the sense of safety I received from evangelicalism's high-control culture that mirrored my father's high-control abuse, I followed my White friends and leaders to the proverbial pool called "conservatism." I sat on the side of this pool with feet swirling in conservative waters. The water was cold but bearable.

In 1991 I moved to Los Angeles to study urban transformation. It was there that I met my first evangelical Democrats. One professor from Arkansas told us to watch for Bill Clinton in the crowded Democratic presidential primary field. That professor was the first evangelical I ever met who voiced approval for a Democratic candidate.

I watched Clinton at the 1992 Democratic National Convention and was mesmerized. Torn, I tuned in to the 1992 Republican National Convention to watch those I had been told were my tribe. I watched as former Nixon speechwriter and presidential candidate Pat Buchanan took to the stage. Buchanan macheted Democrats, accusing them of being "liberals and radicals . . . dressed up as moderates and centrists." Evoking moral repulsion from his traditional base—my spiritual community—he accused the Democratic Party of "cross-dressing."

Buchanan, the man who coined the term "silent majority" in 1969 and partnered with Falwell and Weyrich in support of Bob Jones University in the late 1970s and early '80s, referenced the gains of the civil rights and anti-Vietnam War movements, calling Americans to reject the "discredited liberalism of the 1960s" and the "failed liberalism of the 1970s."[6]

Buchanan trumpeted the triumph of Reagan over communism in the Cold War, and later championed George H. W. Bush's support for anti-abortion policies, prayer in schools, support for

Christian schools (giving a nod to Bob Jones University), and conservative federal judges. He clarified the two sides of America's culture war, placing Clinton and Gore on the side of Satan for supporting LGBTQIA+ rights, public schools, feminism, and the environment.

Buchanan concluded: "There is a religious war going on in this country. It is a culture war as critical to the kind of nation we shall be as the Cold War itself. This war is for the soul of America."[7]

One generation later, the culture war bloomed full when the first African American was elected president of the United States of America. *Brown v. Board of Education*'s desegregation of schools laid the foundations for the desegregation of the whitest house in America—the White House.

I watched 2008 election returns from my best friend Maritza's house in the Bronx. A small multiethnic group of friends and colleagues in ministry all leaned in close to the television as the final returns flashed on the screen. Barack Obama: WINNER!

We erupted into mayhem. We jumped on couches. We hugged each other. We screamed for joy and wept aloud. This was not a mere election result. This was a threshold that none of us ever thought we would live to cross. The nation that once declared people of African descent to be only three-fifths of a human being—the nation that once quantified the monetary value of Black men by how much wealth they could bring to White men—the nation that once declared that Black men "had no rights which the white man was bound to respect"[8] had just elected a Black man to lead the country. When it was announced that Senator Barack Obama would become the forty-fourth president of the United States of America, millions of Americans flooded into the streets in jubilee.

Nearly one year later, September 2009, President Obama rose to the podium in a joint session of Congress to share his healthcare plan with the nation. Early in his speech, he declared that no public funds would be used to cover health care for undocumented immigrants. Rep. Joe Wilson broke decorum, congressional rules, and hundreds of years of precedent and screamed at the president:

"You lie!" Sen. Patrick Leahy said he had never seen anything like it in his thirty-five years in Congress. "But nobody—nobody," the senator said, "ever has done anything like that." Speaking of Obama, Leahy added: "He is the head of government for our country."[9]

In March 2010, on his way to hear President Obama speak about the passage of his signature health care bill, civil rights movement veteran Rep. John Lewis walked with fellow House members through a scene reminiscent of the Little Rock Nine's traumatic steps through the jeering, cursing, spitting crowd of White men, women, and children in 1957. The Little Rock Nine had been on their way to desegregate the local high school. Rep. Lewis was on his way to do the people's business in the people's House when jeering White Tea Party members flanked him and his colleagues as they walked the gauntlet. Suddenly, someone in the crowd screamed the N-word at Rep. Lewis. Someone else lobbed a wad of their spit at Rep. Emanuel Cleaver as another used a gay slur in reference to Rep. Barney Frank.

Politics is simple. It is the question and answer of how the people will live together. The founders of the religious right mounted their culture war to preserve their place at the top of the hierarchy of human belonging—the ruling tier reserved for Christian White men. The religious right's culture war was a continuation of the Civil War, not *Roe v. Wade*. It was catalyzed by Lincoln's Radical Republican shift in American hierarchy through amendments to the Constitution that leveled the legal playing field between former masters and the formerly enslaved for the first time since 1662. In response, southern White men pushed back. They found ways to redeem the hierarchy under new laws while northern Whites looked the other way. That was the compromise: preserve White peace by refusing to see what southern men do both at home and through national policy. Thus, both southern and northern White men waged war to maintain White dominance through peonage, employment discrimination, segregation and redlining, the normalization of the rape and control of Black women, stealing credit for Black inventions and music, and twisting the narrative of our national history such that all things good come from White men—including a White version of Jesus (who was actually Brown).

When ruling is equated with safety, dominance over the other is necessary. From Jonathan Winthrop's "city upon a hill" and the Pequot Massacre, which was his idea, to Donald Trump's grabbing of women's private parts to his Muslim ban to his caging and separation of asylum-seeking families to his LGBTQIA+ military ban and alignment with White nationalist groups, the thematic plumb line of European presence on the soil we call America has been the domination of everybody and everything.

In the days leading up to the 2020 election, we witnessed an escalation of the culture war, from battle cry to the bombs themselves. The Trump administration coordinated its institutional authority toward one goal: voter suppression and eventually blatant attempts to steal votes. In the midst of this mayhem, I had an epiphany. In 2020, people of European descent made up 59.7 percent of the US population. Demographers widely project that by 2045, the White population within the US will drop below 50 percent. Sociologist Dudley L. Poston wrote in a 2020 report: "On the first day of 2020, whites under age 18 were already in the minority. Among all the young people now in the US, there are more minority young people than there are white young people."[10]

Robert P. Jones, in *White Too Long: The Legacy of White Supremacy in American Christianity*, explains that the perceived external threat of racial and cultural change primed White Christians to champion Trump. "In the course of a single political campaign," Jones said, Trump converted White evangelical values voters into nostalgia voters.[11] White evangelicals were not the only White Americans who longed for the good old days when White men ruled. A study conducted by Jones's organization, the Public Religion Research Institute, asked 2,500 adults living in all fifty states, Do you long for the 1950s? The majority of White Americans said yes, while the vast majority of people of color and other minorities said no.[12]

The 1950s was the murder of Emmett Till.

157

The 1950s was the back of the bus and Whites-only water fountains and schools and jobs and lunch counters.

The 1950s was redlining for people of color while White families benefited from the G.I. Bill.

The 1950s preceded the 1964 Civil Rights Act, the 1965 Voting Rights Act, the 1965 Immigration Act, and the 1970 Clean Air Act.

In the 1950s, 59 percent of Black people were living under the poverty line.[13]

The 1950s was before the Stonewall uprising launched the LGBTQIA+ movement.

The 1950s was four decades before the Americans with Disabilities Act.

One evening in the days leading up to the 2020 election, I asked myself, When was the last time men of European descent went anywhere in the world and did not think to themselves, *I should control this space*? The question haunted me. I could not remember a time. I kept tracing back: before the Mayflower, before the slave trade, before Rome, before Greece. Almost three thousand years. Not since before the Greek Empire (before 800 BCE) have men of European descent gone anywhere in the world and *not* sought to dominate it. Now, on the eve of their dethroning, they are thrashing—waging war. They do not know how to be equal. They do not know how to be merely human. They only know war against the image of God in the other. They only know the delusion that they *are* God. They have no common memory of another way to be in the world.

In January 1967, Martin Luther King Jr. flew to Jamaica to finish the manuscript for what would become his final book, *Where Do We Go from Here: Chaos or Community?* One year prior, in 1966, King had witnessed the White backlash against the gains of the movement and began writing the manuscript. He wrote about the profound disappointment of Black America, which was handed the hope of the Civil Rights Act and the Voting Rights Act only to have northern congressional members strike deals with southern members to slow implementation and enforcement. He witnessed the seething rage and growing disillusionment of young

Black men and women who had dared to believe their lives were about to change only to find the ones who made the promises had just bartered their rights away. In the shadow of the Watts riots and reflecting on the rise of the Black power movement, King wrote of the "unregenerate segregationist," that these citizens "have declared that democracy is not worth having if it involves equality."[14]

King was talking about the very men who fathered the religious right: southern segregationists. The rotten core of their movement now stands exposed in our present age. Four years of verbal and political abuse by the executive leader of our nation was papered over by the cultlike loyalty of White evangelicals. They flanked Donald Trump while minimizing his sins and protecting him from accountability. They ignored or echoed daily assaults on truth. They ignored and minimized Trump's collusion with Russia to undercut American democracy. In the name of the culture wars, they hailed their chief for packing federal courts with far-right extremists—some of whom are known members of hate groups. And they rubbed their hands with glee when the GOP Senate broke its own rules to flip the Supreme Court, making it the most conservative it had been since the 1896 *Plessy v. Ferguson* ruling that upheld segregation. And White evangelicals, drunk with power, militarized the police and directed the evisceration of democratic institutions like the Justice Department, the Environmental Protection Agency, public education, the Centers for Disease Control and Prevention, and the Department of Housing and Urban Development.

King reflected in *Where Do We Go from Here?*: "The segregationist goal is the total reversal of all reforms, with reestablishment of naked oppression and if need be a native form of fascism."[15]

I preached the final charge at the mass meeting at St. Paul's Episcopal Church in Charlottesville on August 11, 2017. It was two months after I had transitioned from six years of service at Sojourners, where I organized grasstops leaders to heal what race broke in the world. Over those six years I had trained faith leaders to confront anti-immigrant policy in Alabama, fasted for twenty-two days with the Fast for Families on the National Mall to pressure Congress to pass comprehensive immigration reform, and helped build a bridge for multiethnic churches to partner with the Ferguson movement. I had come to understand my vocation as a call to present my body as a living sacrifice—to show up in the gap and help build a bridge. It was a long journey from the devastating abortion conversation with my mother to Ferguson, but I made it.

I came to understand the history, the warping of our identity, the mangling of Scripture to make God White—to make White men God. My mother saw this, and I began to invite her to witness my journey home to roots of resistance, roots of resilience, roots that stretch back far on this land, roots that have borne witness to it all.

I stood at the podium and reminded the packed church that the Brown, colonized Hebrew priests who were on their way out of seventy years of slavery in Babylon stopped long enough to write down their creation story. As they did, they described their condition: desolate and full of destruction. They commented on their oppressors, who believed the Hebrews were created to be slaves of the gods—gods who lived in the deep waters.[16] The Brown, colonized Hebrew priests painted a word picture of the Supreme God hovering *over* the deep, brooding like a hen broods over her eggs—about to give birth. God enters the darkness and gives birth to light.

As I was speaking, White men in white shirts and khaki pants carrying tiki torches surrounded the church. I was not aware of their presence, only aware that violence could erupt at the Unite the Right White nationalist rally at Emancipation Park the next day.

"I'm not worried," I bellowed to the mass meeting, "because our God cuts the darkness!"

"God ended the Hebrews' oppression, cutting their darkness with light!" I remembered the Fortune family and Henry Lawrence and Lea Ballard and Lizzie and Willa and Sharon. And I remembered Reinaldo and Anita and Austin and Ethel and Dennis. I reminded the crowd that God has already shown us who God is. God set our ancestors free. God had cut their darkness.

The next morning, I joined arms with eighty faith leaders and marched toward Emancipation Park where White nationalists prepared to rally to keep a statue of General Robert E. Lee erected in the city. Each step forward I thought of my ancestors: indentured, enslaved, exploited, removed, and dominated. And I thought of their resistance. I thought of my mother's SNCC organizing and Elizabeth's choice to live a different story than every woman who came before her. And I thought of Lea—I was accountable to Lea.

I stood face to face with a militia man holding a machine gun. As I opened my mouth to pray and sing, I joined the cloud of witnesses that is my family.

"This little light of mine," I roared from a deep place in my bones, "I'm gonna let it shine!"

There was a witness in Emancipation Park that day. Light was there in the darkness. Light bore witness to the martyrdom of Heather Heyer—a young woman mowed down by a White nationalist man who used his car as a deadly weapon. She became light on August 12, 2017. On that same day, Trump revealed the depth of his own darkness when he offered moral cover to Heather's assassin, claiming there were "very fine people on both sides."[17]

That was the moment that led former Vice President Joe Biden to decide to run for president in 2020. Three years later, I organized the evangelical community to engage in public conversations on culture war topics, including abortion. This broke the hypnotic stranglehold the right had on evangelical thought—especially White women and evangelicals of color. Suburban Christian women shifted their loyalty and broke for Biden in the 2020 election, adding to his lead.

Socially distanced Americans watched as returns flashed for the fourth unresolved day since Election Day. On this near-sacred Saturday, the words flashed across our screens: "President-Elect Joe Biden."

On January 6, 2021, the day Congress formally recognized states' certified electoral college votes, White nationalists followed Donald Trump's call to march to the Capitol building and stop the process. Buchanan's culture war became actual war. They stormed the Capitol building. They killed six people total, including two officers. They hunted for congressional leaders, saying they wanted to kill them. They ran the Confederate flag through those near-sacred halls. True to King's words, White nationalists attempted to kill democracy because it demanded equality. But they lost.

On Inauguration Day, Senator Kamala Harris became the first African American, the first South Asian, and the first woman to be elected vice president in our nation's history. Millions of socially distanced Americans wept in front of their televisions when twenty-two-year-old African American National Youth Poet Laureate Amanda Gorman issued her challenge to the nation from the steps of the same Capitol building that White nationalists had tried to destroy. Her poem "The Hill We Climb" is too long to print in its entirety, so I offer these lines that made me gasp when she spoke them:

> For there is always light,
> if only we're brave enough to see it.
> If only we're brave enough to be it.

Are we brave enough to see the light? Are we brave enough to be it?

PART THREE

REPAIR

The 2016 election and its aftermath revealed a great chasm under our feet in the US. Not since the Civil War had our nation been so aware that its unity teetered on a political cliff. According to an April 2017 *Washington Post* report, there was no greater indicator of the way people voted in 2016 than their attitudes on race.[1]

My family's story illuminates how the political construct of race worked to protect the agency of European Americans, especially men, while removing agency from women and men of color who God created to help steward the world. That is the heart of the break—the denial of dignity and the removal of agency to benefit the self. Thus the process of repair matters as much as the intent and its result. The process itself must restore equal capacity to exercise agency to all who have suffered subjugation.

Critical to the process of repair is truth-telling. Truth-telling begins the process of re-membering. In the Christian tradition, truth-telling is confession. Lies and half-truths manipulate power dynamics and maintain one group's control over the other. There can be no repair of relationship between the oppressed and oppression's beneficiaries without the truth being told.

Three months after Trump's inauguration, I visited the Apartheid Museum in Johannesburg, South Africa. The exhibit on the nation's Truth and Reconciliation Commission rocked me. There were three clear objectives:

1. Determine who had perpetrated and been victims of human rights abuses.
2. Determine the requirements for rehabilitation and reparation.
3. Determine which human rights violators would receive amnesty.

Grounded in the Christian call to confession as requirement for repair and in fulfillment of objective 1 and 3, South Africa launched its Truth and Reconciliation Commission. Objective 2 was notably never achieved (more on that in chap. 9). Similar commissions have launched truth-telling processes in the aftermath of atrocities in Bosnia, Rwanda, and in various locations across the US, including Greensboro, North Carolina, and Tulsa, Oklahoma.

Repair requires repentance. Repentance requires reparation.

Reparation is the process of repairing what has been broken through the oppression and subjugation of human dignity. Significant historical precedent exists for offering reparation for particular people groups concerning particular circumstances within the United States. Likewise, significant political arguments have been mounted against reparation, particularly where people of African descent are concerned. Fundamental belief in the way things currently work and the minimization of ongoing inequity has essentially stopped efforts to repair what race broke in our nation.

To move forward requires us to understand the depth of our brokenness as well as to reckon with the reality that our current structures and systems of justice have been tainted by five hundred years of law and policy rigged to favor people of European descent at the expense of all others. If the generational inequity and degradation confronting the US were that of any developing nation, we would see clearly that the prescription for that nation's health requires transitional justice—the process of re-membering and re-forming.

Transitional justice recognizes that normal processes cannot address the overwhelming injustice experienced within countries emerging from periods of conflict and repression. The International Center for Transitional Justice, based in New York City, explains: "Ignoring massive abuses is an easy way out but it destroys the values on which any decent society can be built."[2] Likewise, ignoring abuses tears asunder that which God created whole: memory, people, families, communities, and people groups.

Part 3 will illuminate small-scale precedents of transitional justice within the US and mount a strong faith-rooted case for truth-telling, reparation, and the ethic of forgiveness as a way forward in the face of that which cannot be repaired. Having soaked in the stories of Fortune and her descendants, this section will further examine their connections to the issues of our times and the critical question: How then shall we repair what race broke in the world?

8

Truth-Telling as Reckoning

One month after thousands of White nationalist men and women stormed the US Capitol, killing at least six people while attempting a coup d'état under Trump flags, former President Trump's second impeachment trial began. In the opening arguments, House impeachment managers rolled the tape, illuminating the truth of the horrors of January 6, 2021. Many leading GOP senators turned their eyes, busied themselves, and refused to reckon with reality.

The House managers' opening verdict was unanimous: the evidence was overwhelming. The House managers' case that impeachment proceedings were indeed constitutional was so compelling that Trump's defense team changed its strategy while listening. In the face of House managers' video evidence, emails, and texts detailing the president's direct culpability in the January 6 attempted coup, the defense team shifted its strategy away from denial of Trump's responsibility to the false argument that the Senate does not have the authority to prosecute. Ultimately, the defense counsel rambled, meandered, and made no real point. Still, only seven Republican senators sided with the cogent argument. Despite the evidence, forty-three GOP senators sided with the rambling defense. They voted to block the trial moving forward. But the majority of senators sided with the truth, so the trial advanced.

That vote revealed a fundamental malformation in our national governance. It is not new. It has been with us from the beginning—from the days when my ninth-great-grandmother, Fortune, was sentenced to indentured service, even though the Maryland race law that she was born under did not require it. The law changed *after* she was born, yet a judge—an arbiter of what is supposed to be true and just in our nation—bent the truth of the law to sentence her to generations of powerlessness, exploitation, and rape that she (and we) should not have had to endure.

From the beginning, our nation has bent, twisted, and buried truth in service to European, then White, supremacy. It has hidden its addiction to human hierarchy—the supremacy of White male-ness and pure power. White male addiction to pure power crushed the opportunities for Willa and Lizzie and Henry and Reinaldo and Austin to flourish—to find pockets of air and breath. They were forced to contort themselves into the small boxes set for them. By law, Willa and Lizzie could only be housemaids or field hands in South Carolina.[1] Likely assaulted by men in the houses where they served, according to the family story, the souls of successive generations were gashed by both structural and interpersonal White male lust for power. Henry bore the scars of the Civil War and subsequent White terror. Reinaldo and Anita suffered the degradations of American colonization and eugenics in Caribbean squalor. And Austin navigated daily slashes to his dignity and took them out on his children—who passed that horror down to me.

With hardened apathy, White men and their allied women glance with glassy eyes past suffering generations that lay splayed in White supremacy's wake. White men and their allied women have learned, practiced, and passed down tactics of war in their battle against God for supremacy. Four times in four years, the world witnessed GOP senators—the vast majority southern and White—run re-hearsed plays for power: they projected their own sin onto their perceived opponents, they narrowed their lenses to a pinpoint in a wide panorama of sin, and rather than judging based on merit, they claimed foul on the other side—based on technicalities. In the end, these political tactics suppressed legislators' consciences. Finally, they danced rote steps, moving through motions that placed power in prime positions and granted absolution for racism, sexual assault, exploitation, domination, death, and treason.

On February 13, 2021, the world watched a total of seven GOP senators respond to their consciences, while the other forty-three sealed the coffin of America's delusion of democracy. Forty-three GOP senators muffled the memory of the wailing White Capitol police officer crushed by insurrectionists pushing their way into America's temple of democracy. The same senators blocked recollection of the other souls who died that day. Most lawmakers agreed that Trump was responsible for the attempted coup. Most GOP senators also falsely claimed they lacked jurisdiction to hold him accountable.

Historian Keisha Blain said that the failure to convict Trump "reveals that violence and white supremacy will continue to shape American politics—as they have since the nation's founding." She pointed out that White Americans "have often used violence and intimidation to retain power."[2] Blain referenced antebellum White militias, the rise of the KKK, and the Wilmington massacre as examples.

To Blain's list I add the forced removal of indigenous nations; the Chinese Exclusion Act; the scourge of 4,084 extrajudicial lynchings of African Americans between 1877 and 1950;[3] peonage; the 1921 Tulsa massacre; the Japanese internment camps; the 1961 firebombing of the Freedom Riders Greyhound bus in Alabama; the dogs sicced on children in response to the Birmingham Children's March in 1963; the 1964 assassinations of James Chaney, Andrew Goodman, and Michael Schwerner in Mississippi; the assassinations of Black liberation leaders Malcolm X, Martin Luther King Jr., and Fred Hampton; the political imprisonments of Angela Davis, Assata Shakur, and Leonard Peltier; the infiltration of police departments by White nationalists and subsequent police impunity for streams of hashtagged Black lives from Trayvon Martin to George Floyd; the dismantling of public education, public housing, environmental safety, and workplace equity training; the history books that call enslaved people "workers"[4] and erase the KKK and Jim Crow laws from the collective memories of future generations[5]—all are violence. All are antidemocratic tactics of the White patriarchal war for supremacy. All keep America from becoming America by hiding, suppressing, and killing the truth. And all suppress the image of God on earth.

When I was a child, I loved the game show *Truth or Consequences*. Every week contestants were challenged to answer questions truthfully. If their answer was incorrect, they would have to accept the consequences.

As an evangelical I was taught to value truth and the authority of Scripture. I was taught there are ultimate consequences for all who do not abide by the truth. I was taught Jesus is the truth itself.

But the heritage of White evangelicalism in the US stretches back through Jim Crow segregation to antebellum and colonial slavery to "praying towns" and the Pequot Massacre. All of these regimes required fascist, authoritarian leadership—leadership that always unites racism, nationalism, hard patriarchy, and lies. People of African descent in the US understand fascism intimately. Dr. King wrote in his last book, *Where Do We Go from Here: Chaos or Community?*: "The segregationist goal is the total reversal of all reforms, with reestablishment of naked oppression and if need be a native form of fascism."[6]

African Americans were stunned but not baffled on January 6, 2021, when we, along with the rest of the world, witnessed the noose erected by Trump supporters in the crowd at the White House and the Confederate flag moving through the halls of Congress and the lynch mob searching for Nancy Pelosi—the Catholic woman, third in line to the presidency, who defied and helped dethrone their symbol of White male power.

The 2020 election and Trump's second impeachment acquittal were both a revelation. They revealed the extent to which our nation is rejecting both truth and consequences.

The Ten Commandments proclaim, "You shall not bear false witness against your neighbor" (Exod. 20:16). When lawmakers craft and enforce policy that entrenches racial, gender, religious, sexual orientation, national origin, or ableist hierarchies of belonging, then lawmakers and those who elect them bear false witness against our neighbors. When policymakers break unions and refuse to guarantee a living wage—when the labor of the top 10 percent is valued thirteen times higher than those in the bottom 10 percent—then those who elect the lawmakers bear false witness against our own neighbors.[7] When lawmakers give the top 1 percent a tax cut and pay for it by cutting funding for SNAP and public schools, then we bear false witness against our neighbors.[8] And when one in three Black men are ensnared within America's jails and prisons,[9] but a rich White man who incited an insurrection is acquitted on technicalities by other rich White lawmakers, then America bears false witness against its own citizens—telling poor people, Black people, Brown people: *You are not worthy of equal protection of the law*. We lie.

The apostle Paul lists lying as one of a handful of sins worthy of hell. Lies break and block peace from entering the world. They sow confusion and obstruct the reign of God, which is characterized by *shalom*. At the heart of *shalom* is truth. Truth-telling and integrity are basic requirements for healthy relationships. Without truth, trust is broken. Without trust, relationships are broken—individual, communal, and systemic relationships.

In her book *Until We Reckon: Violence, Mass Incarceration, and a Road to Repair*, Danielle Sered writes, "Acts of individual and structural harm are meaningfully different, but the key elements of accountability—acknowledging responsibility for one's actions, acknowledging the impact of one's actions on others, expressing genuine remorse, taking actions to repair the harm to the degree possible and no longer committing similar harm—apply to both." She issues this challenge: "Just as we ask people who cause interpersonal violence to reckon with their actions, so should we as a society call on ourselves to reckon, too. Until we do, no different future will be possible."[10]

King scribbled his letter from Birmingham Jail on the margins of the newspaper that carried "A Call for Unity." Penned by moderate White clergy, "A Call for Unity" appealed to King and the leaders of the Birmingham movement to slow down and accept incremental change. When he filled the margins of the newspaper, King scribbled on toilet paper rolls. When he ran out, an African American trusty smuggled him scraps of paper. Eventually King's lawyers were able to leave him a pad to write the rest.

King's open letter response was widely published. Written over eight days, King reasoned, "There comes a time when the cup of endurance runs over, and men are no longer willing to be plunged into the abyss of despair."[11] The Birmingham campaign had seen dogs sicced on children while water from fire hoses bore into their backs. The White ministers' call for unity clarified the difference between them and those who could wait no longer. Those White clergy had never experienced the terror of being Black in America. Until they had experienced it, they could not understand why the movement could not wait.[12]

Nearly sixty years after King's letter, George Floyd eked out his last breath while Officer Derek Chauvin knelt on his neck for over nine minutes. Gasping each time, Floyd repeated three words sixteen times: "I can't breathe."[13] Every bit as powerful as King's letter, Floyd's plea released many White Americans from the incomprehension King addressed in 1963.

On May 25, 2020, Floyd—a forty-six-year-old born-again Christian and former sports hero whose lack of opportunity ushered him down a well-grooved path carved by lawmakers for poor Black men (petty drugs, plea deals, and years stolen in jail)—cried the same words that flowed from the strangled throat of Eric Garner almost six years prior. Garner was the first in an epic string of hashtagged Black lives lost to police and vigilante violence since July 2014. In the end, Floyd moaned for his deceased mommy, then died.

Bystanders recorded Floyd's death and released it on social media. The video unleashed a firestorm of racial reckoning across the US and around the world. Over the next two weeks, multiethnic protests filled the streets of more than 140 cities across the US.[14] Fires flared in more than 120 of them. Bob Moses, civil rights architect of the 1964 Mississippi Freedom Summer, said the country seemed to be undergoing "an awakening."[15]

Perhaps the highest point of American consciousness came the day Trump's administration ordered National Guard troops to shoot into a peacefully protesting crowd assembled outside the White House. Guardsmen shot into the crowd, cleared space for Trump to walk across the street, and stand in front of a church he did not attend to hold a Bible that wasn't his own for a photo op. In that moment, Trump showed the world what American fascism looks like.

Don Rose, eighty-nine-year-old former Chicago press secretary to Martin Luther King Jr., marveled that White people's understanding grew in the days after Floyd's death because the police violence usually reserved for Black people was unleashed on them as well.[16] Similar to the plight of White allies for the century after the Civil War, the fascist rule usually reserved for Blacks was levied on Whites perceived to betray the White nationalist project. They, too, posed a direct threat to White power. Using lynching definitions set by sociologists Monroe Work and Florence Work in their widely referenced 1921 Tuskegee Institute study of lynching in America, current-day sociologists have identified 1,297 White people who were lynched from 1882 to 1968.[17]

Scales fell from White eyes in 2020 and in the early days of 2021. We saw who we are and realized we can choose the nation we will be. There is only one condition: we must reckon with the nation we have been—all of it. This requires truth. We must search for the truth. We must listen to the truth. We must tell the truth.

There is a narrative gap in our nation. Wide is the distance between the stories we tell about ourselves and the actual truth of how we got here and who we are. The narrative gap also represents the yawning divide between disparate public narratives of our common story and what it will take to make things right. It is the distance between "Make America Great *Again*" and Martin Luther King Jr.'s "dream" of the Beloved Community.

Narrative shapes worldview. If one's story of America is grounded in the myth of Manifest Destiny and Jonathan Winthrop's "city upon a hill," then one's vision of the future erases, justifies, and spins the sin and oppression that made White American prosperity possible—stolen land, free labor, rape to breed more free labor, and continued exploitation of non-Whites to protect one's destiny on the hill. But if your story of America is shaped by the dream of the Beloved Community, then your vision of the future struggles forward toward a common peace and common justice that our nation has never seen. Our narratives shape our politics— our conversations and decisions about how the *polis* (the people) should live together. Narrative shapes the world.

The first step of transitional justice—the process of transforming a society steeped in oppression into a just democracy—is to shrink the narrative gap. To do this, we must seek the truth, listen to the truth, and tell the truth.

Truth-seeking is a spiritual practice. It requires one to admit they do not already possess the whole truth. They have need. There are things they don't know—things that matter. Truth-seeking requires humility. Humility sees the image of God in the other, the inherent dignity of the other, the mind of the other, the heart of the other—and it respects the will of the other. The practice of humility is the first act of repair. For it was the absence of humility that broke the relationship between people of European descent and the colonized world to begin with. It was the assumption that all who are not like the self are not fully human, not called by God to exercise agency, not capable of stewarding the world. Humility is an act of repentance. Practicing humility heals the European soul.

Truth-listening begins the process of peeling back the death grip of spin and false narratives. Truth-listening leans in. It centers the narratives that rise from the margins and recognizes the expertise of those most affected by oppression. Drawing from humility, truth-listening steps back and invites the other forward.

It recognizes the other's divine call to help steward the guiding story and lay foundations for the guiding vision.

Truth-telling fans the flames of human agency, giving democracy breath and citizens in a democracy the ability to govern themselves toward just peace. It fills the narrative gap with perspective and details usually erased. Truth-telling moves us from the realm of ideas and grounds the transformative process in the reality of what happened. No justice is possible until we reckon with the truth of what happened.

Truth-seeking, truth-listening, and truth-telling are critical to the process of re-membering public memory—reuniting public memory that has been disjointed and dismembered by spin and justification.

The Bible compiles narratives of the oppressed to establish a common public memory. From its first page to its last, more than forty authors from a serially colonized and enslaved people attempt to establish common public memory in a context that breeds fragmentation. While they could have cordoned off the story-telling and story-listening within their own community, the biblical writers often invite immigrants and adopted members to share their common memory as an act of confession of truth that leads to communion.

Genesis 1 was written in the shadow of seventy years of enslavement in Babylon as a rebuke to the worldview of the Hebrews' colonizer. The book of Luke was written to Theophilus (translated "lover of God") to set the record straight under the Roman Empire. Revelation was written in code to a crushed and fragmented colonized people to reconcile their current narrative and to cast a future vision. Throughout biblical narratives, characters build altars, sing songs, and establish common rituals such as the taking of Communion to institutionalize public memory.

Today, individuals engage truth-searching by reading stories, books, and essays, watching movies and documentaries, and soaking in the music that rises from oppressed peoples. But it is not enough to immerse oneself in the stories of the other. A key strategy of White supremacy is to dismember, warp, and erase the memories of peoples of European descent. People deemed "White" in the United States have forgotten who *they* really are. They have forgotten their own histories of oppression and degradation in Europe. They have forgotten why and how they came to this land. God charges the Hebrews again and again to remember that they were once enslaved in Egypt. This is the source of their humility—this is their grounding memory. People of European descent in the US lack such humility because they lack such memory. They have come to believe they are actually White, but Whiteness is a phantom. It is not real. It is constructed by governments and entrenched by common lived experience in relationship to public policy and the cultural mores that grow around them. Whiteness has no common struggle, no common people, no common story. Rather, it floats like a figment, elusive and yet claimed at the same time. Myths and lies are its foundation and beams. And all truth that threatens the constitution of the house called "Whiteness" is eradicated in service to pure power . . . and the promise of it. People of European descent have work to do. They must dismantle the myths of their identity and reckon with their actual origin stories. There is no more powerful way to do this than through the process of uncovering family history.

Family histories tell stories woven by pictures, oral histories, census schedules, ship manifests, immigration papers, newspaper clippings, wills, and military and tax records. Family stories are dynamic, full of movement and verbs, not static hierarchies begging for protection. Family stories are profoundly human, full of texture, unexpected twists, surprises, and secrets—hidden from view to protect illusions of wellness and nobility. For many people of European descent, these secrets protect generations from the shame of falling short of Whiteness. Family stories uncover the things that happened—our untold origin stories that root us in actual time and place and peoples. They have the power to tell us who we really are and how we really got here. They have the power to show us the moment of the break—the moment we were broken and the moment we broke others. We cannot repair the collective until we know when and how we broke it.

My process of re-membering my family story has been pure revelation. It almost hurts to remember the days when I did not know it. I think back to high school and college. As an African American woman in Reagan's trickle-down America and the religious right's Christianity, I had very little mooring—only that which my family was able to give me by sitting me down in front of the television or in the theater watching stories of famous Black people and their struggles. I connected to my story vicariously. Alex Haley's story became my story. The story of *A Woman Called Moses* became my story. They served as a welcome substitute for the massive anchor of family story that I lacked.

I will never forget the first phone conversation I had with my mother when she told me about Hiram and Henry Lawrence. I still have the scribbled family tree. It strikes me now that there were no names included. Only generations and dates. That is how little I knew. But even that was something. Enough to be documented— enough to be re-membered.

Over three decades later and with memberships on Ancestry .com, FamilySearch, My Heritage, 23andMe, Fold3, and African Ancestry, I have been able to piece together the framework of my family's story. Yet there is still so much we do not know. Even as I write this, a DNA genealogist is discovering relatives on the Lawrence line we did not know existed and clarifying our connection to the Fortune family. Each discovery invites more questions. Isn't that the human experience? It is the opposite of the American fable, which levels the tyranny of certainty in the form of cardboard-cutout identities on the backs of Blacks, shrouds Latinos and Asian Americans in confusion, and erases Native Americans outright—all to preserve the simplicity of the myth of Whiteness. Repair requires truth. Truth does not bow to packaged simplicity. Family stories have the power to subvert fabricated hierarchies of human belonging and ground us again in truth.

While individuals re-member through family story, DNA matching, and personal research, civic and religious communities re-member through testimony, ritual, healing circles, book studies, movie nights, film festivals, and the immersive practice of pilgrimage.

William Lloyd Garrison, publisher of the abolitionist newspaper *The Liberator*, wrote about the first time he heard Frederick Douglass speak. Recently emancipated, Douglass stood behind the podium of the 1841 Anti-Slavery Convention in Nantucket. He opened his mouth and testified with the authority of an eyewitness to hell. Douglass's testimony changed Garrison. He wrote:

> I shall never forget his first speech at the convention—the extraordinary emotion it excited in my own mind—the powerful impression it created upon a crowded auditory, completely taken by surprise—the applause which followed from the beginning to the end of his felicitous remarks. I think I never hated slavery so intensely as at that moment; certainly, my perception of the enormous outrage which is inflicted by it, on the godlike nature of its victims, was rendered far more clear than ever.[18]

Testimony has the power to confront, challenge, and change the way we see the world. I witnessed its power while on pilgrimage with fifty other national faith leaders in Montgomery, Alabama, in December 2015. We sat in the conference room of Bryan Stevenson's Equal Justice Initiative. The packed room listened to Stevenson tell the story of people of African descent on US soil from slavery through mass incarceration. Toward the end of his story, he invited Anthony Ray Hinton to the small raised stage. As Hinton told us his story, the room silenced to a hush.

Hinton was mowing the lawn one day in 1985 outside his home in Montgomery. His mother was inside. A police car rolled up and the officers asked him his name. When he told them, they said they were there to arrest him. They placed his hands behind his back, and he struggled, not knowing what he was being arrested for. After telling his crying mother he would be alright, two White officers shoved him into the back of a police car. One sat next to him in the back seat. He asked them what he had done.

The officer said, "Robbery and capital murder."

"What's capital murder?" Hinton asked.

"You're gonna get the death penalty," he said.

"But I didn't do it." He panicked.

"There are five reasons I know you're going to go to jail," the officer said. "One: You're black. Two: We're going to get a white man to say you did it, even if you didn't. Three: The victim is a white man. Four: The judge is a white man. Five: The jury will most likely be an all-white jury. You know what that spells?"

"No." Time stopped as Hinton waited for his answer.

The officer leaned in: "It spells *conviction*."

Hinton's trial lasted one and a half days. He was convicted on the basis of an inaccurate ballistics report that claimed his mother's gun was the murder weapon. It was analyzed by a non-professional who was blind in one eye. He spent thirty years in solitary confinement on death row.

Thirty years.

Fourteen years into Hinton's sentence, Stevenson took up his case and hired three separate forensic experts. They unanimously confirmed that the bullet from the murder weapon did not match the gun in his mother's house. Hinton's innocence was proven, but the courts still would not set him free. Nor would the court give him a new trial. Stevenson's team fought for sixteen more years, all the way to the Supreme Court, which declared in 2014 that Hinton had a right to a new trial.

Hinton was set free in April 2015. Eight months later, he shared with this room full of national faith leaders that he still had trouble stretching out in his new bed. He feels the impact of the thirty years on his body, in his mind, and in his relationships. He shared that his mother died while he was in prison. Now he lives in her house alone. Like any human being, all he wants is to be loved. He forgives the officers who framed him and the courts that unjustly kept him bound—not for their sake, but for his.

Months after his emancipation, the fifty national faith leaders who I had organized to pilgrimage through the story of the confinement of Black bodies on US soil sat in the conference room of EJI encountering Anthony Hinton—a man whose body had absorbed the wrath of systemic white supremacy. We surrounded Hinton, laid hands on him, and prayed the devil back to hell. Tears flowed as we prayed blessings and honor and power back into this man who had it sucked from him by thirty-plus years in solitary confinement. Hinton's testimony changed us forever.[19]

In 2019, Anthony Hinton wrote a book testifying about his experience: *The Sun Does Shine: How I Found Life, Freedom, and Justice.* Read it.

Nations re-member by mounting truth commissions; marking land with monuments and memorials where people, families, and communities were torn asunder; and establishing institutional and cultural common public memory through museums, symposia, and the arts.

I walked through the entrance gate of the Apartheid Museum in Johannesburg, South Africa, and had to choose which entrance I would use: "white," "colored," or "black." The entrance, with its dank, cold bars and turnstile, placed me in the shoes of those upon whom the state leveled these identities until South African apartheid fell in 1994. I walked among the tanks that used to roam the streets of Soweto and through the townships of Cape Town. I felt their ominous threat and read the stories of the men, women, and children who died or went missing at the hands of the apartheid police.

Then I came to the focal point of the museum—the section focused on the Truth and Reconciliation Commission. I read original documents outlining the goals and process, then I sat on the cold cement bench and watched the commission unfold on film. I heard the testimonies of people terrorized and pilfered of loved ones by the South African Police (SAP). I heard former SAP officers detail their own devilish deeds with uncommon transparency. The offer of amnesty lifted the fear of retribution enough to unlock the truth from the mouths of those who committed state-directed murders.

In Germany and in cities across Europe, city governments welcomed artist Gunter Demnig to mark certain streets with brass-plated concrete "stumbling stones" and plaques that remind the general public every single day that a certain Jewish family lived here before the Holocaust: these were their names, this is what happened to them.[20] Germany swore never to forget what it had done lest it repeat the atrocity and the shame of the past. When nations want to forget, they mute the testimony of the land by building over it, renaming it, and reframing it.

In San Antonio, the Alamo sprawls with monuments and mission walls considered so sacred that visitors are prohibited from touching their surfaces. To enter the Alamo is to enter the birthplace of the Republic of Texas. The story Texans are told usually begins in the middle of war, framing the Texans as innocent, bullied settlers battling for freedom from encroaching Mexico. Most Texans don't know that Mexico was a province of Spain until Mexico won its independence in 1821—two years before Stephen Austin was granted land by the Mexican government. Most Texan children are never taught that Austin imagined Texas as a slaveholding province of Mexico and incentivized new settlers to bring more slaves by offering more land if they did.

Mexico, whose economy was built on the backs of enslaved Africans as many as one hundred years before the first Africans walked on Virginia shores, had soured on slavery and had begun to outlaw the institution. Texan schools and monuments and the Alamo itself never mention, even once, that Austin lobbied the Mexican government to keep slavery legal, but they refused and responded by freeing all children immediately in 1827, and emancipating all adults within six months of the law's passage. The Mexican legislature also mandated that living conditions for formerly enslaved Africans in Texas be improved and they be paid for their work.

The writers of Texan textbooks, the curators of Texan museums, the keepers of the Alamo's narrative never mention that Austin instructed White Texans to work around that law by employing the art of spin: he instructed Texans to call their enslaved families "laborers," "workingmen," and "family servants." And nowhere inside the Alamo is it written in any corner of the monument that White Texans went to war against Mexico eight years later in response to Mexico's crackdown on Texan spin. Instead, the Alamo narrators narrow the field of view, focus on the tactical situation of the Alamo battle, and cast the Texans as martyred freedom fighters.[21]

Across the US, public monuments like the Alamo spin fables that twist public memory and tangle it in untruth. Monuments, buildings, and street names cross-stitch seditious narratives into the normative fabric of our lives, casting Confederate soldiers and White nationalists as heroes and men of valor. Colleges and universities register students for classes in buildings named after men who fought to preserve slavery. Figures in church history are dubbed forefathers of Christian faith: the fact that Puritan revivalist Jonathan Edwards not only enslaved people but also wrote an impassioned defense of slavery in 1741 is never questioned.[22] Instead, we are urged to think of him and others like him as products of their time. But in their time, hidden in plain sight, were witnesses of the truth like the Society of Friends who began to openly push back against slavery as early as the 1680s.[23]

Confusion is the author of conflict and separation. Conflict and separation thrive in the shrouded gaps between our narratives. Public monuments, memorials, public art, and protest can all fill our collective narrative gap with light and truth born of eyewitness testimony, credible journalism, historical documentation, and scientific evidence.

On the morning of June 27, 2015, the sun rose over the highway as Christian activist and artist Bree Newsome re-membered the Emanuel Nine—nine Black parishioners gunned down by White supremacist Dylan Roof ten days earlier during a Bible study at Emanuel African Methodist Episcopal Church in Charleston.

Newsome drove from Charlotte, North Carolina, to Columbia, South Carolina, mere miles from the land where Lea was enslaved, where Annie was raped and died, where Lizzie lost her mother, Martha, to medical racism, and where Willa learned to limit her dreams to the confines of White men's homes. When she reached the state capitol, Bree found the Confederate flag raised high over the Capitol grounds. She crept up the flag pole whispering, "Our Father, who art in heaven, hallowed be your name . . ." Police yelled for her to come down, but higher and higher she went. When she reached the top, Newsome snatched the Confederate flag, unhooked it, balled it up, and inched back down the pole. As planned, Newsome was arrested.[24]

It was both art and creative nonviolent protest in the same breath. The bold action of one woman shined light on the truth: we can take the flags down whenever we want to. They are not permanent fixtures. Every day that Confederate flags fly across the South, it is by choice. Newsome's action shined light on a more complex and deeper truth: the Confederate flag is the symbol of an ideology at war against God. To allow the Confederate flag to fly and the statues to tower over people made in the image of God is to war with God for supremacy. "Hallowed be thy name" means "Your name is the highest name. There is no greater authority than you. I have no greater loyalty than to you, God." But to kill is to crush the image of God on earth. There is no way one can honor God and murder an image of God.

Newsome's action snatched the blinders off our nation. Suddenly we saw what we had not seen so clearly in more than one hundred years of post-Reconstruction: White, southern dominion.

But it is not enough to snatch down the monuments and memorials of confusion and injustice. We must fill the gap with permanent installations of truth.

The Whitney Plantation in Louisiana, the National Civil Rights Museum in Memphis, the Equal Justice Initiative's Legacy Museum and National Memorial for Peace and Justice, its soil collection project and the public markers of lynchings, the plaque embedded into the pavement near the spot where Michael Brown died in 2014, the National Museum of African American History and Culture—all contribute to the permanent public memory of the legacy of the legislated lies of racialized and gendered and religious and national and sexualized and ableist hierarchies of human belonging.

Finally, congressional hearings and truth commissions mounted by governments play a vital role in the work of correcting and filling the gap within the fractured and twisted public memory. Drawing on the power of testimony, documentation, data, and scientific evidence, truth commissions and congressional hearings create the official public record necessary to discern effective strategic policies toward repair. The 9/11 Commission, the Kerner Commission, and the 2001 Tulsa Race Riot Commission all leveraged the power of government to lay foundations of common understanding that became points of reference as states instituted programs aimed at accountability and repair.

Twenty days before he died, Martin Luther King Jr. ended his speech at Grosse Pointe High School with a clarion call for the truth to be told: "We shall overcome because Carlisle is right. 'No lie can live forever.' We shall overcome because William Cullen Bryant is right. 'Truth crushed to earth will rise again.'"[25]

Re-membering truth is the first step. The next step is re-membering people and people groups with their own divine call and capacity to steward the world.

9

Reparation as Repentance

I landed in South Africa in January 2017. I had crossed the Atlantic a few times before, but always en route to Europe. It was my first time on the continent of my ancestral homeland. Throughout the transatlantic flight, I imagined my ancestors chained with others who did not speak their language, all packed like cargo below deck. My ancestors survived. That was the miracle. They defied the death ships that carted them and approximately 12.5 million other Central and West African men, women, and children across the Atlantic: 10.7 million survived, and 1.8 million African souls rest at the bottom of the ocean.[1]

My direct ancestors were among those who fought to live. Now I was moving toward their homeland across swirling black burial waters thirty thousand feet below.

I am not sure what I imagined I would see when I stepped foot in South Africa. My extreme ignorance of my people's mother continent was primed by the legal and social erasure of African American connection to our land. Since arrival on North American soil in 1619, our languages were banned. Our dances were banned. Our gatherings were banned. Our faiths were banned. And by the early to mid-1700s, even our names were erased and replaced with the names of Greek gods and mythical creatures like Caesar, Cupid, Venus, and Hero.[2] The African American floated in a netherworld of nonbeing—except for the productivity that Western nations squeezed from our Black bodies to build White wealth.

In simple terms, I expected to see African people in African prints, eating African foods, doing African things. But what I encountered was the aftermath of what happened when we were snatched—the land of our ancestors was seized and it, too, was squeezed dry by European nations that warred over the territories' riches for centuries. The Africans who were left behind were not enslaved. Rather, their land was claimed to add wealth to the coffers of European thrones. The South African peoples and land in particular were utterly degraded. The Dutch rounded up and moved the Khoikhoi and San peoples from their ancestral lands and pushed them into the Eastern Cape. Exploited African migrants from the north and enslaved South Asians from colonized India mined their land for diamonds. In the twentieth century, the Afrikaner government instituted apartheid (meaning "to live apart"). Following the cue of Jim Crow segregation, the Afrikaner government perfected the Jim Crow system, making it nearly impenetrable. Former Khoikhoi land, lush and beautiful, was designated "Whites Only" territory. Indian and multiracial people were rounded up and removed from an area called District 6, previously a community of South Asian and mixed-race people who lived there for generations after slavery. Now District 6 was designated "Whites Only." Apartheid police broke into homes and dragged families out and onto the backs of pickup trucks. Police drove these families to "colored townships," which were cinderblock communities with no grass or trees, no green space. Black South Africans were removed further still and herded onto unpaved dirt fields with nothing but a tin home to give them shelter. They designated these areas "Black townships." Like the slave patrols of colonial and antebellum America, police patrols monitored and sanctioned the movement of Black peoples between townships and to and from their places of work in White areas. Black men were conscripted to mine diamonds while Black women cleaned White families' homes and cared for their children. Dissenters lost employment or were jailed on Robben Island, exiled, or killed.

Apartheid came crumbling down in 1994, when Nelson Mandela was chosen to serve as the nation's first democratically elected president. Having spent twenty-seven years imprisoned for his resistance to the apartheid regime—the first eighteen on Robben Island—President Mandela led the nascent democracy into a process of national reckoning and transformation. While the nation's deep Christian identity compelled leaders to engage a process of truth-telling as confession and amnesty as forgiveness, the commission came to an impasse around the question of reparation. The second objective of South Africa's Truth and Reconciliation Commission, reparations, was never achieved on a wide scale.

In a legal sense, reparations usually involve monetary restitution for loss incurred through oppression. But reparations are more than money. They are also policies and measures enacted in the normal course of governing. Reparations are recognition of and accountability for wrongdoing. They are action by the offending family, community, or government to repair the relationship that has been broken and to restructure the way things work, such that all stand on equal footing from the moment of redress forward.

Inspired by the civil rights movement, Japanese Americans pushed for reparations beginning in the 1960s. In 1988, Ronald Reagan signed the Civil Liberties Act into law. In 1991, George H. W. Bush amended the act, allocating enough funds to ensure each internee received restitution. Interned Japanese Americans each received $20,000 in restitution, a congressional and presidential apology, and an education fund that benefited the children of Japanese American families. Similarly, West Germany paid out 3.45 billion deutsche marks in reparations to Jewish families. The

US aided Jewish reparations by investing in the Marshall Plan, which poured funds into Europe's rebuilding effort after World War II. Finally, Native American nations and tribes have sought reparations in various forms. Some have sought sovereignty, others financial redress, others apology.

In the broadest sense, reparation is all that is required to repair the relationship that has been broken between oppressed and oppressor. Reparation imagines that the hierarchy of human belonging created through oppression is not, in fact, the natural state of things. The hierarchy is constructed and can therefore be deconstructed and designed in a way that makes things right.

The South African Truth and Reconciliation Commission could not agree on how to move forward to redress the oppression of Black South Africans under the apartheid regime. Consequently, the nation's rehabilitation hit an impasse. Though officials removed "Whites Only" signs in 1994, South African segregation now mirrors America's de facto economic segregation. Black townships still overflow with indigenous peoples crammed together in tin homes on barren land. Men, women, and children walk unpaved roads lined with portable toilets beneath a canopy of wires rigged to compensate for the township's lack of electricity. Meanwhile, White South Africans continue to live in beautiful homes surrounded by green trees and green grass, with hillside views of the blue ocean, gold-lined garage doors—actual gold—and razor wire wrapped around the tops of every house. Violence follows inequity, and Cape Town is the most inequitable city on the planet. In short, White South Africans confessed but did not repent.

The US has never confessed. Nor has it repented. African Americans are the only oppressed group to which the US has never made reparation. Rather, through spin, half measures, and obfuscation, the US has covered over, morphed, and entrenched the policies that created the deepest inequities in the US. For example, Henry Lawrence and Lea Ballard's America witnessed the seeds of redlining as a matter of custom and practice in the post-Reconstruction era. By the time of Philip Fortune, Hiram and Ella Lawrence, Lizzie Johnson, and Reinaldo Weekes's generation, customary segregation had been embedded into laws and codes that proliferated the practice of redlining to protect White space and supremacy and to contain people of African descent. It worked. Economists trace America's most indelible, racialized, structural inequities back to segregationist housing policies developed in the shadow of the Civil War and perfected in the nascent years of the twentieth century.[3]

A People without a Land

Milton Dashiell came from an old Maryland family. James Dashiell II acquired hundreds of acres in Somerset County in the 1600s. He cultivated a slave-based plantation that was passed down from father to son for generations. Its wealth established the Dashiell family as Maryland power brokers. James Dashiell II was a judge and lawmaker who eventually served on the Maryland House of Burgesses. The Dashiell plantation was a stone's throw away from land that Fortune's daughter Betty eventually purchased in 1753 from a member of the Day family, which had indentured her mother and sisters. The Dashiells were neighbors of the Fortune family for decades—until Betty fled Maryland's hardening racial hierarchy and mounting violence against free Blacks in the years leading to the Revolutionary War. By 1777, Betty Fortune/Game had resettled in Sussex County, Delaware,[4] an undeveloped region in a southern state bordering the North, at war with itself over slavery.[5]

Generations after Milton Dashiell's ancestor James was a neighbor to mine, and after those neighbors witnessed Betty's removal, Milton Dashiell crafted the local redlining ordinance that laid legal foundations for redlining across the country. In 1910 the Baltimore City Council passed Dashiell's ordinance despite the protests of Black city residents. The *Baltimore Sun* outlined the ordinance at the time:

- That no negro can move into a block in which more than half of the residents are white.
- That no white person can move into a block in which more than half of the residents are colored.

- That a violator of the law is punishable by a fine of not more than $100 or imprisonment of from 30 days to 1 year, or both.
- That existing conditions shall not be disturbed. No white person will be compelled to move away from his house because the block in which he lives has more negroes than whites, and no negro can be forced to move from his house if his block has more whites than negroes.
- That no section of the city is exempted from the conditions of the ordinance. It applies to every house.[6]

Richmond's elite likewise perfected housing inequity. In 1911 the Richmond City Council passed a law that put in place an elaborate web of racial zoning codes.[7] These codes were struck down by the Supreme Court. But each time, Richmond's White leaders came back with new schemes. In *The Color of Law*, Richard Rothstein reveals the scope of this local effort to "isolate white families in white communities."[8] Dashiell's legislative apartheid strategy in Maryland was mimicked in locales across the country, including in Atlanta, Birmingham, Dade County (Miami), Charleston, Dallas, Louisville, New Orleans, Oklahoma City, Richmond (Virginia), St. Louis, and others.[9]

In 1933, when the Federal Housing Authority (FHA) was established to pull the US economy out of the despair of the Great Depression, the FHA drew red lines around Black communities, giving them the lowest rating for mortgages. Now federalized, Blacks were effectively caged into communities that were subsequently neglected and underresourced by city governments. While these measures were reversed over forty years later by the Federal Home Mortgage Disclosure Act (1975) and Community Reinvestment Act (1977), the damage had been done. Forty years of economic apartheid baked inequity into the landscape of our nation.[10] The neglect continues to this day and touches every system and structure that enables flourishing in the US, including housing, transportation, education, water, sewage and sanitation, banking,

business and economic development, and access to gainful employment. As a result, de facto segregation continues to haunt
our schools and churches and boardrooms and neighborhoods
and air and water.

Andre Johnson's *No Future in This Country: The Prophetic
Pessimism of Bishop Henry McNeal Turner* reveals one way the
African American community wrestled with the question of repair in the thick of post-Reconstruction America. In 1891 Bishop
Henry McNeal Turner traveled to Africa for the first time. Turner
had spent the prior decades calling African Americans to love
themselves in the midst of a world ablaze with Jim Crow terror.
When he landed in Sierra Leone he was struck by the cosmopolitan
dignity of African peoples, most of whom spoke several languages.
He marveled at their technologically advanced society, the city's
cleanliness, the majestic cathedrals and churches. In his *Letters
from Africa*, Turner marveled that the buildings "all belonged to
black men."[11] Sierra Leone's "fine buildings" and learned people
all stood before him in great contrast to both the White myths of
African primitivism and the reality of African American squalor.

Traveling at the height of Jim Crow lynchings and peonage,
Turner wrote his letters from Africa only five years before the
consequential *Plessy v. Ferguson* ruling, which effectively nullified
the Fourteenth Amendment, declaring African Americans unworthy of the rights and protections afforded to American citizens.
Turner had no hope that things would or could change for his race
in the US. Yet his pilgrimage to Africa had shown him what full
Black dignity looked like—and that it was possible. So, in 1893,
he convened a national gathering of African Americans aimed at
organizing a mass return to Africa. In his call for the gathering he
wrote, "I do not believe that there is any manhood future in this
country for the Negro, and that his future existence, to say nothing
of his future happiness, will depend upon his nationalization."[12]

By "nationalization," Turner referred to the same movement
that Lincoln championed: the creation of an African American
nation-state in Africa or elsewhere. In pure political terms, this
solution is the only way to guarantee political agency. A people

must have a land upon which they can actualize. America was supposed to be the land of the great democratic experiment—the nation-state crafted on the strength of its ideals, not its ethnic ties. The founding fathers opened the Declaration of Independence with revolutionary words that crafted a new kind of nation: "We hold these truths to be self-evident, that all men are created equal, that they are endowed by their Creator with certain unalienable Rights, that among these are Life, Liberty and the pursuit of Happiness." With these words the founders proclaimed the vision of America—a land where all people have the right to live, to be free, and to flourish. They laid the foundation for the kind of country that America would be—the kind that would organize itself around principle, not ethnic loyalty. But these same founders resisted their own words in practice.

I learned on a pilgrimage to Thomas Jefferson's Monticello plantation that the penman of the first draft of the Declaration of Independence owned more than six hundred people over the course of his life. There were usually about two hundred enslaved people living on his plantation at a given time. Jefferson set aside a few slave dwellings for individual families who worked inside the house or as ironsmiths, but the overwhelming majority of the human beings he owned slept in the fields. He kept scores of children in one small shed where they slept at night. Next to that was a shed for his tools.

Jefferson is revered for his forward-thinking ingenuity, yet he could not see his way past his double mind. He claimed to desire the gradual abolition of enslaved people, but he refused to set free the people he owned. Toward the end of his life, he was faced with a choice: free the remaining 130 enslaved souls or sell them to pay off his debt. He sold them into the Deep South. The people and families and community he owned, rather than he himself, paid the penalty for his debt.

The Fourteenth Amendment moved White America from ambiguity about who America is for to the unambiguous granite rock of constitutional law: America is for all who are born here or naturalized here, Congress and the states proclaimed. Nonetheless, southern White state and local legislators effectively wove a web of Jim Crow laws and policies that blocked people of African descent from all avenues that led to flourishing. They crafted laws in a way that guaranteed White people the right to flourish, but locked Blacks out of the franchise. Turner understood this and did not believe Whites were capable of repentance. So he called African Americans to take things into their own hands and leave.

Derrick Bell, one of the fathers of modern critical race theory, picks up Turner's argument to explain why White America is incapable of repentance. In his 1992 book, *Faces at the Bottom of the Well*, Bell explains the critical role African Americans have played in stabilizing the US from the beginning. Without Blacks, Bell surmises, class warfare would have broken out between poor Whites and the White elite. But, in times of economic upheaval— from the turbulent years leading up to the Revolutionary War, the post–Civil War years and the southern droughts of the late nineteenth century, the deep economic inequality of the 1920s, the Vietnam War's recession, or the grotesque inequity and corruption revealed by the Great Recession of 2007–2009—the White ruling class consistently diverted the attention of working and poor Whites from the injustice of the economic gap between them and the top 1 percent. They pointed the finger at Black, indigenous, and other people of color who served as a perpetual scapegoat that fueled what Bell calls "racial bonding" between poor and rich Whites. This racialized bond is a potent political force that Bell asserts has kept America from disintegrating into balkanized states.[13]

That said, even Bell sees no hope in nationalizing African Americans in another land. Bell shares a fable of a fictionalized expedition of thousands of African Americans who tried to settle an uninhabited island that had appeared about nine hundred miles due east of South Carolina in the middle of the Atlantic. An armada of ships full of African Americans set sail from the land of their enslavement. Brown faces looked eastward, full of the hope of self-actualization. They are dumbfounded when the island that held their hopes becomes shrouded in mist and sinks back into the sea before their eyes. They called it Afrolantica. Its loss could have broken their hope, but it did not. Rather, in Bell's fable, the armada returned to America's eastern shores having been awakened to one critical truth: they already possess the power to self-actualize. They had organized the armada. They had set out on the sea. They braved uncharted waters. They can brave America.[14]

What will it take to brave America? The answer to that critical question is becoming clear in the years since Bell wrote *Faces at the Bottom of the Well*. He wrote it in an era when segregationist rebuttals to civil rights gains were in the crafting stage, before their full impact was levied on our communities. Since then, the fruit of those early years has been revealed: American prisons and jails are bursting from a 500 percent increase in population from 1980 to 2021,[15] resulting in a *New York Times* report declaring 1.5 million Black men "missing" from Black communities.[16] Policies developed in the 1980s and '90s snagged Black men in the Jim Crow net of convict leasing and continue to rob them of family developing years—using them again to supply the White economy with free and low-cost labor and to fill prison beds traded on the stock market.[17]

Likewise, a stand-your-ground law was adopted in 2005 in Florida, and versions of the law now exist across the US legal landscape. The law offers impunity to anyone who kills someone and claims they feared for their life. In the past, this impunity was limited to the inside of one's home. Stand-your-ground laws expanded impunity to outside the home. Ostensibly developed to serve battered women, these laws have failed Black women,[18] while courts have referenced the law in jury deliberations in ways that have benefited White men. George Zimmerman walked free after murdering Trayvon Martin. His defense? He feared for his life. Martin had no weapon—only a bag of Skittles and a bottle of Arizona Iced Tea. The world watched the river of hashtagged deaths of Black and Brown men, women, and children flow past their social media feeds for the next several years. The vast majority of cases have never seen the inside of a courtroom, and if they did, the perpetrator was rarely convicted. Not only is a river of lives gone, but a river of fathers is gone, and a river of contributors to households, businesses, governance, and culture is gone.

Likewise, land upon which we could have flourished has been consistently seized and transferred from our families' legacies to the coffers of White governments and families. At the turn of the twentieth century, Anthony Crawford was a fifty-six-year-old leader in the Black community of Abbeville, South Carolina. Farming on his rich land garnered him and his multigenerational family a prosperous living that overflowed to bless his community. The proceeds from Crawford's 427 acres helped fund a local church, school, and several farms. One day in the harvest season of 1916, Crawford got into a dispute over the price of cottonseed with a White storekeeper. He refused to do business with the storekeeper and was arrested. A mob of three hundred White townspeople dragged his body from the jail. They beat him. They strung him up. Then they blocked Crawford's family from retrieving the body. Crawford's body hung on that tree for days—as a warning to all the other Black townspeople about what happens to Black people who think they are equal. That was not good enough for the White mob. They drove the Crawford family from Abbeville and seized their land—427 acres—gone from the Crawford family legacy. That's 427 acres gone from the Black Abbeville community. Gone.[19]

Sometimes the seizure happens at the hands of mobs, other times at the hands of the government. Hiram Lawrence owned several homes on one block in the Elmwood community of Philadelphia. He leveraged his land in this marshy area on the outskirts of the city to welcome displaced southern African Americans who were migrating north in flight from southern terror. All of those homes were my family's legacy. My great-grandfather's leadership and hospitality were our legacy. The city of brotherly love seized that legacy and forced Great-Grandpop Hiram to sell his land to them for pennies on the dollar. Our family birthright was gone. A vital community resource was gone. In its place, a gas station and parking lot now sit adjacent to the I-95 interstate near the Philadelphia airport. Likewise, Lea Ballard lost her land to the city of Camden, South Carolina. They, too, claimed the power of eminent domain. I don't know the details. I only possess correspondence to Willa from a lawyer and from the City of Camden. She tried for years to get her great-grandmother's land back to no avail.[20]

William A. Darity Jr. and A. Kirsten Mullen open the question of reparations in their book *From Here to Equality* with a profound thought: Had the original promise of a land grant to the formerly enslaved in the amount of forty acres and a mule been kept, "it is likely that there would be no need for reparations to be under consideration now." They continue: "If the forty acres had been allocated roughly to families of four, each ex-slave would have received ten acres of land. Since there were approximately 4 million freedmen, a total of 40 million acres of land should have been allocated to formerly enslaved blacks."[21] How different could our lives have been had the government allowed people of African descent to accumulate wealth—had Betty Fortune never had to flee her land in Maryland, had Henry and Harriet never been chased out of Kentucky, had Hiram's land never been claimed by eminent domain, had Lea's land never been claimed by eminent domain, had Reinaldo and Anita not been relegated to the swamplands of annexed and Jim Crowed Puerto Rico . . . how different would our lives be if my generation had been able to build on generations of wealth accumulation? What could we have contributed to the world had our forebears been given the foundation from which to fly? Instead, we moved and survived and built what we could, passing down what we could: a locket, a picture, a single two-story row house in ghettoized and gutted South Philadelphia. It was enough to survive the struggle, but it was not enough to fly.

Others were not so lucky. They did not survive at all.

Journalist Ta-Nehisi Coates writes, "With segregation, with the isolation of the injured and the robbed, comes the concentration of disadvantage. An unsegregated America might see poverty, and all its effects, spread across the country with no particular bias toward skin color. Instead, the concentration of poverty has been paired with a concentration of melanin. The resulting conflagration has been devastating."[22] While income is garnered through labor, wealth accumulates across generations.[23] People of African descent have been systematically and structurally blocked from accumulating and passing on wealth. Thus, the median base of wealth for White families is ten times that of Black families,[24] and White college graduates possess seven times the wealth of Black college graduates.[25] The Samuel DuBois Cook Center on Social Equity produced a report in 2018 that challenged prevailing policy myths regarding how to close the racial wealth gap in the US. The authors clarify:

> There are no actions that black Americans can take unilaterally that will have much of an effect on reducing the racial wealth gap. For the gap to be closed, America must undergo a vast social transformation produced by the adoption of bold national policies, policies that will forge a way forward by addressing, finally, the long-standing consequences of slavery, the Jim Crow years that followed, and ongoing racism and discrimination that exist in our society today.[26]

Repair will require repentance—full repentance—national repentance, state-based repentance, city-based repentance, the repentance of families and individuals. Repentance will require reparation and restitution.

Imagine two brothers are playing with a toy. The toy was a gift to the older brother from his grandmother. The younger brother steals the toy and claims it as his own. The children's mother overhears the fight and never addresses it. Instead, the boys continue to fight, till the younger one punches his brother into submission. He keeps the toy and plays with it at the dinner table that night, and the mother still does nothing. The younger brother gets to keep the toy. End of story.

What kind of relationship between those two brothers might exist from that point forward? Will it be characterized by trust, mutual accountability, and fairness? Or will it be fundamentally broken? What will it take to make the relationship right? What responsibility does the parent hold for the relationship between the brothers? How does the parent's governance impact the siblings' relationship? The simple answer is this: The parent's governance has the power to bless or curse the relationship between siblings. If skewed in favor of one sibling or another, the lack of boundaries within the household will lay foundations of distrust, manipulation, and domination and will break the relationship between siblings. The establishment and enforcement of equitable boundaries lays foundations for trust, shared agency, and mutual flourishing of both siblings.

Who is the parent in the story of the US? It is not the US government. Colonizing governments of Britain, Spain, and France, as well as the subsequent US government, are the younger brothers who stole land, labor, and compensation from indigenous, African, Asian, and Latinx peoples. If the US government is not the parent, who is? Who has the authority to determine how the people will live together in the US? By what authority can the US be led to make things right? In a democracy, the greatest authority is the voters themselves. When the vast majority of people in that democracy claim to be people of faith, as in America, then the voters must leverage their votes in deference to a higher authority than their own comfort or fear. They (we) must answer to God— the parent of all humanity—the one who the prophet Micah tells us will "arbitrate between strong nations" (4:3).

The first page of the first book of the Bible contains a foundational text of all Abrahamic faiths. The writer of Genesis 1 declares, "Then God said, 'Let us make humankind in our image, according to our likeness; and let them have dominion over the fish of the sea, and over the birds of the air, and over the cattle, and over all the wild animals of the earth, and over every creeping thing that creeps upon the earth'" (1:26). These revolutionary words established the inherent dignity of all humanity and the divine call

198

and capacity of all to exercise stewardship of the world—a status singularly reserved for kings and queens in previous civilizations. Freedom to flourish is a basic right of humankind. The first paragraph of the Charter of the United Nations begins: "We the peoples of the United Nations determined to save succeeding generations from the scourge of war, which twice in our lifetime has brought untold sorrow to mankind, and to reaffirm faith in fundamental human rights, in the dignity and worth of the human person, in the equal rights of men and women and of nations large and small."[27] Likewise, the first line of the Universal Declaration of Human Rights declares: "Whereas recognition of the inherent dignity and of the equal and inalienable rights of all members of the human family is the foundation of freedom, justice and peace in the world . . ."[28]

The fastest and surest way to limit or crush human flourishing is through oppression or poverty. Human hierarchies of belonging are the precursor for both. They are the source of shattered societies and broken people groups and economic disparity. They are antithetical to faithful protection of the image of God on earth. In Fortune's story, we bear witness to the intersectional nature of American hierarchies of human belonging. In those 1662 and 1664 Virginia and Maryland laws, racial, gender, and citizenship-status hierarchies of belonging were crafted. Inextricably intertwined, the three oppressions worked together to legally establish and protect White male social and economic supremacy in Fortune's world.

Recall from chapter 1 that in early colonial Virginia, to be counted a British citizen, one's father must have been a British citizen. Elizabeth Key challenged her slave status in court in 1656 based on the fact that her father, who was also her master, was a British citizen. Therefore, she should not have been enslaved. Key won her case and others followed. To avoid losing their free labor, legislators in the House of Burgesses changed the law concerning citizenship status in 1662. They shifted from English common law to the Roman law of *partus sequitur ventrem*, which determines citizenship through the status of the mother. This enabled White men to continue to rape their enslaved women, produce free labor, and breed generations of free labor. Maryland followed two years later, establishing its own first slave laws. In Maryland's laws, as with Virginia, the only class of people who never received legal penalty for interracial relations was White men. The same laws that established Blackness also established Whiteness, womanness, and immigrant status for the first time in early colonial America.

Human hierarchies of belonging broke America to the bone through the establishment of inequitable dominion—disparate capacities to exercise agency and impact the world. Therefore, the *process* of repair matters as much as the intent and the amount of restitution. The process must recognize, engage, and submit to the agency of the broken ones. These broken ones must determine the requirements of their own flourishing.

The land lay cracked for three years. Famine had overtaken. David, king of Israel, prayed the kind of prayers that desperate leaders pray when they reach the end of themselves. The people were looking to him and he had nothing but empty hands and compromised land. One day David heard God's voice like a hush in the wind: "There is bloodguilt on Saul and on his house, because he put the Gibeonites to death" (2 Sam. 21:1). The people of Israel had sworn to spare the Gibeonites in war, but Saul had tried to commit genocide against them.

Notice that David did not call together his own council to figure out how to fix the situation. Instead, he enters a reparative process. The process itself is the starting point for healing between the two people groups. So, David called the Gibeonites and began a process of repentance.

Reparation is repentance. To repent, one must understand how one broke the relationship in the first place. In this case, Saul led the nation of Israel to attempt to commit genocide against the Gibeonites. Saul led them to disregard the image of God in the Gibeonites—to disregard their God-given call to exercise dominion over their own land and people and lives. And Saul broke relationship with God when he dared to usurp God's singular authority to ordain the day of each Gibeonite's death. David repented by calling the Gibeonites. He did not continue the injury by usurping their authority to exercise dominion again. He did not continue the break in relationship by "fixing" the problem from on high. He brought them in close. He spoke with them—the first step in mending relationship. Then he did something radical—something revolutionary.

"David said to the Gibeonites, 'What shall I do for you? How shall I make expiation, that you may bless the heritage of the LORD?'" (2 Sam. 21:3). He repeats it again one verse later: "What do you say that I should do for you?" Expiation was a necessary requirement in cleansing bloodguilt. Yet, notice: David asks. He does not tell them how he will pay for Saul's sin. In the asking, David recognizes the Gibeonites' divine call to exercise dominion in the world—and over this moment. They tell David exactly what repair will require. The Gibeonites have already had their council session. They know what repair will take. The Gibeonites demanded the death of seven of Saul's sons. Understand, no one is advocating death as repair in the US. But the principle we can glean is this: repair will be costly. It will cost families their manufactured peace. It will cost the oppressors, their descendants, and those who benefit from their sin assumptions of entitlement. It will cost lifestyles built on the quicksand of sin. Ultimately, it will cost the centering of White sensibilities.

Notice also that David does not negotiate. He does not ask questions to see how much he can get the Gibeonites to step back from their demand. Even in this costly phase of repair, David remains committed to mending Israel's relationship with the Gibeonites by honoring the image of God in them and their divine call to exercise dominion over this moment. This is Israel's act of repentance. David does what they ask of him.

But the story does not end there. Rizpah, a descendant of Esau, had been Saul's sex slave. She had been forced to bear two of Saul's children. Then she was forced to watch her sons die for Saul's sins. When her son's bodies were lifted on stakes above the city, Rizpah laid down sackcloth and performed ritual mourning nonstop. She did not let the birds of the air or the beasts of the field eat the bodies of her sacrificed sons. This enslaved woman—oppressed twice and triple shamed—exercised profound agency in this desperate act of love. Rizpah's agency moved King David to exercise mercy on her (2 Sam. 21:10–12).

The essence of the Hebrew concept of *shalom* is radical connectedness. *Shalom* is when all things are in radical, connected relationship with each other. David gathered the bodies of the men in Rizpah's family, including Saul, and buried them together (2 Sam. 21:13–14). With this act, David brought her family together in death. David did not let disconnection continue in perpetuity. He stopped the cycle of separation, shame, and violence in his generation. With her family reconnected in death, shame was lifted from Rizpah's shoulders.

And what was God's response to David's acts of *shalom* building? "After that, God heeded supplications for the land" (2 Sam. 21:14).

The repentance of people of European descent in the US and across the post-colonizing world will require similar submission to the strategies of the subjugated in order to transform our world through structures and ways of living together that protect and serve the flourishing of all. It will also require nations skilled in the art of the deal to dump deals and to go the extra mile—to do all that it takes to repair what race broke in the world.

The Black Manifesto

In April 1969, one year after the assassination and burial of Martin Luther King Jr., the Black Economic Community Development Conference convened in Detroit. James Forman was present. Forman was a veteran of the civil rights movement, having served as executive secretary of SNCC (1961–1966) and having helped organize the Freedom Rides as well as the Birmingham, Albany, and Selma campaigns. When my mother, Sharon, helped launch the Philadelphia SNCC office, she was personally trained by Forman in church outreach and organizing. In the course of the gathering in Detroit, Forman helped craft a list of demands that became known as the Black Manifesto. Recognizing the central role of the White church in initial and ongoing enslavement and colonization of people of African descent, the Black Manifesto made a direct demand to White churches and Jewish synagogues calling on them to issue payment to the Black community in the amount of $15 per African American in the US, totaling $500 million. (Today's equivalent would be $110 per African American, totaling $5.17 trillion.)[29] The drafting committee did not imagine a check for $15 being mailed to each African American. Rather, they demanded the money be used to fund a restitution program for Black farmers who had been dispossessed of their land due to White southern terror. They called for the funds to be used to establish major publishing companies, television networks, and research hubs, as well as a training center for the next generations of organizers. The Black Manifesto also called for the funds to be allocated to institutions that strengthen the capacity of welfare recipients and laborers to organize and collaborate with leaders and businesses in Africa to strengthen the capacity of our African brothers and sisters to decolonize their nations.

Movement for Black Lives

One year after the Ferguson movement catalyzed the twenty-first-century push for civil rights, the Movement for Black Lives, a consortium of fifty organizations and networks dedicated to the flourishing of people of African descent, convened in person and online in 2015. The loose network came together to chart its vision for the Black community in the twenty-first century. I followed proceedings online from my home in Washington, DC. It was pure love and pure power. It was the daughters, grandsons, and great-grandchildren of the generations that pushed the US to the Civil Rights Act and Voting Rights Act. This movement centered the intersectional oppressions of young Black queer women, thereby including all who may have been left out in previous generations' patriarchal visions. The Movement for Black

Lives (M4BL) launched its vision in 2016. It included a section focused on reparations. M4BL did not focus on any single institution nor on reparations for antebellum slavery. Rather, M4BL called for reparation for harm from colonialism and enslavement through redlining, mass incarceration, and surveillance. The following should be included in any plan for reparations crafted by governments, businesses, or any other institution. M4BL also developed forty concrete policy recommendations with the capacity to actualize the following vision:

1. Reparations for the systemic denial of access to high quality educational opportunities in the form of full and free access for all Black people (including undocumented and currently and formerly incarcerated people) to lifetime education including: free access and open admissions to public community colleges and universities, technical education (technology, trade and agricultural), educational support programs, retroactive forgiveness of student loans, and support for lifetime learning programs.

2. Reparations for the continued divestment from, discrimination toward and exploitation of our communities in the form of a guaranteed minimum livable income for all Black people, with clearly articulated corporate regulations.

3. Reparations for the wealth extracted from our communities through environmental racism, slavery, food apartheid, housing discrimination and racialized capitalism in the form of corporate and government reparations focused on healing ongoing physical and mental trauma, and ensuring our access and control of food sources, housing and land.

4. Reparations for the cultural and educational exploitation, erasure, and extraction of our communities in the form of mandated public school curriculums that critically examine the political, economic, and social impacts

of colonialism and slavery, and funding to support, build, preserve, and restore cultural assets and sacred sites to ensure the recognition and honoring of our collective struggles and triumphs.

5. Legislation at the federal and state level that requires the United States to acknowledge the lasting impacts of slavery, establish and execute a plan to address those impacts. This includes the immediate passage of H.R. 40, the "Commission to Study Reparation Proposals for African-Americans Act" or subsequent versions which call for reparations remedies.[30]

H.R. 40

With the echoes of the Berlin Wall's crash reverberating in the background and in the shadow of the blockbuster film *Glory*, which introduced America for the first time to the critical role of Black Civil War soldiers in winning the war, Rep. John Conyers (D-Michigan) submitted House Resolution 40 (H.R. 40) for consideration in 1989. The bill was simple. It called for a commission to study the impact of slavery then and now and consider how the US could pay reparations. Conyers submitted the resolution every year for nearly thirty years. Every single time, it was blocked from passage. Conyers died in 2017. Since then, Rep. Sheila Jackson Lee has introduced the bill every year. As of the writing of this chapter, the bill is being considered by the Judiciary Committee, in preparation to be brought to the House floor for a vote. It is expected to pass the House. From there it will move to the Senate, and we will pray.[31]

When the prophet Isaiah cried out to Israel, he warned them that they were posing as if they sought God and delighted to know God's ways. They were fasting and praying, but at the same time they were oppressing their workers, beating them, and serving their own interests on their fast day. The prophet announces to the people the cry of God to them:

> Is not this the fast that I choose:
> to loose the bonds of injustice,
> to undo the thongs of the yoke,
> to let the oppressed go free,
> and to break every yoke? (Isa. 58:6)

The prophet calls the people to share their bread with the hungry, to bring the homeless into their homes, to cover the exposed, and to remove oppression and exploitation from among them (58:7–9).

He calls them to stop trying to shift blame. Perhaps they complained: "My family never owned slaves. Why should I have to pay reparation?"

Isaiah calls them to stop going through empty motions and to actually do the work of repair.

And when the nation has done all of this, Isaiah says, "then your light shall rise in the darkness and your gloom be like the noonday. . . . Your ancient ruins shall be rebuilt; you shall raise up the foundations of many generations; you shall be called the repairer of the breach, the restorer of streets to live in" (58:10, 12).

What could it look like for government, businesses, churches, and other institutions to begin to let the oppressed go free in the United States of America? Perhaps it would look like the transformation of the US from a five-hundred-year-old hierarchy of human belonging into a circle where all govern together and have equal access to flourishing.

Only when we do this, then and only then, can we call ourselves repairers of the breach.

10

Forgiveness and the Beloved Community

Elazar Barkan, my professor and author of the landmark treatise *The Guilt of Nations: Restitution and Negotiating Historical Injustices*, stood at the front of our class of about six around a large conference table in the middle of the small Ivy League room. I was a few weeks into my second of three terms in the master's program in human rights at Columbia University's Graduate School of Arts and Sciences. The class was titled "Peace."

"What do you think of forgiveness?" Barkan asked the group of White women and me.

I raised my hand and volunteered: "I think forgiveness is essential."

Barkan stiffened as his eyes seemed to squint, as if trying to understand the words coming from my mouth.

"Without forgiveness," I continued, "there is no path to reconciliation."

Barkan, who founded the Institute for Historical Justice and Reconciliation in The Hague, leaned in and pushed back.

I paraphrase here, because his response surprised me so much that I only remember the general gist and how I felt. Here is the gist: to demand that survivors of oppression forgive their oppressor is to dominate them a second time.

Here is how I felt: befuddled.

Forgiveness is a Christian concept—one that entered the world through the person of Jesus, who taught his followers to pray, in the context of Roman-occupied and colonized Israel: "And forgive us our debts, as we also have forgiven our debtors" (Matt. 6:12).

Barkan explained that forgiveness of a nation or people that has oppressed exposes survivors to further victimization through reengagement with oppressors. Victims do not have to reconcile with their oppressors, Barkan insisted.

And I agree.

But forgiveness has been misunderstood.

In the ethical tradition of the person of Jesus, forgiveness is not repair, nor does forgiveness require it. Rather, forgiveness is a component of repair, along with truth-telling and repentance; yet it is independent from each of the others. It does not require truth-telling. It does not require repentance.

Twenty years before I sat at the conference table in Barkan's classroom, I sat on the floor under a table in a hotel conference room—weeping. I had just heard a talk on forgiveness at a Christian conference and I felt like my soul was cut open. All the hurt and damage done to me at the hands of a trusted one who molested me as a child was laying bare in the form of my tears, which would not stop. My friend found me in the conference room and joined me under the table. She literally just sat with me. Then through snot and puffy eyes, I repeated the phrase that rung like a bell in my ears since the keynote speaker Ney Bailey uttered the words: "Forgiveness is to set the prisoner free, only to realize the prisoner was you."[1]

I realized for the first time in my life that I was emotionally imprisoned by the wrong done to me. I wanted the wrongdoer to suffer. I had withheld forgiveness. But I was the one who was trapped in the moment of their transgression. They had moved on—not me. I needed a way to cut the tie.

There, on the floor, under the conference table, I imagined the perpetrator sitting across from me on the floor. I uttered the words, "I forgive you."

Forgiveness is pure power. It is choice—an act of agency by survivors most often brutalized through the erasure of agency. Forgiveness is the act of snatching back the mind and soul from the ties created by oppressors' lying teeth that often tell their victims, "You need me. You cannot win against me. You must deal with me. You must bow to me. I am God."

Forgiveness cuts the ties between oppressed and oppressor. This may seem contrary to the goal of repair, which is connection. But forgiveness sees what is. Forgiveness looks full into the unrepentant exploiter, enslaver, and abuser, and it rejects the lie that one's future is dependent on the graces of the unrepentant individual or nation. Rather, forgiveness stares down oppressive nations and men and says, simply, "I have agency. I do not need you. I choose to cut the tie that binds us together in the spiritual realm. I release you from your debt to me—your debt of dignity, your debt of equal protection of the law, your debt of leadership that cares for all its citizens, your debt of an eye for an eye, your debt—because I do not need you. I have God. God will move heaven and earth and democracy to fill my need. You can go now. . . . Now." Forgiveness walks forward and lives and heals and loves and votes, understanding that one's former oppressor is not God. God is God. Flourishing is possible, because God *is*.

With this understanding of forgiveness, we close our journey with one final question: What is the role of forgiveness in the quest to heal what race broke in the world?

Forgiveness demands an object. A wrong has been done and someone or some corporate body has done it. In the context of race and colonization, European nations embarked on an age of discovery. Discovery does not break the world. Claiming discovery of lands long inhabited by indigenous peoples breaks the world. Lies break the world. Leveraging those lies to lay legal claim to land and treasure not beholden to your laws breaks the world. Belief in the myth of Western supremacy breaks the world. To gaze upon the men and women who greeted your ship and, in that moment, claim *terra nullius* ("empty land") in order to lay legal claim breaks the world. Looking in the faces of Brown men and women who dress and build and dance and eat and speak differently from you and telling them they are uncivilized—and therefore hold no legal claim to the land they had cultivated for thousands of years before you "discovered" it—that breaks the world. These original sins laid the legal, social, moral, and theological foundations for the genocide, rape, theft, exploitation, dehumanization, domination, family separation, and death that followed for the next five hundred years.

To talk about forgiveness, we must first understand the nature of guilt. In 1945, the German philosopher Karl Jaspers launched a series of lectures exploring the nature of Germany's national guilt. World War II had just come to an end, and the question haunted all Germans: Who is guilty? To be both accountable and forgiven to any degree, one must first be guilty. To answer this question, Jaspers believed it was important not to paint guilt with a broad, unscrupulous brush. To do so would be to leave room for denial, pushback, and academic debate that prevents the establishment of measures that repair what oppression broke. In the interest of mindful discernment, Jaspers crafts a schema of national guilt categories:[2]

1. **Criminal guilt** is applied only to those who break the law. Writing as the Allied nations were establishing the Nuremberg trials, Jaspers does not limit "the law" to that which is reflected in the nation's laws at the time of the offense. He recognizes that the tendency of the oppressive state is often to legalize oppression, as in the case of slavery and lynching (to this day the US does not have a national law that explicitly criminalizes lynching). Jaspers expands his legal purview to incorporate international law and natural law—principles understood to be true that form

the foundation for international law and many national constitutions.[3]

2. **Political guilt** concerns all citizens of a modern nation or state that has committed an atrocity. The idea is that those citizens elected or allowed their government to commit the named atrocity. Whether they were for or against it, it was done in their name. Therefore, national sanctions or economic repercussions hold all citizens accountable for their active support, passive complicity, or failure to push back hard enough to stop it.[4]

3. **Moral guilt** "exists for all those who give room to conscience and repentance." Jaspers continues: "The morally guilty are those who are capable of penance, the ones who knew, or could know, and yet walked in ways which self-analysis reveals to them as culpable error—whether conveniently closing their eyes to events, or permitting themselves to be intoxicated, seduced or bought with personal advantages, or obeying from fear."[5]

4. **Metaphysical guilt** is akin to what we call *survivor's guilt* or *moral injury* today. It is the guilt that eats at the soul when one was present at the scene of atrocity—even if present to fight it. Metaphysical guilt taunts the conscience with the guilt of surviving while others lay dead. Metaphysical guilt is the mindful realization that one has encountered evil. As a result, that evil made its own mark on one's soul—becoming a part of one's story and a possibility again for one's future. Jaspers explains that there were multiple opportunities for Germans to stand in the way of oppression in 1933 and 1934 and 1938. Many did stand in the way, and they were executed. They sought and found death. Those who survived did so because they acted anonymously.[6] "We survivors did not seek [death]. We did not go into the streets when our Jewish friends were led away; we did not scream until we too were destroyed. We preferred to stay alive."[7]

For the purpose of this chapter, I focus on political guilt and forgiveness. First, we must acknowledge there are at least two kinds of just responses to guilt: (1) *retributive justice*, which demands retribution or punishment for wrongdoing, and (2) *reparative justice*, which seeks strategies to repair the relationship that has been broken by injustice.

The call for retribution rises from the soil of domination, the soil of "either they win or I win," the soil of White nationalism, which demands purity and purges all that is not deemed pure from the polis—locking undesirables away in prison, shipping prisoners to distant work farm islands in the Caribbean or Australia or creating an entire state to house British prisoners—Georgia. The end goal of retributive justice is a perfect society full of perfect people. Accordingly, retributive justice rises from a narcissistic logic that demands perfection in life and places the self as the measure of perfection. Retributive justice sees and treats people as if they are a single unit, being born, living, and eventually dying in a vacuum disconnected from context, family, or community—unable to learn, to grow, to be transformed, or to be redeemed. Fear is the tie that binds the retributive society.

Donald W. Shriver Jr., author of *An Ethic for Enemies: Forgiveness in Politics*, lists some punitive responses to wrongdoing: terror, vindictiveness, retaliation, punishment, restitution, protest, and passivity.[8] I would argue that it's debatable whether restitution is a retributive or a reparative strategy. I suppose from the point of view of the one who is required to restore what has been taken, it may feel punitive. But from the point of view of the oppressed— the one from whom the thing was stolen—the oppressor is not centered at all. Instead, the oppressed one is centered. From the oppressed point of view, restitution restores both the wronged and the relationship back to health. That said, I agree with Shriver that restitution calls for the restoration of things that have been all too often lost forever. Restitution can diminish tragedy, Shriver argues, but in the end it is often impossible.

Desmond Tutu puts flesh on the bones of the punitive process, explaining the dynamics that exploded in Rwanda. "The top dog wanted to cling to its privileged position and the underdog strove to topple the top dog. When that happened, the new top dog engaged in an orgy of retribution to pay back the new underdog for all the pain and suffering it had caused when it was top dog."[9] Punitive justice can never lead to peace. It may "purify" the land of all enemies, but it cannot connect us. It cannot repair.

By contrast, reparative justice sees the offender as a human being. It also sees the self as a human being. It sees all as living and moving and doing life within a complex web of relationships that require respect and trust. It sees all as fallible and sees injustice as a break in human relationship. It seeks first to restore the oppressed, the relationship, and the one who has lost their way. The end goal of reparative justice is the inextricably well-connected society: human and imperfect but committed to protecting and restoring each other through just processes that protect the ties that bind together the reparative society.

The United States and its legal landscape were crafted by European men who were the products of the retributive British Empire. Original colonists built their wealth through the free labor of formerly incarcerated criminals shipped from Britain to the colonies to help empty Britain's overfull jails and to provide free labor. Within thirty years of Britain's investment in the transatlantic slave trade, colonists applied an even more brutal web of punitive laws meant to control enslaved Africans and protect White supremacy. Slaveowners chopped off ears, fingers, feet, and genitalia if enslaved men, women, or children offended the master or attempted escape. Upon the founding of the United States, colonial retributive mores were leveled full on the backs of Blacks and Native Americans. A breach of racial hierarchy by one would bring the wrath of the master or the cavalry on many. In Lea's and Lizzie's post-Reconstruction era, this violence translated into lynching, convict leasing, and peonage, lowering the bar of criminality and sentencing Black boys and men to uncounted years in prison for sitting on a park bench for too long. It translated into race riots and massacres and public lynchings. In Reagan's America, the bar of criminality was lowered again, and Black men were swept up and shoved into prisons and held for fifteen years for holding a dime bag of weed. In Trump's America, a lack of documentation was transformed from a civil offense requiring a fine and actions to obtain documentation into a criminal offense that led to immediate imprisonment and deportation—permanent separation from one's family.

As a nation, we have never turned from our bent toward retribution. But in recent years, we have begun to round a corner. Public history projects like the Equal Justice Initiative's Legacy Museum and National Memorial for Peace and Justice bear witness to the depths of evil born on US soil by our lust for retribution. Mix that bent with racialized bias, and our nation's retributive lust led to nearly 4,084 lynchings of Black men, women, and children from 1877 to 1950.[10] And it continues to fuel disparate applications of death penalty law to this day.

We cannot repair what race broke in the world by applying the logic of retribution. That logic was both the seed and the sun that grew our White supremacist, violent society. To seek truth-telling and reparation alone would not change the game. It would reveal truth and level the playing field. But the game would still aim for perfection—not connection. There is no guarantee we would not end up in the same place—suffering under the oppressive weight of domination two or three or ten generations later. Reparative justice would change the game at the core, so that the quest for perfection would fall by the wayside and the tenth generation would reap the fruits of connection and plant seeds that deepen it.

Shriver wrote in 1995, in the shadow of the felled Berlin Wall and the first democratic election in South Africa, "Real political recovery from catastrophic, unjust suffering involves some really new relationships with enemies and their descendants."[11]

He continued reflecting on the state of relations between African Americans and those of European descent in the US: "General Grant himself soon ordered his troops to cease their celebratory gun salutes: 'The war is over, the rebels are our countrymen again, and the best sign of rejoicing after the victory will be to abstain from all demonstrations.'"[12] Likewise, Shriver recalled the warning that King gave in a 1964 speech in St. Louis: "We must learn to live together as brothers or perish together as fools."[13]

Political forgiveness, as Shriver conceives it, is not a carte blanche license for oppressors to oppress. It is not a free pass to escape accountability for oppression. Rather, political forgiveness is how enemies can live together in common space after conflict. It is located in the distance between the "eye for an eye" and licentiousness. Shriver, quoting author Susan Jacoby, "advocates a wisdom that societies persist in a 'balance between compassionate and retributive impulses.' Once they are committed to such balance, 'individuals and societies turn their attention to the question of what forms of retribution, and which forms of forgiveness, afford the opportunity of an existence that encompasses both justice and love.'" Shriver riffs on the theme, calling for "just love and loving justice."[14]

Forgiveness as Reparative Justice

In *No Future without Forgiveness*, Tutu calls us to the vision of *ubuntu*, a sense of universal care for humanity. He calls us to remember the Allied powers' Marshall Plan, which helped to rebuild our enemies' nations after World War II. He reminds us of the global unity we feel when natural disasters strike and nations unite to help one another. In these moments we are catching a glimpse of *ubuntu*. The African term means *I am because we are*. "It speaks to the very essence of being human," says Tutu.[15] It paints a picture of the collective interdependence of all humanity. Tutu continues: "God has set in motion a centripetal process, a moving towards the Centre, towards unity, harmony, goodness, peace and justice; one that removes barriers."[16]

Ubuntu imagines oppressed and oppressor both present in the end—connected and interdependent. That end—a radically connected end—requires some measure of forgiveness. As an Anglican bishop, Tutu draws from the person of Jesus to build his imagination of what *ubuntu* will look like: "Jesus says, 'And when I am lifted up from the earth I shall draw everyone to myself,' as he hangs from His cross with out-flung arms, thrown out to clasp all, everyone and everything, in a cosmic embrace, so that all, everyone, everything, belongs."[17]

The far-flung love of Jesus is a direct challenge to the reigning Western supremacist philosophies and governance of the Roman Empire. The Romans were deeply influenced by the Greek philosophers, including Plato, who invented the concept of race. Plato imagined race as the various metals that people groups were made of. Race ordered society, determining how different people groups contribute to the republic.[18] Plato's student Aristotle introduced explicit human hierarchy, arguing in his *Politics* that some races are created to rule while other races are created to be slaves. Aristotle did not understand race to be determined by the color of a people group's skin, but he did understand it to be a determining factor of intelligence and whether a people group was "supreme" (his language) or created to be enslaved. Early in his treatise, Aristotle declares that the Barbarians are a people group created to be enslaved. Later, Aristotle says any group that allows itself to be ruled demonstrates that it is an inferior race. To be fully human in Aristotle's imagination was to be Western, male, and able-bodied.[19] The Roman Empire was built on the philosophical and political foundations of Greek philosophers, including Aristotle. When they conquered a non-Western people, they saw those people as racially inferior.

In this context, Jesus teaches his followers to pray:

> Our Father in heaven,
> hallowed be your name.
> Your kingdom come.
> Your will be done,
>   on earth as it is in heaven.
> Give us this day our daily bread.
> And forgive us our debts,
>   as we also have forgiven our debtors.
> And do not bring us to the time of trial,
>   but rescue us from the evil one. (Matt. 6:9–13)

Christians are taught this prayer in Sunday school. We place our little palms together in front of our little hearts. We close our eyes and we pray the Lord's Prayer by rote. Rarely does the Sunday school teacher inform the children of the context of that prayer, as Obery Hendricks does in his book *The Politics of Jesus*.

Hendricks explains that Jesus is teaching his followers to pray for the end of Caesar's reign and the beginning of God's. The prayer for daily bread is a prayer for the end of the people's suffering under the colonized oppression of Rome. They were starving. Bread was their staple food, yet there was not enough. According to Hendricks, it was common custom for Caesar to send his soldiers to roll their cart through the streets and toss bread to the starving crowds. That practice was called "the daily bread."[20] When Jesus teaches us to pray that God, not Caesar, provide our daily bread, he is calling for the end of Caesar's reign.[21]

Then Jesus says, "Forgive us our debts, as we also have forgiven our debtors." The Greek word for "forgive," Hendricks explains, can also be translated "to release." To forgive is to release those who owe a debt to you—to cut the tie that binds you together and to send them away. Jesus calls the people to pray that they will be released from their debt. This is a prayer for Jubilee— that economic system instituted by God when God governed the people of Israel in Leviticus 25:8–55. Jubilee came every forty-nine years. In the fiftieth year, all debt was forgiven, all property returned, all enslaved people set free. This is as much promise as it is prayer. The king of the kingdom of God has come to earth and *can* release them!

Then Jesus calls the people to do something even more radical. He calls them to release Rome from its debt to the Hebrews. In the year Jesus was born, Rome crucified five hundred northern Galilean resisters each day for several days. Rome spread salt on the lands of those they conquered to prevent them from being able to grow their own food, making them dependent on the empire. Cut the tie, Jesus is saying! Turn your back on Rome! Turn your face to God. Look to God for your daily bread. Look to God to move heaven and earth to release you from your debt to Rome.

217

Look to God to pay back all that Rome stole from you—not only in the by and by but on earth as it is in heaven. Forgive Rome. Release Rome so that you may actually be filled. I believe he is saying, "You don't need Caesar for daily bread; God is the God who rained manna from heaven! You do not need empire to live! You do not need Caesar to survive." Later in Matthew's Gospel, Jesus multiplies the bread loaves and feeds five thousand people. Forgive Rome so that you may actually receive what you need.

Consider for a moment all that Rome owed the Hebrew people: they claimed sovereignty over the land, took away the health of the land and the Hebrews' ability to grow their own food, and exercised agency over their lives and families—Hebrew husbands and sons were lynched by crucifixion as warning against potential insurrectionists, and their daughters and wives no doubt absorbed sexual violence from the ever-present Roman guard. Rome owed the people the belief and structures and laws that protect, cultivate, and serve the image of God within them. Rome owed the people recognition of and freedom to exercise agency—to make decisions that impact the world—to help steward the world. Rome owed the people the joy of thriving and living without trauma and oppression. Rome owed Hebrews their families, actual fathers and sons that its military killed, imprisoned, or mutilated. Rome owed the people tax money that they should never have had to pay, due to Rome's corrupt tax-collecting system. Rome owed the people more than it could repay. Even with redress, fathers and sons crucified for rebellion could never be returned. Even with redress, the land could never be restored to the soil that was there before Roman soldiers tossed salt on it. Even with redress, Rome would not pay back every single family all of the land and livestock sold to pay Rome's corrupt tax collectors. No, if the people demanded *all* that Rome owed them—an eye for an eye—then the people would have waited forever. They would have lived and died in want, need, hunger, and frustration.

But if the people turned to God—if the people believed in the rule of God—if the people understood that the moral arc of the universe may be long but it bends toward justice—if the people understood that they don't need Rome to have their needs met, that there is a new kingdom coming—if the people understood the reality that they are made in the image of God and that means they have the intrinsic right and capacity to exercise agency—if the people understood that they are created with the spiritual authority to move and push against the kingdoms of men together, because the kingdom of God has come to earth as it is in heaven—if the people understood that if they had the power to live according to the truth of the peaceable kingdom of God in the here and now, God would release them from their debts to Caesar—if the people walked in this truth, then they would hunger no more.

And that is what happened. Brown Jesus died at the hands of the Roman Empire.

Jesus's followers ran and hid in caves and attics. Acts 2 shows us what happens when God's reign is unleashed on earth: Tongues are loosed and colonized people, forced to speak one common trade language, suddenly speak each other's indigenous languages! And they understand each other. Connection! The people come together and share their resources, and Scripture says no one had need. Connection! Colonized people bridge racial and ethnic divides imposed by the powers. Connection! The people organize and live in a way that defies Rome's sovereignty over their bodies and families and land and freedom. Connection! And members of the enemy's military are forgiven and accepted into the fold. Connection!

Rome was not a democracy. The people had little power to impact governance, so they built an alternative society that operated according to the values of the kin-dom of God—the brotherhood and sisterhood of all humanity. The United States is a capitalist democracy, so the people *are* able to impact governance through the powers of the vote and the dollar. Faith-rooted movements such as abolitionism, suffragism, and the civil rights movement all called their followers to walk and live in the here and now according to the truth of the kingdom of God—to exercise agency, to choose suffering now on the road to freedom from oppressive rule, to live as if the peaceable God is reigning now, to accept the consequences levied by the kingdoms of men, understanding that the earthly kingdom's power is limited. It has an expiration date. But the reign of God is forever.

Heeding this call, abolitionists boycotted sugar and broke the law to leverage their homes as safe houses on the Underground Railroad. Heeding this call, suffragists organized and marched and went to jail and refused to eat until women got the vote. Heeding this call, Fannie Lou Hamer attempted to register to vote in Mississippi and was jailed and beaten by policemen till her body went stiff, preparing to die.[22] But she had already turned her back on empire. She did not need them to be well. She did not need the nod of White men to live free. She lived free, because God told her she was free indeed. Bloody and bruised, Hamer sang through the jail bars:

> Paul and Silas began to shout, let my people go!
> Jail door open and they walked out, let my people go![23]

And civil rights foot soldiers offered to pray with White churches that barred them from common worship and arrested them when they tried to attend White churches in Mississippi. They tried to pray with Sheriff Jim Clark, who was responsible for murdering their fellow Black resisters in Selma. At the heart of nonviolent action is this truth: The peaceable kin-dom already exists. We will suffer the violent backlash of the kingdoms of this world as we lean into and follow God's reign, but on the other side is glory. We manifest the kingdom by living it.

Neither Rome nor the United States can pay back all that they took from those they subjugated. They simply cannot pay it all. They don't have it to give. Even if they did, it would not matter. This is a call to decenter oppressive nations and their timelines. Oppressive nations and states are not the ultimate determiner of human flourishing. God is. In the Christian tradition, Brown Jesus is committed to releasing the burdens of oppression for all who walk with him.

We turn our backs on the powers that dare to believe they are the source of rights and flourishing. We live the truth of our rights and we lock arms in the communion of common struggle and we find flourishing in our connectedness. Then we turn to the God who owns cattle on a thousand hills and we call on God to ante up. "O, God," we cry. "You pay the debt."

Do we still push for reparations and restitution? Yes. Because the relationship between oppressed and oppressor cannot be repaired until the one who has committed harm has acknowledged their wrongdoing, apologized, and changed course to live and move in the opposite direction. Reparation and restitution are repentance. Repentance is necessary for repair.

The measure of forgiveness offered by the oppressed is found in the distance between that which the wrongdoer is able to offer to repair the relationship and that which they owe.

We forgive for our own empowerment. We forgive for our own healing.

As we close, it is important to recognize two hefty questions that need to be considered when oppressed people decide to forgive in today's America: How do we forgive when the oppressor continues to oppress? And how do we deal with the shame and stigma of oppression on our souls?

I grew up visiting my grandparents Junius and Willa in their South Philadelphia neighborhood, Point Breeze. My mother and father, Sharon and Dennis, would pile me and my two sisters, Hollie and Merry, in the back of the Buick and drive us from the suburban neighborhood of West Oak Lane to visit Grandmom and Grandpop. South Philly had its own particular vibe. Streets built for horses and buggies were so narrow that 1970s Buicks and Cadillacs lined the sidewalks on the opposite side of my grandmother's street, South Chadwick Street—across the street from Child's Elementary School.

This street was once lined with trees, a thick canopy of protection from extreme heat and heavy rain, filtering each breath over South Philly's African American community. When my mother was a little girl, trees lined Child's School and every city block.

Nestled in the comfort and chaos of three generations sharing a three-story house on Dickinson Street, little Sharon used to go outside when the moon rose over Point Breeze and she would say "good night" to the tree across the street. She would talk to the tree. She had a relationship with that tree. Then one day she woke up and the tree was gone. Slowly, all the trees disappeared from Point Breeze—even Child's School was left barren. Black residents were never told why the trees were taken from them. They were not consulted or given the chance to petition for the trees to stay. White city leaders exercised dominion over Black residents and took their trees. Meanwhile, trees in the White communities slightly north went untouched.

Old-timers whispered that the city didn't want to keep up tree maintenance in the Black communities. But a 2019 article on Philadelphia's PBS affiliate revealed that Italian immigrants integrating Black South Philly at the time petitioned the city to remove the trees. They wanted to be able to lean out of their windows and see what was happening, to call out to people on the streets.[24] The city never asked the neighborhood's long-time Black residents what they wanted. Rather, they accommodated Whiteness. In subsequent years, heat islands sprawled across the southern swath of the city along with other Black and Brown neighborhoods throughout Philadelphia, drawn by unshaded black roofs, blacktop parking lots, and exposed concrete streets. Homes became ovens, and fans and air conditioners ran on overdrive, pushing particulates into unfiltered air. Hundreds of people died who did not have to.[25]

My generation of children ate the fruit of environmental racism. We played double Dutch jump rope, hopscotch, and jacks on bubbling tar streets and hot concrete—warped and cracked by rain water that stagnated with no roots to absorb it. We had an increased chance of suffering from asthma, lung disease, heart disease, and cancer with such few trees to filter toxic air rising from our homes and the one-hundred-fifty-year-old refinery just one mile away producing the bulk of the city's toxic waste.[26] We did not know trees once lived among us. We didn't know that we, too, were worthy of their protection and filtration. We simply played and made do.

When the occasional car tried to pass, we would all move to the side and wave them by. The old-timers sat in folding lawn chairs in front of their row houses or they sat directly on their front steps, talking to one another from stoop to stoop, across and up and down the street. The Point Breeze community was largely African American since the 1930s when Willa and Junius's generation migrated north in the Great Migration. Most families in the area hailed from the same communities in Virginia and South Carolina.

At night the children sat on the steps and talked outside. I will never forget one night when I sat on the steps of the home next to Grandmom's house, talking with new friends who had just moved in. We marveled at the moon. The full moon seemed to be suspended in the sky with clouds slowly floating across its face. It would hide, then come out again. The older brother—about my age, nine years old—spoke in a voice that signaled that what he was saying was sacred and secret knowledge—I was to hold and keep this knowledge and never forget.

"That is the Friendship Moon," he said.

If you meet under this moon, you will be friends forever.

It was a long time before I ever saw that moon again, though I have looked for it. I don't know what ever happened to that little boy. Yet in my memory that was the magic of South Philadelphia—a community teeming with life and families and old-timers on front steps.

Decades later, I worked as a campus minister specializing in racial reconciliation in Los Angeles. My cousin Allen Jenkins had become the pastor of St. Barnabas Bethsaida United Methodist Church in Philadelphia and invited me to preach one Sunday. We hadn't been back to the neighborhood since Grandmom Willa passed a decade before. St. Barnabas is located six blocks from my grandmother's house. As we drove away, all we saw were gutted row homes—the aftermath of decades of drug epidemics and city neglect. Literally no windows, boarded up doors, and burned out, gutted edifices.

"Where are all the people?" I thought. "Where is the community?" I'm still learning the story. This is what I know.

On our visits in the year after Grandpop Junius passed, sometimes I would watch my mother's brother, Uncle Richie, take furniture out of Grandmom Willa's home. She would cry, begging him not to take her couch, her watch, her coffee table. I never understood why he did this. I was a little girl, but I understood that he was hurting his mother. "Why would he do that?" I thought. I loved Uncle Richie. He used to hold me when I was a baby. He was always attentive and always present when we visited.

Songwriter and poet Richard Lawrence, my Uncle Richie, became addicted to heroin in the mid-1970s. Willa's furniture fed his habit. What I didn't know then was that heroin had proliferated in the neighborhood. Young men who sang doo-wop on street corners in the 1950s and 1960s were now trying to figure out how to survive between heroin hits.

In 1994, Nixon's domestic policy adviser and Watergate co-conspirator John Ehrlichman confessed to a reporter that in 1969, when Nixon's presidential campaign vowed to mount the first war against drugs in US history, the goal was not public health. The goal was a racialized political win in the shadow of the civil rights movement. "The Nixon campaign in 1968, and the Nixon White House after that," said Ehrlichman, "had two enemies: the antiwar left and black people." He continued:

> You understand what I'm saying? We knew we couldn't make it illegal to be either against the war or black, but by getting the public to associate the hippies with marijuana and blacks with heroin, and then criminalizing both heavily, we could disrupt those communities. We could arrest their leaders, raid their homes, break up their meetings, and vilify them night after night on the evening news. Did we know we were lying about the drugs? Of course we did.[27]

Heroin was pumped into Point Breeze through the mafia, police, and small dealers. Heroin addiction took over. Richie thumped to the floor and died in his bedroom in my grandmother's house on South Chadwick Street on March 28, 1975.

Crack was pumped into Point Breeze in the late 1980s and 1990s. Around that time, my Grandmom Willa was diagnosed with Alzheimer's. She did not recognize my mother, and neighbors would find her wandering the neighborhood sometimes, unkempt and wearing her bathrobe. On March 11, 1992, she was found on the floor in her home. She had been punched to death by a crack addict who had pillaged her for all she had.

As I write this, my body tingles under the weight of this layered trauma.

Richie and Willa are only two of millions of stories of loss to heroin and crack during the drug war years. In those years communities like Point Breeze suffered the trauma of losing leaders and potential leaders, safety, businesses, and jobs. Renters suffered the trauma of slumlords refusing to fix homes in the depreciating neighborhood. And survivors suffered more trauma when they heard city officials whisper "urban renewal." They knew what that meant: "Negro removal," as Mindy Thompson Fullilove says in her book *Root Shock: How Tearing Up City Neighborhoods Hurts America, and What We Can Do about It.* With the introduction of the Housing Act of 1949, urban renewal paved the way for the progressive retooling of cities across the US, preparing them for a postwar economy.[28] By the early 2000s urban renewal meant eviction. It meant the displacement of historical markers, and with that, common memory. Urban renewal meant higher taxes and foreclosures. Urban renewal meant ethnic cleansing of Black communities to make way for affluent Whites.[29]

Once a bustling mixed-income community full of African-descended men, women, and children whose grandparents were born enslaved, who migrated north to escape Jim Crow terror and poverty, decades later these families have suffered more layers of oppression from slumlords, police brutality, mass incarceration, and death by heroin and crack.

Resmaa Menakem, a trauma therapist and author of *My Grandmother's Hands: Racialized Trauma and the Pathway to Mending*

Our Hearts and Bodies, describes the impact of compounded racialized trauma: "As many researchers now believe, the ongoing violations of the Black body and heart have resulted in widespread trauma. This racialized trauma shows up as an array of adaptive but dysfunctional behaviors, including hypervigilance, heightened anxiety and suspicion, ADD/ADHD, Obsessive-Compulsive Disorder, and addiction."[30] Menakem names several other manifestations of trauma in Black bodies. "Healing trauma involves recognizing, accepting, and moving through pain—clean pain," Menakem says. "It often means facing what you don't want to face—what you have been reflexively avoiding or fleeing. By walking into that pain, experiencing it fully, and moving through it, you metabolize it and put an end to it."[31]

My own weight gain began when my mother and father, Sharon and Dennis, divorced and we moved away from the comfort of my grandmother and other family in Philadelphia to live with my mother's new love, Ernie Harper, and his three children. They lived in a small rural town outside Cape May, New Jersey, called Erma. We were the only Black family within a fifteen-mile radius. I gained ten pounds in my first year there and scores more over the years under the White gaze—trying to feel normal but never really fitting in. Our family was struggling and coping. My coping methods were White evangelical religion and ice cream: both disconnected me from my body, so that I could escape the pain that Menakem says we must face.

In 2020, three things happened: (1) I detoxed from sugar and all flour and changed the way I ate, (2) I began seeing a somatic therapist, and (3) I signed the deal to write this book. Oh, and I went into lockdown to keep from getting or spreading COVID-19. The lockdown forced me to face the pain. I became acquainted with the ways our bodies actually communicate with us, telling us what is wrong. I became aware of small traumas that I usually would have buried, facing them one at a time and moving through them. Menakem talks about "clean pain"—pain that is not compounded and impacted, folded in on itself.[32] He says the goal is to get to the point where you are no longer having to wade through the compacted mess, but instead have worked through past pain and are living in the present, dealing with one clean pain at a time.

When I started writing this book in August 2020, I sat down to write the chapter on Henry Lawrence and decided to look up the land that Hiram, his son, lost to eminent domain in 1950s Philadelphia. I found the land on a Zillow map and realized the prices were much more affordable than I imagined. I checked my grandmother's house, which we lost to foreclosure in 2014. It was for sale! It turned out to not be available, but I still felt drawn to the neighborhood. I remembered the gutted buildings of the early 2000s. Now, it seems new homes were coming up everywhere. And the community was full of White people, dogs, and cafes. My body buzzed with grief, but it would not let me stop looking. Over the next three months, I took trips to Point Breeze to view homes until I settled on a home, one block from my grandparents' house. My great-grandmother Ella Fortune Lawrence lived one block further.

I have felt drawn to this place, and I've hardly known why. Even as I write this, I feel like I am onto something. My whole body is buzzing. Perhaps the layered trauma of this land is the same layered trauma that has lived in my body. Over the last year, I have been wading through that trauma and becoming reunited with my body. I feel a new level of healing rising in my body—living on the land and confronting the pain—the pain of the community and within my soul.

Chapter 10 in Menakem's *My Grandmother's Hands* begins with a quote from Tyra Banks: "Take responsibility for yourself, because no one's going to take responsibility for you."[33] It is my responsibility to heal from trauma. No one else except me can heal my traumatized body. I must live according to the truth of Brown Jesus, as much for my own healing as for the repair of our broken world. I must embrace the truth that my body matters to the God who created every inch and loves me and has the power to restore my body and soul to health without the powers of Whiteness giving the nod.

Toward the end of his book, Archbishop Tutu says, "According to Jesus we should be ready to [forgive] not just once, not just seven times, but seventy times seven—without limits—provided, it seems Jesus says, your brother or sister who has wronged you is ready to come and confess the wrong they have committed, yet again."[34] How else can we get to the beloved community?

The Call to the Beloved Community

There is a print by John August Swanson called *Psalm 85*.[35] It is a picture of the tree of life in the middle of a colorful field ripe for the harvest. Sunbeams shine down while Brown community members play and work in the field and climb the tree. The verses of the psalm are written between the rows and in the sunbeams. The passage reads:

> Steadfast love and faithfulness will meet;
> > righteousness and peace will kiss each other.
> Faithfulness will spring up from the ground,
> > and righteousness will look down from the sky.
> > (Ps. 85:10–11)

The Hebrew word for "love" (*hesed*) actually means "merciful kindness." The word for "faithfulness" (*'emeth*) figuratively means "truth" or "trustworthiness." The word for "righteousness" (*tsedeq*) means "equity" or "justice." The word for "peace" (*shalom*) refers to the radical wellness of all relationships in creation. If we substitute these sharper meanings of the text, this is how it reads:

> Merciful kindness and truth will meet;
> > equity and the radical wellness of all relationships in
> > creation will kiss each other.
> Trustworthiness will spring up from the ground,
> > and justice will look down from the sky.

This is the biblical vision of what Martin Luther King Jr. called the Beloved Community. The King Center describes that vision as "a global vision, in which all people can share in the wealth of the earth. In the Beloved Community, poverty, hunger and homelessness will not be tolerated because international standards of human decency will not allow it. Racism and all forms of discrimination, bigotry and prejudice will be replaced by an all inclusive spirit of sisterhood and brotherhood."[36]

There are two paths set before the oppressed: One path leads to rage, compounded pain, sickness, and death. The other leads to the Beloved Community. On that road there is truth-seeking, truth-listening, and truth-telling. There is reparation and equity. And there is mercy—release. For the sake of my body and soul and the bodies and souls of my family's descendants to the tenth generation from me, I choose the Beloved Community.

For readers in European bodies, you also have a choice. You can continue your war for supremacy against the image of God on earth. You can resist God's Beloved Community; resist truth, resist equity, resist justice, and resist mercy. You can try to maintain your space at the top of a crumbling racial hierarchy. You won't be there long. You are already in the global minority. Within one generation you will be in the minority in the United States as well. When that day comes, you can wage war or you can lean into truth, lean into repentance and repair, and allow yourselves to be released—forgiven.

Only then can we find a new way of being together in the world.

I can almost hear my seventh-great-grandmother Fortune Game/Magee, who walked this land ten generations ago and absorbed the wrath of its first race, gender, and citizenship laws into her traumatized body. In my mind's ear, I hear her whisper, *Yes, child. Yes . . .*

Acknowledgments

It's amazing to think that this project began with a phone call thirty years ago. I still have the scribbled family tree that my mother dictated to me over the phone. Sitting in the lighting booth of an off-Broadway musical, waiting to start the show and run the lights, I gazed at that rudimentary tree. It looked more like hieroglyphics than a family tree, but it was mine. Drawn in early 1991, my tree had no names, only relationships like "Grandfather," "Great-grandfather," "Great-great-grandfather." Each name had approximate years when they walked in this world. That's it. That's all we knew before the search began, before Ancestry.com, before the trips to the National Archives, and before the pilgrimages. I began to understand the impact of local and national politics on my ancestors' lives. All we had was a scribbled tree. Along the way my mother and I shared discoveries. She shared with me the stories she lived and the stories passed down to her. Before I thank anyone else, I must thank my mother, Sharon Lea Lawrence Harper. She has been my constant companion on this learning journey for three decades. It is an honor to gift her with this book.

I am grateful for my agent, Howard Yoon, who, along with his associate Jay Venables and interns, combed through the original *Fortune* proposal and asked all the right questions. They offered suggestions and praise, and they "got it." Howard became the project's most passionate champion and brought the project to Brazos.

I owe much to the team at Brazos, including Baker Publishing Group's CEO and president Dwight Baker, marketing director Jeremy Wells, contracts manager Jean Entingh, Paula Gibson (queen of fonts), and Eric Salo, whose meticulous work helped hone this work to the shape you see today. I am especially indebted to senior acquisitions editor Katelyn Beaty, who hounded me for nearly a year for the proposal, then championed *Fortune* with the passion of Joan of Arc within the Brazos team. She walked with me through completion of the manuscript, giving me enough space to find the book's voice but enough guidance to identify critical questions. In the end, I am humbled by the passionate commitment to this project and its call to repair what race broke in the world—championed by the Brazos team of mostly European-descendant followers of Jesus. They give me hope.

Along the way there are others: mentors, elders, and sage friends whose wisdom and guidance stirred my thinking and helped connect dots. I must thank Rev. Dr. Brenda Salter McNeil, who was among the first to teach me the art of reaching across racial barriers. As well, I thank Dr. Ruby Sales (also known as Momma Ruby). My mother's friend from their SNCC days, Momma Ruby taught me to think more critically and not to fear the truth.

This book was more challenging to write than I imagined. After thirty years of research, I imagined I was ready to simply write it down. I was not. I did not calculate two critical factors that would rise up like leviathans in 2020, threatening to sidetrack my writing at each turn: (1) I spent the 2020 election season organizing faith communities to ally with communities of color, and (2) I was bum-rushed by the raw reality of the trauma that much of my family has survived. These brutal stories would not have been written without the steady counsel of my coaches, Amy Tatsumi and Medria Connolly. They helped me to recognize ancestral trauma carried in my body. They taught me to honor and to release it.

I am indebted to Dr. Velina Hasu Houston, Dr. Endesha Ida Mae Holland, and Eric Trules, who taught me to tell a compelling story while earning my MFA in Playwriting at the University of Southern California. I am grateful for John Slade, Nikki Hevesy, Renée Roqué White, Brent Blair, Danny Strong, Scarlett Lam, Nyna Shannon Anderson, Bobby Goodman, Laura Raynor, and the community of theater artists who walked with me through my first forays into family research while writing and producing my play *An' Push da Wind Down* at the University of Southern California School of Theatre. Written before the benefit of Ancestry.com and DNA research, this full-length play drew from a combination of mentoring by Cherokee community leaders Kay Cope, Alisa Cauldwell, and Virginia Carey, as well as historical and cultural research and a playwright's imagination of what life might have been like for the Lawrence line before their presence is recorded in Ohio County, Kentucky, circa 1842. These brilliant and accomplished artists and mentors taught me to respect the story and tell it with unflinching truth and without compromise to unleash its power.

My conversations with Rev. Dr. Otis Moss III and Rev. Dr. Reggie Williams on the *Freedom Road* podcast and on my Instagram Live Kitchen Table Convos showed me how I had understood pre-slavery African history through the filter of the White gaze. They challenged me to dig deeper.

I offer my gratitude to Jimmy McGee. In my early years of working out issues of race, I was content to help a White organization do a little better. McGee challenged me, calling out how very far from the Beloved Community was our individualistic evangelical idea of "racial reconciliation." Jimmy also served as the director of the two-year Pilgrimage for Reconciliation within a national evangelical ministry. I write extensively about this pilgrimage and its impact in *The Very Good Gospel*. It changed my life and faith and exposed me to the challenge of international peace building and the biblical concept of *shalom*.

In like manner, I am indebted to the Warehouse community and South African peace-builder Rev. Rene August, who invited me to spend a week on Robben Island, off the coast of Cape Town, with her and fifty other global faith leaders. Over the course of one week, we retraced Nelson Mandela's journey and wrestled with the question of racial repair. At the end of that week, over a lovely meal with Warehouse executive director Craig Stewart and his family, the idea came to me that true repair must move from a transactional legal paradigm to a relational one. Rather than agreeing on an amount of a check, we must trace the offense back to its genesis to reverse the harm. That idea stuck and serves as the foundational premise of this book.

I am indebted to the beautiful communities of the North American Institute for Indigenous Theological Study (NAIITS) and Eloheh Village, which taught me the concept of colonization. Through their stories, I began to understand that my own story is not simply the story of race. It is an extension of the ongoing story of colonization. The political construct of race is simply a tool of domination in the hands of colonizers. In the logics of colonization, genocide clears the land for White consumption and flourishing. I've come to understand that slavocracy is fundamentally the economic system crafted to help White bodies thrive.

Along the way there have been sojourners and guides on the journey toward family discovery. I must thank CeCe Moore's DNA Detectives Facebook Group, full of generous hearts and sharp minds who help untangle the web of clues hidden in our DNA. And I must thank Glenda Guess, who brought me to speak to faith and civic leaders in Henderson County, Kentucky, then rallied her friends to embark on a mini pilgrimage to the land where the Lawrence line lived in Ohio County, Kentucky. It meant everything to stand on their land—to see it—and to see all of the majestic White graveyards and the Black graves hidden behind small churches in the mountains. Thank you for searching gravestones with me on that rainy day. I will never forget you or your love for me and my family.

I am blessed with many friendships and communities that midwifed *Fortune*. Maritza Crespo carried *Fortune* in her heart and prayers. She prayed me through the rough and challenging patches and now shares in the joy. Catherine and Rev. Dr. Scot Sherman and Dr. Elizabeth Rios offered their respective homes as writing caves. Dr. Rios and her husband Hiram also traveled with me to

Loíza, Puerto Rico, in search of information on my Weeks ancestors. David Dault read the very first draft of the introduction and
helped me find the book's voice. Kirsten Powers has been a fierce
advocate for me and this project at every step. The Freedom Road
Global Writers Group offered sacred space to write with a faithful online community of writers whose work and feedback has
sharpened my craft and encouraged me forward each week. Special
thanks particularly goes to Amy Kenny and Junita Calder, Writers
Group members who, after listening to early drafts, consistently
took the time to send detailed written suggestions to strengthen
the text you hold. And thank you Meighan Stone for your support and encouragement. The Samuel DeWitt Proctor Conference
introduced me to the brilliance of Dr. Mindy Thompson Fullilove.
Our community of partners, such as Auburn Senior Fellows, Jim
Wallis and the Sojourners team, Red Letter Christians, Evangelicals 4 Justice, and Voices Project, have offered invaluable opportunities for this extrovert to work out thoughts before committing
them to the page.

I am blessed with an incredible team full of smarts and heart at
FreedomRoad.us. Katie Zimmerman, Dr. Liz Rios, Jazmine Steele,
Katie Norris, Christina Kedaj, and Irma Weeks have all contributed their exceptional administrative, communication, graphic
arts, research, and support skills in partnership with Brazos to
ensure the message of *Fortune* was engaged by the broad Freedom
Road community and our passionate, dedicated launch team!

I offer thanks to my family. When my DNA results returned
from AfricanAncestry.com, I wept aloud. It was the first time in
ten generations that we knew which tribe we descend from on
our mother continent. While we do not yet have the full picture,
we know my matrilineal line stretches to the Hausa and Yoruba
people. My Aunt Najuma says her early research of the Weeks
side also stretches to the Yoruba. Within the Yoruba and many
West African tribes, the griot keeps the stories of the people. Re-
positories of oral history, the griots serve as advisors, storytellers,
historians, and poets. Griots steward their people's collective story
with vulnerability and fierce truth. They understand this simple

truth: only the truth can heal our world. I am from a family of griots. My mother has been the keeper of the stories in her Lawrence, Fortune, Jenkins, and Ballard lines. My Aunt Najuma has kept the stories of the Weeks/Weekes line. I pray that this book helps answer questions and fill in blank spaces for my sisters, Hollie and Meredith. The next generations hold the stories now. We have listened to and taken in our elders' words and have confirmed and sharpened the pictures. I pray I have carried the stories well. I pray the generations after me walk them forward. Luna, Razi, Dove, Junie, Hassan, and all your many cousins, step-siblings, and half-kin—that is your charge.

Finally, I honor Fortune, my seventh-great-grandmother. I honor Maudlin Magee, her mother. I honor Sambo Game, Fortune's father. Three hundred and thirty-five years ago, their bodies absorbed the eviscerating lashes of colonization, slavocracy, patriarchy, and White nationalism. They moved through a world just beginning to construct racial, gender, and citizenship hierarchies. Their lives, legal trails, and tax records bear witness to the trauma of that nascent era when evil still gestated in the womb of America. Through it all, they remembered who they were. They passed down family names, leaving a bread crumb trail for future generations to find their way back to their genesis—the time before the law held them down, the time when we were free, the time when we were simply and magnificently human. I thank them. I honor them. I bless them—all the generations before them and all the generations to come.

Notes

Acknowledgments of Country

1. Helen C. Roundtree and Thomas E. Davidson, *Eastern Shore Indians of Virginia and Maryland* (Charlottesville: University Press of Virginia, 1997), 105.

2. John Norwood, *We Are Still Here! The Tribal Saga of New Jersey's Nanticoke and Lenape Indians* (Moorestown, NJ: Native New Jersey, 2009), 10, available at https://nanticoke-lenape.info/images/We_Are_Still_Here_Nanticoke_and_Lenape_History_Booklet_pre-release_v2.pdf.

Introduction

1. "The First Africans," Historic Jamestowne, accessed June 17, 2021, https://historicjamestowne.org/history/the-first-africans.

2. A database of slave ship voyages from Africa in 1619 shows that for all ships bound for Mexico that year, the principal place of purchase was Luanda, Angola. See "Trans-Atlantic Slave Trade Database," Slave Voyages, accessed July 8, 2021, www.slavevoyages.org/voyage/database.

3. Sweet Honey in the Rock, "Wade in the Water," *Live at Carnegie Hall* (Rounder Records, 1988), recorded live in New York, November 7, 1987, available at http://youtu.be/9NCHAwSru3c.

Chapter 1: Fortune

1. Helen C. Roundtree and Thomas Davidson, *Eastern Shore Indians of Virginia and Maryland* (Charlottesville: University Press of Virginia, 1997), 3.

2. Roundtree and Davidson, *Eastern Shore Indians*, 86–87.

3. Roundtree and Davidson, *Eastern Shore Indians*, 84–125.

4. T. Stephen Whitman, *Challenging Slavery in the Chesapeake: Black and White Resistance to Human Bondage, 1775–1865* (Baltimore: Maryland Historical Society, 2007), 5.

5. Whitman, *Challenging Slavery in the Chesapeake*, 7.

6. Paul Heinegg, *Free African Americans of Maryland and Delaware: From the Colonial Period to 1810* (Baltimore: Clearfield, 2000), 138, available at http://www.freeafricanamericans.com/Farmer-Guy.htm.

7. "Trans-Atlantic Slave Trade Database," Voyage ID 9863, Slave Voyages, accessed April 21, 2021, www.slavevoyages.org/voyage/database#results.

8. "Trans-Atlantic Slave Trade Database," Voyage ID 9863.

9. Interview with Ibrahima Seck by Lisa Sharon Harper, "On Freedom Road: The Roots of U.S. Exploitation of Immigrant Labor—Slavery and Peonage," *Freedom Road* (podcast), July 3, 2019, https://freedomroad.us/2019/07/on-freedom-road-the-roots-of-u-s-exploitation-of-immigrant-labor-slavery-and-peonage.

10. Carson Gigg, *A Supplement to the Early Settlers of Maryland* (Annapolis: Maryland State Archives, 1997), 248; Thomas Daniel Knight, "Six Generations: The Family of George Magee," Scotch-Irish Society of the United States of America, newsletter (Spring 2012), 11, http://www.scotch-irishsocietyusa.org/wp-content/uploads/2018/10/SIS NewslSpring12.pdf.

Starting with King Henry VIII's reign, Irish lands were confiscated from Gaelic clans and Irish-Norman dynasties, and then colonized by English settlers, extending the reach of the English crown. Plantation rule continued under Queen Mary I and Queen Elizabeth I and accelerated when the king of Scotland rose to the English throne in 1603 and became King James I. He opened more land for Scottish settlers in Ireland. Irish Catholics of the Ulster region rose up in rebellion in 1641. English and Scottish settlers—men, women, and children—were locked in houses where they were burned alive. Scholars estimate twelve thousand died and many more lost their homes. Though the massacre ended, the war for English supremacy over Irish land continued for decades. See John Marshall, *John Locke: Toleration and Early Enlightenment Culture* (Cambridge: Cambridge University Press, 2006), 58n10. By 1682 Scottish Presbyterians' resistance to imminent Catholic English rule under James II had grown to a fever pitch, leading many Scots to leave Ireland for the New World.

11. Heinegg, introduction to *Free African Americans of Maryland and Delaware*, available at http://www.freeafricanamericans.com/Intro_md.htm.

12. Ross M. Kimmel, "Blacks before the Law in Colonial Maryland" (MA thesis, University of Maryland, 1974), chap. 3, https://msa.maryland.gov/msa/speccol/sc5300/sc5348/html/chap3.html.

13. Kimmel, "Blacks before the Law," chap. 3.

14. Kimmel, "Blacks before the Law," chap. 4.

15. "A Love Story Carved in Callum's Family Tree," *Baltimore Sun*, June 22, 2005, https://www.baltimoresun.com/features/bal-to.objects22zjun22-story.html.

16. Paul Heinegg, email correspondence, September 4, 2019.

17. Kimmel, "Blacks before the Law," chap. 3.

18. Heinegg, *Free African Americans of Maryland and Delaware*, 128, available at http://www.freeafricanamericans.com/Farmer-Guy.htm.

19. Kimmel, "Blacks before the Law," chap. 3.

20. Heinegg, *Free African Americans of Maryland and Delaware*, 128 (see "Fortune Family"). And primary source copy of deed for Betty Game's land, retrieved from Somerset County Courthouse land records archives.

21. J. Hall Pleasants, "The Lovelace Family and Its Connections: Todd, Day, Bickerton, Hubbard, Dallam, Gorsuch," JSTOR Early Journal Content, accessed April 21, 2021, https://archive.org/stream/jstor-4243832/4243832_djvu.txt.

22. Heinegg, *Free African Americans of Maryland and Delaware*, 128.

23. Paul Heinegg, email correspondence, September 4, 2019.

24. Paul Heinegg, *Free African Americans of Virginia, North Carolina and South Carolina: From the Colonial*

Period to about 1820, available at http:// freeafricanamericans.com/Fagan_George .htm. Note: The records for these siblings appear approximately twenty-one to thirty-one years after their birth, indicating documentation as they enter society following their indentured service. All of their service ended before the approximate end of Sarah's indenture. When their indentures ended, they would not have been able to reconnect with their mother, since she was still indentured.

25. Obituary for Mildred Delores Jeter Loving, available at Tribute Archive, accessed August 2, 2021, https://www .tributearchive.com/obituaries/1897921 /Mildred-D-Loving.

Chapter 2: The Lawrences

1. Plato, *The Republic* 8, trans. Benjamin Jowett (Mineola, NY: Dover, 2000), 203–29, http://classics.mit.edu/Plato/re public.9.viii.html.

2. Raoul Peck, *Exterminate All the Brutes* (HBO Max, 2021).

3. Alexis de Tocqueville, *Democracy in America*, in George Wilson Pierson, *Tocqueville in America* (Baltimore: Johns Hopkins Press, 1938), 598.

4. "The Removal of the Muscogee Nation," National Museum of the American Indian, accessed April 21, 2021, https://americanindian.si.edu /nk360/removal-muscogee/during.html.

5. Josephine Smith, morning devotional, NAIITS Annual Symposium on Indigenous Theology, June 6–8, 2013, Tyndale University, Toronto, Ontario.

6. "Pennsylvania, Death Certificates, 1906–1967," Ancestry.com, accessed September 7, 2021, https://www.ancestry .com/imageviewer/collections/5164/im ages/42342_645856_0545-02560?pId =604583241 (subscription required).

7. See "Dawes Final Rolls," Oklahoma Historical Society, accessed April 21, 2021, https://www.okhistory.org

/research/dawesresults.php?fname=&lna me=Barnett&tribe=Cherokee&roll num=&cardnum=&action=Search and https://www.okhistory.org/research /dawesresults.php?fname=&lname =Smith&tribe=Cherokee&rollnum =&cardnum=&action=Search.

8. "U.S. World War I Draft Registration Cards, 1917–1918," Ancestry.com, accessed July 8, 2021, https://www .ancestry.com/search/collections/6482.

9. "Confederate Company Muster Roll (1861–1865)," National Archives, carded records showing military service of soldiers who fought in Confederate organizations, compiled 1903–1927, documenting the period 1861–1865, Pub. No. M319, Content Source: NARA, National Archives ID: 586957, Record Group 109, Kentucky, Roll 0131, Fold3 .com, accessed September 7, 2021, https://www.fold3.com/image/121347985 (subscription required).

10. "Alexander T. Hines Confederate Oath of Allegiance Record," National Archives, carded records showing military service of soldiers who fought in Confederate organizations, compiled 1903–1927, documenting the period 1861–1865, Pub. No. M319, Content Source: NARA, National Archives ID: 586957, Record Group 109, Kentucky, Roll 0131, Fold3.com, accessed September 7, 2021, https://www.fold3.com /image/121348010 (subscription required).

11. "Map of White Supremacy's Mob Violence," Plain Talk History, accessed April 4, 2021, https://plaintalk history.com/monroeandflorencework /explore/map2/#6.5/38.119/-84.659.

12. As of 2019 (before Ancestry .com changed its algorithm), Ancestry .com DNA matches for Harper had a full page of fourth-cousin Lawrence surname matches, many of whom have no African DNA found. Lawrence matches are still

present, but not as many are listed. This would indicate that Jonathan Lawrence is their common ancestor.

13. 1860 Census, Caney Ohio, Kentucky; Roll. M653_390; Page: 729; Family History Library Film: 803390. Accessed via Ancestry.com.

14. Compiled Military Service Records of Volunteer Union Soldiers Who Served with the U.S. Colored Troops, 54th Massachusetts Infantry Regiment (Colored), National Archives at Washington, DC, Microfilm serial M1898, Microfilm roll 19.

15. "Dawes Final Rolls," Oklahoma Historical Society, accessed September 7, 2021, https://www.okhistory.org/research/dawesresults.php?fname=&lname=Hines&tribe=Cherokee&rollnum=&cardnum=&action=Search.

16. Henry Lawrence, Certificate of Civil War Ancestry, issued by African American Civil War Museum, Washington, DC, July 7, 2012.

17. Henry Lawrence, Declaration for Original Invalid Pension (1886), National Archives at Washington, DC.

18. Henry Lawrence, 1st Lieutenant, Company I 116th Regiment U.S. Colored Infantry, Pension Application Papers, National Archives at Washington, DC.

19. BYU Communications News, "Racial Discrimination in Union Army Pensions Detailed by New Study," Brigham Young University, February 9, 2010, https://news.byu.edu/news/racial-discrimination-union-army-pensions-detailed-new-study.

20. Henry Lawrence, Invalid Pension Approval (November 1899–January 1900), National Archives at Washington, DC.

21. Henry Lawrence, Invalid Pension Approval (November 1899–January 1900), National Archives at Washington, DC.

22. Henry Lawrence, Invalid Pension Approval (August 10, 1899–January 13, 1900), National Archives at Washington, DC.

23. BYU Communications News, "Racial Discrimination in Union Army."

Chapter 3: Lea

1. Paul E. Lovejoy, *Transformations of Slavery: A History of Slavery in Africa* (London: Cambridge University Press, 2012), chap. 2.

2. "Christopher Columbus," History.com, updated October 7, 2020, https://www.history.com/topics/exploration/christopher-columbus.

3. See "Trans-Atlantic Slave Trade Database," Voyage ID 42987, Slave Voyages, www.slavevoyages.org/voyage/database#results; and David Keys, "Details of Horrific First Voyages in Transatlantic Slave Trade Revealed," Institute of the Black World 21st Century, August 27, 2019, https://ibw21.org/editors-choice/details-of-horrific-first-voyages-in-transatlantic-slave-trade-revealed.

4. "Telling the Complicated History of Charleston, South Carolina," CBS News, February 24, 2020, https://www.cbsnews.com/news/charleston-south-carolina-complicated-history; "An African American Museum in Charleston Is Finally Being Built," CBS News, December 21, 2019, https://www.cbsnews.com/news/african-american-museum-in-charleston-to-tell-history-of-enslaved-people-in-united-states.

5. "The Quaker Settlers during the Royal Period (1729 to 1775)," Royal Colony of South Carolina, accessed July 8, 2021, https://www.carolana.com/SC/Royal_Colony/sc_royal_colony_quakers.html.

6. See U.S. Quaker Meeting Records, 1681–1935, "Richmond and Cedar Creek Monthly Meetings, Minutes 1739–1773," Ancestry.com, accessed April 21, 2021, https://www.ancestry.com/imageviewer/collections/2189/images/42483_1821100519_4152-00354 (subscription required).

7. See 1800 Census, "Kershaw District, South Carolina," National Archives and Records Administration, Washington, DC.

8. L. Glen Inabinet, "'The July Fourth Incident' of 1816: An Insurrection Plotted by Slaves in Camden, South Carolina," Proceedings of the Reynolds Conference, University of South Carolina, December 2–3, 1977, available at http://slaverebellion.info/index.php ?page=an-insurrection-plotted-by-slaves -in-camden-south-carolina.

9. "The African Slave Trade and South Carolina," Sciway, accessed April 21, 2021, https://www.sciway.net/hist /chicora/slavery18-2.html.

10. Dina Gilio-Whitaker, "The Untold History of Native American Enslavement," ThoughtCo, updated March 3, 2021, https://www.thoughtco .com/untold-history-of-american-indian -slavery-2477982.

11. Acts of the South Carolina General Assembly, "1740 South Carolina Slave Code," no. 670 (Columbia, SC: South Carolina Department of Archives and History, 1740), 1, available at http:// www.teachingushistory.org/tTrove /documents/Scansof1740SlaveCodes .pdf.

12. See Igor Derysh, "'Experimental Concentration Camp': Whistleblower Alleges Women Face Hysterectomies in ICE Detention," *Salon*, September 15, 2020, https://www.salon.com/2020/09 /15/experimental-concentration-camp -whistleblower-alleges-women-face -hysterectomies-in-ice-detention.

13. Bob Zellner, interview by Lisa Sharon Harper, filmed by the Justice Conference US on the Freedom Road Greenville University Justice Pilgrimage, "The History of Race in America," Facebook video, 53:12, May 16, 2018, https:// www.facebook.com/thejusticeconfer enceUS/videos/10155336445442385.

Part Two: Degradation and Resistance

1. Timothy Tyson, *The Blood of Emmett Till* (New York: Simon & Schuster, 2017), 54–55.

Chapter 4: Lizzie

1. Eric Foner, "Rooted in Reconstruction: The First Wave of Black Congressmen," *The Nation*, October 15, 2008, https://www.thenation.com/article /archive/rooted-reconstruction-first-wave -black-congressmen.

2. Isabel Wilkerson, *Caste: The Origins of Our Discontents* (New York: Random House, 2020), 133.

3. Wilkerson, *Caste*, 160.

4. Richard Rothstein, *The Color of Law: The Forgotten History of How Our Government Segregated America* (New York: Liveright, 2017), viii.

5. "Convict Lease System," Digital History, accessed April 21, 2021, http:// www.digitalhistory.uh.edu/disp_text book.cfm?psid=3179&smtid=2.

6. David M. Oshinsky, *Worse Than Slavery: Parchman Farm and the Ordeal of Jim Crow Justice* (New York: Free Press, 1996), 58.

7. Oshinsky, *Worse Than Slavery*, 59–60.

8. Oshinsky, *Worse Than Slavery*, 58.

9. Oshinsky, *Worse Than Slavery*, 62.

10. "On Freedom Road: The Roots of U.S. Exploitation of Immigrant Labor—Slavery and Peonage," *Freedom Road* (podcast), July 3, 2019, https:// freedomroad.us/2019/07/on-freedom -road-the-roots-of-u-s-exploitation-of -immigrant-labor-slavery-and-peonage.

11. "South Carolina Hurricanes and Tropical Storms," South Carolina Department of Natural Resources, SC State Climatology Office, accessed July 27, 2021, https://www.dnr.sc.gov/climate /sco/Tropics/pastTracks/ts8_1908.php.

12. Joy DeGruy, *Post Traumatic Slave Syndrome: America's Legacy of Enduring Injury and Healing* (Milwaukie, OR: Uptone Press, 2017), 134.

13. DeGruy, *Post Traumatic Slave Syndrome*, 134.

14. DeGruy, *Post Traumatic Slave Syndrome*, 135.

15. Maya Angelou, "Still I Rise," in *And Still I Rise: A Book of Poems* (New York: Random House, 1978), 41.

Chapter 5: Reinaldo y Anita

1. "Barbados History," Global Security, July 16, 2017, https://www.global security.org/military/world/caribbean /bb-history.htm.

2. "World Directory of Minorities and Indigenous Peoples—Barbados," Refworld, May 2008, https://www.ref world.org/docid/4954ce3023.html.

3. Ben Johnson, "West Country Duking Days," Historic UK, accessed July 9, 2021, https://www.historic-uk .com/HistoryUK/HistoryofEngland /West-Country-Duking-Days.

4. "World Directory of Minorities and Indigenous Peoples—Barbados," Refworld, May 2008, https://www.ref world.org/docid/4954ce3023.html.

5. "Barbados Plantation History," CreoleLinks.com, accessed September 7, 2021, https://creolelinks.com/barbados -plantation-history.html.

6. Maris Corbin, "An Old Quaker Burial Ground in Barbados," *Journal of the Friends Historical Society* 60, no. 1 (2003), https://journals.sas.ac.uk/fhs /article/view/3412/3364.

7. "Ancestry DNA Story for Lisa Sharon," under "Lesser Antilles African Americans," Ancestry.com, accessed July 9, 2021, https://www.ancestry.com /dna/origins/share/f4474805-d84f-4a46 -9d06-c0115de01e1c; and https://www .ancestry.com/dna/origins/9769CE5C -466C-4FF1-BBD7-2DB664CCAC01/de

tails?branch=11.18_1.5.1&time=1750 (subscription required).

8. "Caribbean Histories Revealed: Slavery and Negotiating Freedom," National Archives (UK), accessed April 21, 2021, http://www.nationalarchives.gov .uk/caribbeanhistory/slavery-negotiating -freedom.htm.

9. Karl Watson, "Slavery and Economy in Barbados," BBC, last updated February 17, 2011, http://www.bbc.co .uk/history/british/empire_seapower /barbados_01.shtml.

10. Vincent Hubbard, *A History of St. Kitts: The Sweet Trade* (Oxford: Macmillan Caribbean, 2002), 10.

11. Cited in Carl Bridenbaugh and Roberta Bridenbaugh, *No Peace beyond the Line: The English in the Caribbean 1624–1690* (New York: Oxford University Press, 1972), 301, quoted by "Conditions in the Sugar Works," International Slavery Museum, accessed July 9, 2021, https://www.liverpoolmuseums.org.uk /conditions-sugar-works.

12. Keith Mason, "The World an Absentee Planter and His Slaves Made: Sir William Stapleton and His Nevis Sugar Estate, 1722–1740," *John Rylands University Library of Manchester Bulletin* 75, no. 1 (1993): 126.

13. Tito Ayala, interview by Lisa Sharon Harper, Facebook video, 22:45, June 25, 2019, https://www.facebook.com/lisa sharonharper/videos/1021987755246 8579.

14. Luis M. Diaz Soler, *History of Enslaved Africans in Puerto Rico* (San Juan: University of Puerto Rico Editorial Universitaria, 1970), 145–46.

15. "The Loiza Aldea Yearly Patron Saints Day: Saint James the Apostle and Vejigantes," Elyunque, accessed April 21, 2021, http://www.elyunque.com/veji gante.htm.

16. Najuma Weeks, recorded interview with author, November 28, 2020.

17. Najuma Weeks, interview.
18. Don Weeks, recorded interview with author, June 15, 2021.
19. University of the West Indies TV, "From Apology to Action: Caricom's Call for Reparatory Justice," Facebook video, 1:38:27, July 6, 2020, https://facebook.com/story.php?story_fbid=27613729011 4969&id=1092567170812001&_rdr.

Chapter 6: Sharon

1. The content in this chapter concerning Sharon is informed by the author's recorded interview with Sharon L. Lawrence Harper, December 26, 2020.
2. See Sherry Howard, "A Dream Book of Lottery Numbers," Auction Finds, https://myauctionfinds.com/2010/03/30/a-dream-book-of-lottery-numbers.
3. Martin Luther King Jr., *Where Do We Go From Here: Chaos or Community?* (Boston: Beacon Press, 1968), 122.
4. "Table 2: Poverty Status by Family Relationship, Race and Hispanic Origin," at "Historical Poverty Tables: People and Families—1959 to 2019," US Census Bureau, accessed April 21, 2021, https://www.census.gov/data/tables/time-series/demo/income-poverty/historical-poverty-people.html.
5. John Lewis, "Speech at the March on Washington," Washington, DC, August 28, 1963, available at Voices of Democracy, https://voicesofdemocracy.umd.edu/lewis-speech-at-the-march-on-washington-speech-text.
6. Student Nonviolent Coordinating Committee, "The Story of SNCC," pamphlet, 1966, page 8, available at Civil Rights Movement Archive, https://www.crmvet.org/docs/sncc66.pdf?source=post_page.
7. "Meredith March against Fear (June 1966)," Bob Fitch Photography Archive, Stanford Libraries, https://exhibits.stanford.edu/fitch/browse/meredith-march-against-fear-june-1966.

8. Recorded interview with Charles McLaurin at the Fannie Lou Hamer Foundation office, May 16, 2018, while on the "Gospel and the Politics of Race" Freedom Road Pilgrimage in partnership with Greenville University. Access to recording available upon request. Stokely Carmichael's "Black Power" speech (Greenwood, Mississippi, July 28, 1966) can be found at Encyclopedia.com, https://www.encyclopedia.com/history/dictionaries-thesauruses-pictures-and-press-releases/black-power-speech-28-july-1966-stokely-carmichael.
9. Recorded interview with Charles McLaurin, May 2018, "The Gospel and the Politics of Race," Freedom Road Pilgrimage in partnership with Greenville University.
10. "'Black Power' Speech (July 28, 1966, by Stokely Carmichael)," Encyclopedia.com, accessed April 21, 2021, https://www.encyclopedia.com/history/dictionaries-thesauruses-pictures-and-press-releases/black-power-speech-28-july-1966-stokely-carmichael.
11. "'Black Power' Speech (July 28, 1966, by Stokely Carmichael)."
12. Paul Laurence Dunbar, "We Wear the Mask," in *The Complete Poems of Paul Laurence Dunbar* (New York: Adansonia, 2018), 54, available at https://www.poetryfoundation.org/poems/44203/we-wear-the-mask.

Chapter 7: Lisa

1. Randall Balmer, "The Real Origins of the Religious Right," *Politico*, May 27, 2014, https://www.politico.com/magazine/story/2014/05/religious-right-real-origins-107133.
2. Michael Cromartie, ed., *No Longer Exiles: The Religious New Right in American Politics* (Washington, DC: Ethics and Public Policy Center, 1993), 26.
3. Randall Balmer, *Thy Kingdom Come: How the Religious Right Distorts*

Faith and Threatens America (New York: Basic Books, 2007), 16.

4. "Martin-Quinn Scores," http:// mqscores.lsa.umich.edu/measures.php, citing data from Andrew D. Martin and Kevin M. Quinn, "Dynamic Ideal Point Estimation via Markov Chain Monte Carlo for the U.S. Supreme Court, 1953–1999," *Political Analysis* 10, no. 2 (2002): 134–53, http://mqscores.lsa.umich.edu /media/pa02.pdf.

5. "A False 'Scream,'" editorial, *New York Times*, March 11, 1985, section A, page 18, https://www.nytimes.com/1985 /03/11/opinion/a-false-scream.html.

6. Pat Buchanan, "Pat Buchanan 1992 Republican National Convention Address," C-Span, streaming video, 35:32, August 17, 1992, https://www.c-span.org /video/?31255-1/pat-buchanan-1992 -republican-convention-address.

7. Pat Buchanan, "1992 Republican National Convention Address."

8. *Dred Scott v. John F. A. Sanford*, 60 U.S. 393 (1856), available at Legal Information Institute, Cornell Law School, https://www.law.cornell.edu/supreme court/text/60/393.

9. Molly K. Hooper, "You Lie: Rep Wilson Apologizes for Yell," *The Hill*, September 10, 2009, https://thehill.com /homenews/house/58035-you-lie-mccain -calls-on-wilson-to-apologize.

10. Dudley L. Poston Jr., "Three Ways That the U.S. Population Will Change over the Next Decade," PBS Newshour, January 2, 2020, https://www .pbs.org/newshour/nation/3-ways-that -the-u-s-population-will-change-over-the -next-decade.

11. Robert P. Jones, *White Too Long: The Legacy of White Supremacy in American Christianity* (New York: Simon & Schuster, 2020), 15.

12. Alex Vandermaas-Peeler, Daniel Cox, Maxine Najle, Molly Fisch-Friedman, Rob Griffin, Robert P. Jones,

"Partisan Polarization Dominates Trump Era: Findings from the 2018 American Values Survey," Public Religion Research Institute, October 29, 2018, https://www .prri.org/research/partisan-polarization -dominates-trump-era-findings-from-the -2018-american-values-survey.

13. "Table 2: Poverty Status by Family Relationship, Race and Hispanic Origin," at "Historical Poverty Tables: People and Families—1959 to 2019," US Census Bureau, accessed April 21, 2021, https://www.census.gov/data/tables/time -series/demo/income-poverty/historical -poverty-people.html.

14. Martin Luther King Jr., *Where Do We Go From Here: Chaos or Community?* (Boston: Beacon Press, 1968), 11–12.

15. King, *Where Do We Go From Here?*, 12.

16. Most scholars believe the book of Genesis was written by four sets of authors and compiled into one coherent book after the return from the Babylonian exile. Genesis 1 is believed to be the final part of the book of Genesis to be added to that canon. Written by a company of priests exiting the Babylonian exile and about to enter their own rule in the temple, they stopped to write down their creation story. The Babylonian creation story bears striking resemblance to the Hebrew story penned in Genesis 1, but there are important differences.

For the full text of Enuma Elish, the Babylonian creation story, see Joshua J. Mark, "Enuma Elish—The Babylonian Epic of Creation—Full Text," World History Encyclopedia, May 4, 2018, https://www.worldhistory.org/article /225/enuma-elish---the-babylonian-epic -of-creation---fu. For my reflections on the critical differences between the two stories, see Harper, *The Very Good Gospel: How Everything Wrong Can Be Made Right* (Colorado Springs: Water-Brook, 2016), chap. 2.

17. Glenn Kessler, "The 'Very Fine People' at Charlottesville: Who Were They?," *Washington Post*, May 8, 2020, https://www.washingtonpost.com/poli tics/2020/05/08/very-fine-people-char lottesville-who-were-they-2.

Part Three: Repair

1. Thomas Wood, "Racism Moti-vated Trump Voters More Than Author-itarianism," *Washington Post*, April 17, 2017, https://www.washingtonpost.com /news/monkey-cage/wp/2017/04/17/rac ism-motivated-trump-voters-more-than -authoritarianism-or-income-inequality.

2. "Transitional Justice," Interna-tional Center for Transitional Justice, accessed April 21, 2021, https://www .ictj.org/about/transitional-justice.

Chapter 8: Truth-Telling as Reckoning

1. Isabel Wilkerson, *Caste: The Origins of Our Discontents* (New York: Random House, 2020), 133.

2. Keisha Blain, quoted in "This Ac-quittal Sends Three Dangerous Messages to Future Presidents," *Politico*, February 13, 2021, https://www.politico.com/news /magazine/2021/02/13/impeachment-vote -history-roundup-468998.

3. Equal Justice Initiative, *Lynching in America Report: Confronting the Legacy of Racial Terror*, 3rd ed. (Mont-gomery, AL: Equal Justice Initiative, 2017), 4, https://lynchinginamerica.eji .org/drupal/sites/default/files/2020-09/09 -15-20-lia-cap.pdf.

4. Zoë Schlanger, "Company Apolo-gizes for Texas Textbook that Calls Slaves 'Workers': We Made a Mistake," *Newsweek*, October 5, 2015, https:// www.newsweek.com/company-behind -texas-textbook-calling-slaves-workers -apologizes-we-made-380168.

5. Emma Brown, "Texas Officials: Schools Should Teach That Slavery Was

'Side Issue' to Civil War," *Washington Post*, July 5, 2015, https://www.wash ingtonpost.com/local/education/150 -years-later-schools-are-still-a-battlefield -for-interpreting-civil-war/2015/07/05 /e8fbd57e-2001-11e5-bf41-c23f5d3face1 _story.html.

6. Martin Luther King Jr., *Where Do We Go From Here: Chaos or Commu-nity?* (Boston: Beacon Press, 1968), 12.

7. Juliana Menasce Horowitz, Ruth Igielnik, and Rakesh Kochhar, "Trends in Income and Wealth Inequality," Pew Research Center, January 9, 2020, https:// www.pewresearch.org/social-trends /2020/01/09/trends-in-income-and-wealth -inequality.

8. "Republican Plans to Cut Taxes Now, Cut Programs Later Would Threaten Food Assistance through SNAP," Center on Budget and Policy Priorities, November 6, 2017, https:// www.cbpp.org/research/federal-budget /republican-plans-to-cut-taxes-now-cut -programs-later-would-threaten-food.

9. See "Criminal Justice Fact Sheet," NAACP, accessed June 18, 2021, https:// naacp.org/resources/criminal-justice-fact -sheet.

10. Danielle Sered, *Until We Reckon: Violence, Mass Incarceration, and a Road to Repair* (New York: New Press, 2019), 237.

11. Martin Luther King Jr., "Letter from a Birmingham Jail," in *Why We Can't Wait* (New York: Signet Classic, 2000), 70.

12. King, *Why We Can't Wait*, 69–70.

13. Manny Fernandez and Audra D. S. Burch, "From 'I Want to Touch the World' to 'I Can't Breathe,'" *New York Times*, November 5, 2020, https://www .nytimes.com/article/george-floyd-who -is.html.

14. Derrick Bryson Taylor, "George Floyd Protests: A Timeline," *New York Times*, January 6, 2021, https://www

.nytimes.com/article/george-floyd -protests-timeline.html.

15. Ellen Barry, "7 Lessons (and Warnings) from Those Who Marched with Dr. King," *New York Times*, June 17, 2020, https://www.nytimes.com/2020 /06/17/us/george-floyd-protests.html.

16. Barry, "7 Lessons (and Warnings)."

17. Douglas O. Linder, "Lynchings: By State and Race, 1882–1968," Famous Trials, accessed April 21, 2021, https:// famous-trials.com/sheriffshipp/1083 -lynchingsstate. These statistics were compiled by Monroe and Florence Work in their 1921 sociological analysis of lynchings. For more information on Monroe and Florence Work, see https:// plaintalkhistory.com/monroeandflor encework/welcome.

18. Garrison, preface to *Narrative of the Life of Frederick Douglass: An American Slave* by Frederick Douglass (Garden City, NY: Anchor Books, 1973), x.

19. Anthony Hinton, speaking at Sojourners Faith Table Retreat at Equal Justice Initiative (EJI), Montgomery, AL, December 15, 2015, story available at https://www.facebook.com/photo.php ?fbid=10208167861693628&set=t.121392 7451&type=3.

20. http://www.stolpersteine.eu/en /home.

21. "Stephen F. Austin," Wikipedia, last updated June 14, 2021, https://en .wikipedia.org/wiki/Stephen_F._Austin.

22. Kenneth P. Minkema, "Jonathan Edwards's Defense of Slavery," *Massachusetts Historical Review* 4 (2002): 23–59, http://www.jstor.org/stable/250 81170.

23. Donna McDaniel and Vanessa D. Julye, *Fit for Freedom, Not for Friendship: Quakers, African Americans, and the Myth of Racial Justice* (Philadel-

phia: Quaker Press of Friends General Conference, 2009), 3–42.

24. Tariro Mzezewa, "The Woman Who Took Down a Confederate Flag on What Came Next," *New York Times*, June 14, 2020, https://www.nytimes.com /2020/06/14/us/politics/bree-newsome -bass-confederate-flag.html.

25. Martin Luther King Jr., "The Other America" (speech, Grosse Pointe High School, Detroit, Michigan, March 14, 1968), available at http://gphistorical .org/mlk/mlkspeech/index.htm.

Chapter 9: Reparation as Repentance

1. Aaron O'Neill, "Estimated Share of African Slaves Who Did Not Survive the Middle Passage Journey to the Americas Each Year from 1501 to 1866," Statista.com, February 24, 2021, https:// www.statista.com/statistics/1143458/an nual-share-slaves-deaths-during-middle -passage.

2. See Nic Butler, "Recall Their Names: The Personal Identities of Enslaved South Carolinians," Charleston County Public Library, October 2, 2020, https://www.ccpl.org/charleston-time -machine/recall-their-names-personal -identity-enslaved-south-carolinians.

3. See Richard Rothstein, *The Color of Law: A Forgotten History of How Our Government Segregated America* (New York: Liveright, 2017).

4. Paul Heinegg, *Free African Americans of Maryland and Delaware: From the Colonial Period to 1810* (Baltimore: Clearfield, 2000), 128, available at http:// www.freeafricanamericans.com/Farmer -Guy.htm.

5. Douglas Harper, "Slavery in Delaware," Slavery in the North, accessed April 21, 2021, http://slavenorth.com /delaware.htm.

6. Garrett Power, "Apartheid Baltimore Style: The Residential Segregation Ordinances of 1910–1913," *Maryland*

Law Review 42, no. 2 (1983): 299–300, https://digitalcommons.law.umaryland.edu/mlr/vol42/iss2/4.

7. Benjamin Campbell, *Richmond's Unhealed History* (Richmond, VA: Brandylane, 2012), 142.

8. Rothstein, *Color of Law*, 44–45.

9. Rothstein, *Color of Law*, 45.

10. Campbell, *Richmond's Unhealed History*, 143.

11. Henry McNeal Turner, *African Letters* (Nashville: A.M.E. Sunday School Union, 1893), 33, available at Documenting the American South, https://docsouth.unc.edu/church/turneral/turner.html.

12. Henry McNeal Turner, *Respect Black: The Writings and Speeches of Henry McNeal Turner*, ed. Edwin S. Redkey (New York: Arno, 1971), 176, cited by Andre Johnson, "The Emigration and Propaganda Campaign of Henry McNeal Turner," paper presented to the National Communication Association, University of Memphis, November 15–18, 2007, 2.

13. Derrick Bell, *Faces at the Bottom of the Well: The Permanence of Racism* (New York: Basic Books, 1992), 10–11.

14. Bell, *Faces at the Bottom of the Well*, 39–57.

15. "Criminal Justice Facts," Sentencing Project, accessed April 21, 2021, https://www.sentencingproject.org/criminal-justice-facts.

16. Justin Wolfers, David Leonhardt, and Kevin Quealy, "1.5 Million Missing Black Men," *New York Times*, April 20, 2015, https://www.nytimes.com/interactive/2015/04/20/upshot/missing-black-men.html.

17. Whitney Benns, "American Slavery, Reinvented," *Atlantic*, September 21, 2015, https://www.theatlantic.com/business/archive/2015/09/prison-labor-in-america/406177.

18. E.g., the emblematic case of Marissa Alexander in 2012. See Charles Broward, "NAACP Weighs In on What They Say Is a 'Stand Your Ground' Case against Jacksonville Woman," *Florida Times-Union*, April 21, 2012, https://www.jacksonville.com/article/20120421/NEWS/801254470.

19. "Lynching of Anthony Crawford," Wikipedia, updated January 18, 2021, https://en.wikipedia.org/wiki/Lynching_of_Anthony_Crawford; and "Abbeville," YouTube video, 7:22, published by "Equal Justice Initiative," July 17, 2017, https://youtu.be/-HHY_4f5nds.

20. Letter to Willa B. Lawrence from Attorney Richard W. Lloyd, October 23, 1975.

21. William A. Darity Jr. and A. Kirsten Mullen, *From Here to Equality: Reparations for Black Americans in the Twenty-First Century* (Chapel Hill: University of North Carolina Press, 2020), 208.

22. Ta-Nehisi Coates, "The Case for Reparations," *Atlantic*, June 2014, https://www.theatlantic.com/magazine/archive/2014/06/the-case-for-reparations/361631.

23. William Darity Jr., Darrick Hamilton, Mark Paul, Alan Aja, Anne Price, Antonio Moore, and Caterina Chiopris, "What We Get Wrong about Closing the Racial Wealth Gap," Samuel DuBois Cook Center on Social Equity, April 2018, https://socialequity.duke.edu/wp-content/uploads/2019/10/what-we-get-wrong.pdf.

24. Kriston McIntosh, Emily Moss, Ryan Nunn, and Jay Shambaugh, "Examining the Black–White Wealth Gap," Brookings Institution, February 27, 2020, https://www.brookings.edu/blog/up-front/2020/02/27/examining-the-black-white-wealth-gap.

25. Michaela Broyles, "A Conversation about the Racial Wealth Gap and How to Address It," Brookings Institution, June 18, 2019, https://www.brookings.edu/blog/brookings-now/2019/06/18/a-conversation-about-the-racial-wealth-gap-and-how-to-address-it.

26. Darity et al., "What We Get Wrong."

27. "United Nations Charter," United Nations, accessed April 21, 2021, https://www.un.org/en/about-us/un-charter/full-text.

28. "Universal Declaration of Human Rights," United Nations, accessed April 21, 2021, https://www.un.org/en/about-us/universal-declaration-of-human-rights.

29. Fifteen dollars in 1969 would equal $110 today (due to inflation). At about 47 million in the US who identify as Black, that total would come to $5.17 trillion at $110 each. See "Inflation Calculator" at https://smartasset.com/investing/inflation-calculator#xiyvXpuUQh; and Christine Tamir, "The Growing Diversity of Black America," Pew Research Center, March 25, 2021, https://www.pewresearch.org/social-trends/2021/03/25/the-growing-diversity-of-black-america.

30. "Reparations," Movement for Black Lives, accessed April 21, 2021, https://m4bl.org/policy-platforms/reparations.

31. Commission to Study and Develop Reparation Proposals for African Americans Act, H.R. 40, 117th Congress (2021–2022), https://www.congress.gov/bill/117th-congress/house-bill/40.

Chapter 10: Forgiveness and the Beloved Community

1. Ney Bailey, keynote speech at Campus Crusade for Christ, Northeast Christmas Conference, Philadelphia, Pennsylvania, December 1989.

2. Karl Jaspers, *The Question of German Guilt*, trans. K. B. Ashton (New York: Fordham University Press, 2000), 25–26.

3. Jaspers, *Question of German Guilt*, ix, 49–50.

4. Jaspers, *Question of German Guilt*, ix–x, 55–56.

5. Jaspers, *Question of German Guilt*, 57–58.

6. Jaspers, *Question of German Guilt*, x–xi, 65.

7. Jaspers, *Question of German Guilt*, 66.

8. Donald W. Shriver Jr., *An Ethic for Enemies: Forgiveness in Politics* (New York: Oxford University Press, 1995), 31.

9. Desmond Tutu, *No Future without Forgiveness* (London: Rider, 1999), 208.

10. Equal Justice Initiative, *Lynching in America Report: Confronting the Legacy of Racial Terror*, 3rd ed. (Montgomery, AL: Equal Justice Initiative, 2017), 4, https://lynchinginamerica.eji.org/drupal/sites/default/files/2020-09/09-15-20-lia-cap.pdf.

11. Shriver, *Ethic for Enemies*, 5.

12. Shriver, *Ethic for Enemies*, 5.

13. Martin Luther King Jr., speech at St. Louis University, St. Louis, Missouri, March 22, 1964, quoted in *St. Louis Post Dispatch*, March 23, 1964, page 3A.

14. Shriver, *Ethic for Enemies*, 31, quoting Susan Jacoby, *Wild Justice: The Evolution of Revenge* (New York: Harper & Row, 1983), 361–62.

15. Tutu, *No Future without Forgiveness*, 34.

16. Tutu, *No Future without Forgiveness*, 213.

17. Tutu, *No Future without Forgiveness*, 213.

18. Plato, *The Republic* 8, trans. Benjamin Jowett (Mineola, NY: Dover, 2000), 203–29, http://classics.mit.edu/Plato/republic.9.viii.html.

19. Aristotle, *Politics*, trans. Benjamin Jowett (Kitchener, Ontario: Batoche Books, 1999), 4, 9, 79.

20. Obery M. Hendricks Jr., "The Politics of Jesus," keynote speech, The Gospel and the Politics of Race Conference, Princeton University, 2008.

21. Obery M. Hendricks Jr., *The Politics of Jesus: Rediscovering the True*

Revolutionary Nature of Jesus' Teachings and How They Have Been Corrupted (New York: Three Leaves Press, 2006), 104–5.

22. See Charles Marsh, *God's Long Summer: Stories of Faith and Civil Rights* (Princeton, NJ: Princeton University Press, 1997), 10–21.

23. Fannie Lou Hamer, "Go Tell It on the Mountain, Let My People Go," on *Lest We Forget*, vol. 1, *Movement Soul: Sounds of the Freedom Movement in the South, 1963–1964*, 1980, Folkways Records.

24. Ryan Briggs and Catalina Jaramillo, "Philly's Low-Income Neighborhoods Have Fewer Trees and the City's Free Tree Program Isn't Helping," WHYY (PBS affiliate), July 24, 2019, https://whyy .org/articles/phillys-low-income-neighbor hoods-have-fewer-trees-and-the-citys-free -tree-program-isnt-helping.

25. Irina Zhorov, "Tackling the Heat Island Problem in Concrete Jungles," WHYY (PBS affiliate), June 28, 2017: https://whyy.org/segments/tackling-the -heat-island-problem-in-concrete-jungles.

26. Linda Villarosa, "Pollution Is Killing Black Americans: This Community Fought Back," *New York Times*, July 28, 2020, https://www.nytimes.com /2020/07/28/magazine/pollution-phila delphia-black-americans.html.

27. Dan Baum, "Legalize It All: How to Win the War on Drugs," *Harpers Magazine*, April 2016, https://harpers .org/archive/2016/04/legalize-it-all.

28. Mindy Thompson Fullilove, *Root Shock: How Tearing Up City Neighborhoods Hurts America and What We Can Do about It* (New York: New Village Press, 2016), 57.

29. See Fullilove, *Root Shock*, 71–100.

30. Resmaa Menakem, *My Grandmother's Hands: Racialized Trauma and the Pathway to Mending Our Hearts and Bodies* (Las Vegas: Central Recovery Press, 2017), 129.

31. Menakem, *My Grandmother's Hands*, 165.

32. Menakem, *My Grandmother's Hands*, 165–67.

33. Tyra Banks, quoted in Menakem, *My Grandmother's Hands*, 137.

34. Tutu, *No Future without Forgiveness*, 220–221.

35. John August Swanson, *Psalm 85*, 2003, https://www.johnaugustswanson .com/default.cfm/PID%3d1.2-16.html.

36. "The Beloved Community," King Center, accessed April 21, 2021, https:// thekingcenter.org/about-tkc/the-king -philosophy.

Index